ALSO BY ADRIAN BURGOS, JR.

Playing America's Game: Baseball, Latinos, and the Color Line

CUBAN STAR

CUBAN STAR

*How One Negro-League Owner
Changed the Face of Baseball*

ADRIAN BURGOS, JR.

🖑 HILL AND WANG
A DIVISION OF FARRAR, STRAUS AND GIROUX
NEW YORK

Hill and Wang
A division of Farrar, Straus and Giroux
18 West 18th Street, New York 10011

Distributed in Canada by D&M Publishers, Inc.
Printed in the United States of America
First edition, 2011

Library of Congress Cataloging-in-Publication Data
Burgos, Adrian, 1969–
    Cuban star : how one Negro-league owner changed the face of baseball /
Adrian Burgos, Jr.—1st ed.
        p.   cm.
    Includes bibliographical references and index.
    ISBN 978-0-8090-9479-0 (alk. paper)
    1. Pompez, Alex, 1890–1974.   2. African American baseball team
owners—Biography.   3. Baseball scouts—United States—Biography.
4. Cuban American—Biography.   I. Title.

GV865.P66B87 2011
796.357092—dc22
[B]
                                                            2010038497

Designed by Jonathan D. Lippincott

www.fsgbooks.com

1   3   5   7   9   10   8   6   4   2

To Dolly, Miranda, and Julia

CONTENTS

PREFACE

Some stories seemingly wait for specific historians to uncover, research, and write. For me it was the life of Alex Pompez, the Harlem
numbers king who became professional baseball's greatest importer
of Latin American talent. His burial plot in the expansive Woodlawn
Cemetery was right across the street from the Bronx apartment where
my maternal grandmother lived. Woodlawn's marvelous headstones,
family crypts, and mausoleums long intrigued me. On childhood visits
to my grandmother's apartment I often gazed into the cemetery and
wondered about the life stories of those buried there: war heroes who
date back to the American Revolution, New York City's well-known
families, along with the famous entertainers Irving Berlin, George M.
Cohan, and Duke Ellington and the historical figures Elizabeth Cady
Stanton and Madame C. J. Walker. Most of their stories have been
told. The story of Pompez, one of Woodlawn's lesser-known occupants,
piqued my curiosity.

His life story embodied both the dreams deferred and the promise
of America's game with a twist. He was an Afro-Cuban-American who
rose to reign as a Harlem numbers king and then remade himself strictly
as a baseball entrepreneur and talent evaluator of the highest order.
I became acutely aware of Pompez's contribution to baseball history
while researching my first book on how Latinos were affected by baseball's color line. Interestingly, his role had typically been described as
part of two distinct chapters, as if his story didn't bridge the era of Jim
Crow segregation and the onset of baseball integration. In fact, his
name kept popping up in three discrete historical literatures: Negro

leagues, Latinos in baseball, and Harlem. Yet the dots were never fully connected. As I eventually discovered, the story of his forebears and his time in Harlem threaded these stories together and illuminated the forces and actors who shaped who he was and how he became baseball's numbers king.

Pompez was a trailblazer who over the span of seven decades—from his Negro-league days through his major-league scouting work—opened pathways for talent from once-insignificant baseball territories. His Cuban Stars were the first Negro-league team to tour Puerto Rico and the Dominican Republic, and they were also the first to acquire talent from these two baseball-loving societies—decades before the major leagues dipped into these talent pools. Equally significant, his approach to the incorporation of individuals from these and other Spanish-speaking societies in the 1950s and 1960s prefigured the best practices major-league teams would adopt in the late twentieth century: Spanish-language classes in spring training, formal and informal mentoring, and careful selection of housing for young players, among others.

This book provides an inside look at the sporting world and communities within which Pompez operated. His story not only complicates how most scholars have written about race in America and the working of the color line—what the African American intellectual W.E.B. DuBois astutely predicted would be the problem of the twentieth century—but also what we think we know about the process of dismantling baseball's color line. Simply put, many did not quite know what to do with the fact that he was a black Latino, a "mulatto" who was bilingual. Attempts to place his story within traditional notions of race and identity led to a conundrum: Was it a story of a Cuban, a black man, an American, or some combination of the three? Historians have also not fully explored the people, events, and circumstances that shaped who Pompez was as a man. This book unravels much of the mystery that surrounds his time in Harlem's numbers racket, his work as a sports entrepreneur, and his involvement in the desegregation of organized baseball. His story is of an individual who lived in between what others viewed and some sought to maintain as well-defined spaces: black-white; legal-illegal; good-criminal; citizen-foreigner. He was all of these, often at the same time.

. . .

On February 27, 2006, the Baseball Hall of Fame announced that Pompez, along with sixteen other Negro-league figures, had been selected for induction by a special Negro-league committee. His election meant he would have a plaque among baseball's immortals in the Hall of Fame gallery, joining the handful of players whose careers he had touched: Orlando Cepeda, Martín Dihigo, Monte Irvin, Willie McCovey, Juan Marichal, and Willie Mays.

I had the distinct honor of serving on the committee that elected Pompez to this hallowed hall. Only a select few Latinos are immortalized in Cooperstown, from both baseball's segregated and integrated eras. He actually bridges the two eras, capturing the story of baseball's color line and those who finally traversed it. Pompez was a Negro-league team owner, briefly NNL (Negro National League) vice president, and a major-league scout who became the first Latino director of international scouting for any organization, and his story encapsulates the arc of race, opportunity, and America's game. As someone who was black and Latino, he encountered race in nearly all of its complexities when it came to baseball in the Americas. That racial beliefs followed wherever he traveled and persisted regardless of his station in life is captured in former Cuban baseball team owner Emilio de Armas's description of Pompez to the journalist Robert Heuer: *"Él era mulatto, pero todovía era buena gente"* (He was black, but he was still a good person). Such comments were often standard fare, not extraordinary expressions of personal animus or racial hatred. The words remind us that leaving the United States for the Spanish-speaking Caribbean did not mean Pompez entered into a race-free zone, lands where all were color-blind and race neutral; that place did not exist then, nor does it now. This reality did not sour him. Most who knew him recall his warm smile, endearing personality, and determination, qualities that convinced most prospects and parents to place their trust in him.

The once-excluded Negro-league executive made the smoothest transition of all Negro-league owners to baseball's integrated era. He was much more than an evaluator of talent who scouted Latin America and the black baseball circuit for the Giants. A witness to the rise and fall of the Negro leagues, the hardening of racial fault lines in the

American South, the limitations of color blindness within the Cuban nation-building project, and the harsh realities of both southern and northern forms of segregation, he drew on this vast experience to counsel African American and Latino prospects about the rules of social engagement. This represents an understudied part of baseball's integration story: the unique expertise honed through involvement in the Negro leagues and Caribbean baseball brought to bear on the entry and development of black and Latino players into organized baseball. Indeed, over his twenty-five years with the Giants, his recommendations spurred the organization to acquire the Negro-league stars Monte Irvin and Willie Mays while personally participating in the signing of McCovey, Cepeda, and Marichal.

He never fully escaped his past as a numbers king, however. His inclusion in the Hall of Fame's 2006 class had its dissenters. Some stated that his reign as a Harlem numbers king while a Negro-league owner should have disqualified him. A Kansas City–based sportswriter decried him as "a notorious mobster," "a racketeer," a member of Schultz's mob, and the "No. 1 numbers man in Harlem." To such dissenters, that period in his life forever constrains the possibility of his redemption. In their view numbers kings were vultures who preyed on the dreams of the less fortunate in Harlem's black and Latino communities; a few attached that label to Pompez and his baseball career, claiming he also took advantage of the baseball aspirations of Latinos for his own gain. Grave inconsistency, complained some baseball enthusiasts, especially since the major leagues' all-time hit leader, Pete Rose, remained permanently ineligible due to his gambling on baseball. A reflection of the "hobgoblin of consistency" in Hall of Fame elections historically, wrote noted baseball historian John Thorn in a *New York Times* op-ed piece of Pompez's election while Rose remained barred.[1] Other dissenters disputed his impact within baseball, minimizing his contribution to two of the more significant transformations in U.S. professional baseball during the twentieth century: its integration and its Latinoization.

The biggest howl came from those disappointed that Buck O'Neil was not included in the 2006 class. Opinion pieces and editorials cried foul. *Sporting News* writer Dave Kindred labeled it "an outrage." Keith Olbermann's *Countdown* on MSNBC named the snubbing of O'Neil the number one story for its February 28 show. The same questions were asked repeatedly: How could the special committee elect seventeen Negro-league figures yet manage to leave out O'Neil? Worse yet, how could they include Pompez and not O'Neil? "Buck has a lot of fans on this committee," observed Ray Doswell, attempting to illuminate the difficult choices committee members faced. "I think even the people who didn't vote for him are his fans, but they decided to vote with their conscience and the high standards of the Hall of Fame." "Those high standards, by the way," Olbermann opined, "permitted them to yesterday elect Alex Pompez, a former racketeer in the Dutch Schultz crime family, who once owned the New York Cubans and later scouted for the New York Giants."[2] Thus, in lamenting O'Neil's exclusion Olbermann denigrated Pompez's inclusion, impugning him as one of Schultz's men, a mobster.

The *Countdown* host conferred his show's ignoble award of "Worst Person in the World" to the entire committee. In so doing, my name was drawn into the controversy. A lifelong baseball fan who played high school and collegiate ball before engaging in the scholarly study of baseball history, I never imagined finding myself in the middle of a Hall of Fame controversy. But there my name was, scrolling through on *Countdown* along with those of the other eleven committee members. A flurry of e-mails followed, many claiming a grave injustice had been done. An alumnus of my university expressed shame in sharing an affiliation. Some called us cretins and ignoramuses, while others used less colorful nouns.

The dissenters are wrong on both the numbers and the baseball fronts. To equate Pompez with Dutch Schultz as "notorious mobsters" or to insinuate the two were partners in crime is specious. Enjoying access to political fixers and those who roamed halls of justice in New York City that Pompez could only dream of as a black Latino, Schultz overtook Harlem's numbers scene with reckless abandon. Their modus operandi was distinct—so concluded the retired New York City police detective turned academic historian of black organized crime Rufus Schatzberg, who contended that Schultz and his coterie introduced gun violence into the numbers game in Harlem.[3] Not only did Schultz transform Harlem's numbers into something far more nefarious, he did so by paying off police and public officials with money generated from Harlem's numbers—an act that reminded Harlem residents that whiteness could engender privileges for even criminal kingpins. Simply put, Schultz and Pompez were not partners; they were not equals. The two years spent in Schultz's outfit after his hostile takeover represented the nadir of Pompez's involvement in both the numbers racket and professional baseball.

Dissenters are also off base on the baseball front; Pompez was the most significant force in the incorporation of Latino talent for much of the twentieth century. He was a trailblazer: his Negro-league teams expanded black baseball's talent pool beyond Cuba; he directly addressed the cultural barriers Latino players encountered through an innovative approach; he introduced the best lot of Latino players into U.S. professional baseball when one combines his time in the Negro leagues and the major leagues. Equally important, he took a different tack when it came to acquiring Latino players, this most evident in contrasting him with the Washington Senators. The major leagues' most active organization in Latin America during its segregated era, Washington merely extended Latino prospects a chance to break into organized baseball—no signing bonus and, typically, just a one-way ticket to a spring training tryout. Pompez offered Latino players much more. First as a Negro-league owner and then as a Giants scout, he attended to the cultural barriers that might hinder their success, whether it was making housing arrangements that sought to alleviate cultural isolation and foster greater familiarity with English or creating English-language classes for Latino prospects at Giants minor-league spring training in the early 1960s. He did not seek out Latinos as a cheaper source of talent; they were his central base. And he welcomed them all, from the darkest to the lightest. He even worked with organized-baseball insiders such as the Senators scout Joe Cambria to secure opportunities for Latinos to creep across the racial divide before organized baseball abolished its color-line system. Forged in his decades in the Negro leagues, this approach would make him the most successful recruiter of Latino talent in U.S. professional baseball.

Pompez may not have invented what we can label a "Latino" approach, but he perfected it within the baseball world, where it placed him at a distinct advantage. Largely shaped by the experience of growing up in the U.S. South and within the Cuban émigré community, he envisioned the Americas as a broad, interconnected cultural terrain where others saw hard and fast lines of separation. Thus, he went beyond strict allegiance to his Cuban nationality to reach out to others from throughout Latin America as he used his multicultural background and bilingual skills to acquire talent throughout the English- and Spanish-speaking Americas. This, I contend, was a key to his longevity in professional baseball, and why he was able to successfully reinvent himself several times, to have multiple rises and falls and, ultimately, redemption. His attention to what Latin Americans would encounter within—and beyond—the baseball world was driven by his own experience. He was not a foreigner in a strange land; he was native to the United States, familiar with its evolving social rules when it came to race and place.

Reaction to Pompez's election into the Hall of Fame among Negro leaguers who had played for him and those he had signed for the Giants was quite distinct from that of the dissenters. They saw recognition of their history and the honoring of a key participant within that history. "I'm glad Alex Pompez is going to the Hall of Fame," Felipe Alou, the San Francisco Giants' manager in 2006, declared to the *San Jose Mercury News*. "You have to know the man. The man was bigger than the numbers." "He was quite a man," Alou expounded in another interview. "He helped a lot of Latin players make the transition to baseball in America. I know he helped me." Juan Marichal was similarly effusive, telling New York *Daily News* sportswriter Bill Madden, "He was like a father to us all." Orlando Cepeda turned emotional when I asked him to reflect upon Pompez's enshrinement on the evening following the induction ceremony. "People just don't know how much he did for us," he explained. "How hard it was then and all he did to make sure we had a chance."[4] These players added nuance where others sought to impugn Pompez's character and paint him as a Schultz-type mobster. They knew the heart of the man; they understood he had endeavored to smooth their path into the Negro leagues and, later, the majors. It was the times, players from Rodolfo Fernández to Buck O'Neil himself told me over the course of my researching Pompez's story, in explaining his time as a Harlem numbers king. And most understood the context of that time: of the ubiquity of segregation; the resilience needed to press forward; the work involved in transforming America's game into an integrated institution. That history and what Pompez contributed to it is what these ballplayers understand far better than does the press or the fans angered by his enshrinement. It is that story—of the Harlem numbers king who ranked among baseball's greatest talent scouts and who facilitated the entry of the game's greatest generation: its integration pioneers—I hope these pages have done justice.

CUBAN STAR

PART I

RISING STAR

Cuban baseball magnate Abel Linares took great pride in his All Cubans team having been the first Cuban professional team to tour the United States, in 1899. Renamed the Cuban Stars in 1905, the team developed over the next decade into the most formidable and respected Cuban club in U.S. professional baseball. In fact, the success of Linares's Stars had done much to reclaim the Cuban name in baseball stateside, where the first documented "Cuban" team was the 1885 Cuban Giants, a team composed almost entirely of U.S.-born blacks.[1] So the news that Alex Pompez had launched another team that would operate under the "Cuban Stars" name justifiably sent Linares into a rage.

Feeling his brand name pirated and his market encroached upon, Linares moved into action. He sent an irate cable to Puerto Rican baseball promoter José Ezequiel Rosario, who had organized the slate of exhibitions for the upstart team. In it Linares claimed that his team was the "authentic" Cuban Stars and that history was on his side: his team had toured the United States first, and his squad was "the same that played in the Cuban championship and who traveled to the United States every year."[2] Rosario was quick to extend an invitation to Linares in the form of a challenge: the Puerto Ricans would host a game between the two Cuban Stars teams where they could battle for the rightful claim to the name. Ever confident, the Cuban entrepreneur accepted the challenge.

Linares arrived in Puerto Rico with his team, which was literally full of Cuban stars. The aggregation included future Hall of Fame pitcher José Méndez and slugging outfielder Cristóbal Torriente. It also included pitcher Adolfo Luque, who would go on to win nearly two hundred games in a twenty-year major-league career. Local promoters billed the match-up as one to determine the "authentic" Cuban Stars and "the imposters." The billing no doubt built up the excitement of the challenging team's owner, the brash young Cuban-American Alex Pompez. This was an unexpected moment to make an early impression with his newly formed lineup. Unlike Linares, few of his players had yet to establish themselves as stars in the Cuban League. Nor did they have extensive experience barnstorming in the States. For José María Fernández, Julio Rojo, Bernardo Baró, and Bartolo Portuando, among other talented finds of Pompez's, the subsequent tour of the States was their first year of many participating in the U.S. black baseball circuit.

The contest in San Juan was close. Despite the fact that Pompez's squad was still in the process of coalescing as a unit, his team delivered the victory over Linares's veteran club. Puerto Rican sportswriter Luisin Rosario described the game's significance: "After a great advertising campaign in the press came the clash between the 'authentics' and the 'imposters' with the disgrace for the 'authentics' who were defeated by the 'imposters' by a score of 3 to 2. With that defeat, the fear of the authentics increased considerably." Pompez's upstart team had gained a rightful claim to the Cuban Stars name and its twenty-six-year-old owner began to exhibit his flair for drama. An indignant Linares demanded a rematch. "Not enough time," Pompez coyly responded. His triumphant Cuban Stars had to set sail to start its inaugural campaign in the States; this year there would be two Cuban Stars teams touring the circuit.[3]

The son of a Cuban-born lawyer, Alex Pompez would travel a different path than his father when it came to their professions and social activities. His father, José González Pompez, participated in social and political circles that connected him directly to the father of the Cuban nation, José Martí, and other titans of the Cuban independence movement in the late nineteenth century; José Pompez also served in the Florida statehouse as an elected representative. His son would make his mark on history through participation as a Harlem numbers king and in operating a Negro-league professional baseball team for over thirty years. Much changed in the world from the time the father immigrated to the United States, was naturalized in 1879, and died in 1896 and the time his son would rise atop Harlem's sporting world. Jim Crow segregation emerged to characterize race relations in Florida, precluding the possibility that the son could follow in the footsteps of the father and serve in the statehouse. Cuba gained its independence from its Spanish colonial ruler, giving Cuban exiles and their progeny a choice of whether to return and rebuild the land of their ancestors or to make their futures in stateside communities. For those who chose to remain in Florida, the deterioration of race relations, along with worsening of economic conditions in the early twentieth century, would again raise the question of whether to migrate or remain. By 1910, Alex Pompez decided to leave Tampa behind and to cast his lot with those venturing not south to Cuba but north to Harlem.

Baseball would be there through it all for Pompez. The game was never too far away, reigning as the sport of choice among Cubans in Key West, where he was born, and in Tampa, where he lived through most of his adolescence. Time spent in Havana as a teenager "infected" him with the passion for the game. But rather than become a major player on the field, he was destined to succeed off the baseball diamond, first as a Negro-league team owner in New York and then as a scout for a major-league team. That he spent his first thirty-four years in professional baseball as an owner in the Negro leagues was telling of the opportunity available for Cubans of his background: someone who was more than Cuban, more than black.

The communities Pompez grew up in featured a mixture of anti-colonial politics, cigar-making, baseball, literature, and music that exposed them to the evolving sensibilities about what it meant to be Cuban, a Negro, and a first-generation U.S.-born Latino. The son of Cuban émigré parents came to count himself among "people of the darker races." In his day he was a Cuban Negro; today we might call him an Afro-Cuban-American. This meant often not fitting comfortably in either camp: too Cuban to garner the full acceptance of U.S.-born blacks; too much a "Negro" for lighter-skinned Cubans to unequivocally embrace him as one of their own. From entries in the U.S. Census to port-of-entry papers, official documents alternately described him as

Negro, Cuban, African, and black. He was a regular traveler between the United States and the Caribbean, and his citizenship status also caused confusion. Official papers would occasionally list him as a Cuban citizen; a few of these documents contained marginal notations that he was indeed a U.S. citizen. What was certain in his travels was that he was not confused with a white Cuban. Indeed, the possibility of achieving acceptance as white in Florida or elsewhere in the States remained closed off to the son of an educated, lighter-skinned Cuban father and a "mulatto" mother. He would have to make his own way, however he could.

1

ROOTS AND ROUTES

The crowd gathered at the dock in Key West buzzed with excitement as they awaited the arrival of their special invited guest aboard the steamer *Olivette*. Once José Martí was spotted disembarking from the *Olivette*, the marching band struck up the music and the crowd waved their Cuban flags. Among those greeting Martí stood José Francisco Lamadriz, veteran of Cuba's first war for independence and president of the Convención Cubano. The two engaged in a warm embrace with tears in their eyes. "I am embracing our past revolutionary efforts," Martí stated. "And I embrace our new revolution," responded Lamadriz.[1]

The joyous reception hid the labor a committee of local club leaders had put forward to bring about Martí's visit. A group of cigar factory workers had insisted Martí visit their community following his successful stay in Tampa, where he recruited support for his revolutionary organizational effort. Among those involved in organizing Martí's visit to Key West was José González Pompez, who had established himself within the Florida isle's circle of figures active in the Cuban independence movement. He along with other committee members solicited donations to cover the cost of Martí's trip to Key West by going door-to-door and visiting cigar factories. Their task of rallying interest in Martí's budding organization, Partido Revolucionario Cubano, involved more than the usual advocacy. For starters, only one of the committee members, Serafín Bello, was an established leader from one of the dozens of Cuban revolutionary clubs in Key West.[2] Moreover, the Key West community had seen leaders, glib speakers, and organizers come and go; each arrived with lofty goals, delivering speeches, and in need of a lot of financial support. Angel Peláez, the committee's elected president, described the heady days in preparation for the Cuban apostle's visit: "There was a difficulty, and that was the impossibility of the committee going to all the factories within a short time, because nearly all of the members were poor workers, [they were] on the committee in the spirit of patriotism and without pay. Each day meant for them a loss of one day's salary, which was their bread, the life of their family." Pompez intervened to provide a partial solution to the transportation issue committee members faced, supplying a *carretón*, a small mule-drawn cart, to carry the cigar workers as they traveled from factory to factory. Their effort definitely seemed worth it as they looked out onto the wharf and saw the cheering multitude greet the guest of honor.

For José Pompez, participation in the visiting committee was part of his contribution to *la causa* of freeing the island of his birth and from where he had fled Spanish colonial rule. He and other Cuban exiles came to see Key West as a democratic laboratory for what they desired for their native land. Unlike Cuba, Key West had an economy devoid of slavery and a political system that allowed all adult male citizens the opportunity to participate electorally. Florida laws on eligibility for voting, moreover, provided Cuban émigrés the possibility to practice their democratic rights of electoral participation. Requirements called for a declaration of intent to naturalize along with six months' residence for county elections and a year's residency to become eligible to vote in state elections.[3] Such possibilities had drawn Pompez to Key West after filing his declaration of intent on September 4, 1879.[4] Key West was where he would fall in love with and marry Loretta Mendoza Pérez and where the couple would start a family.

That baseball, the numbers, and cigars would largely impact the life of Alex Pompez is little surprise, considering the Cuban émigré communities of Key West and Tampa. In these communities Cubans forged a culture that was an amalgam, created through economic exchange and the flow of workers and entrepreneurs who adopted practices from different locations within the Americas. The result was a culture they claimed was distinct from that of their island's colonial rulers, Spain. A young Alex witnessed the migrations of Cubans between Cuba and Florida driven by mobilizations around nationalist insurgency, the rise and fall of cigar work at factories, and the emergence of baseball as the Cuban national game on sandlots in their *colonias* formed in the States. These events would shape his worldview and that of others as to the possibilities for individual and collective remaking, of participating in the making of something new, of becoming Cuban and fighting for one's own nation wherever one resided. Those lessons would be part of Pompez's inheritance from his father and those of his father's generation.

Baseball Takes Root

War and migration marked the span between 1868 and 1898 for Cubans. The Ten Years' War produced little tangible results for the insurgents. The Pact of Zanjón ended armed hostilities but produced a fragile peace. Upset that the pact did not abolish slavery, insurgent leaders Antonio Maceo and Calixto García, among others, refused to sign. Armed hostilities renewed on August 26, 1879. The Guerra Chiquita (Little War) that ensued also failed to yield independence, but it did produce the gradual abolition of slavery, a planned eight-year transition period from forced labor to free labor. Tens of thousands of Cubans who supported independence continued to flee the island's political turmoil in either self-imposed or government-ordered exile during this thirty-year span. These migrations included a number of families whose offspring would significantly impact Cuban baseball throughout the Americas.

Spanish ruling authorities, concerned with baseball's association with subversives, kept close tabs on the colony's baseball scene. The colonial government first banned baseball in 1869 but soon rescinded the ban. Another ban followed in 1873. After the Ten Years' War, authorities continued to suspect the game was more than a North American import and that it possibly served as paramilitary exercises preparing Cubans for battle against colonial forces. Lingering suspicions prompted officials to intensify monitoring of the game: all social organizations, including baseball clubs, were required to officially register to legally hold private meetings. In 1876, colonial authorities forbade the names Yara and Anacaona: the former invoked the Grito de Yara that initiated the Ten Years' War, the latter a Taina princess who resisted the first

Spanish arrivals to the island.[5] Cubans continued to embrace the game nonetheless. They took baseball wherever they migrated, forming baseball clubs and creating local amateur and semiprofessional teams. The Aloma brothers (Ignacio and Ubaldo) from Cienfuegos typified the way Cubans transported the game. In 1891, the brothers relocated their sugar plantation from Cuba to San Pedro de Macorís in the Dominican Republic. Once there, they organized the first two baseball clubs in the country. Cubans likewise spread the game to other parts of Caribbean, including the Yucatán region of Mexico and Venezuela.

Many Cubans would make Key West their home while the struggle for Cuban independence persisted. Individually and collectively, their actions unveiled the vaunted place baseball occupied in Cuban culture and its links to the insurgency.[6] A shift in cultural orientation among self-identified Cubans quickened in the late 1840s. Those supportive of national independence increasingly sent their children to educational institutions in the United States instead of Spain. Baseball subsequently arrived in Cuba in the early 1860s, before armed hostilities erupted between Cuban insurgents and Spanish colonial forces. Whereas in the United States the Civil War and military mobilization facilitated baseball's spread across the nation, the game's introduction in Cuba resulted from a migration of students who studied in the United States and transported baseball equipment and knowledge back to Cuba as part of the cultural baggage they acquired. Credited with introducing the first bat and ball to the island, Nemesio Guilló underscores this cultural shift within the Cuban elite. In 1858 Guilló arrived in Mobile, Alabama, to attend Springhill College. Six years later he returned to Cuba. Among the belongings the young man brought back was baseball equipment, which Cuban newspapers later described as "the first to be seen in Cuba."[7] Guilló was not alone. Dozens of Cubans learned to play the sport while pursuing their studies in the States. Esteban Bellán stood most prominent among them. A teenage Bellán arrived in New York City in 1865 to study at Rose Hill College (present-day Fordham University), where he earned the distinction of being the first Cuban to play college varsity baseball in the States in 1868 and three years later appeared as the first Latin American to play major-league ball when he joined the National Association's Troy Haymakers.

Further evidence that baseball had begun to sink deep roots within Cuban culture abounded. The game took root wherever Cuban émigrés migrated. In Key West, they formed their own league and received visits from island-based Cuban teams. A local league established in 1887 would include four teams: Azul, Punzó, Intrépido, and Progreso. The names gave a clear indication of the nationality and political stances of the émigrés, referring to the colors of the Cuban League's Habana (Azul) and Almendares (Punzó) and also to their fearless spirit and belief in progress. In 1888, the Island Habana baseball club visited Key West. But that squad was not the first Cuban team to pay a visit to the Cuban colony. Seven years early, the Fe baseball club had made the trip across the straits to play against the local competition.[8]

For members of Cuban émigré communities in Key West and elsewhere, baseball provided more than recreation and diversion; it helped define them as a people. Cubans viewed baseball as as much their game as that of the United States. Cuban nationalists envisioned baseball as an expression of their culture, one that distinguished them from the Spaniards who controlled Cuba. The baseball clubs they formed made their politics obvious, bearing names like Yara, Progreso, and América. Additionally, Cubans founded the baseball periodicals *El Score*, *El Baseball*, and *El Pitcher*, among others, which followed their budding baseball scene on the island, where a professional league took form in 1879, as well as in the émigré communities. The flurry of publications and the practice of exchanging information among journalists in the States and on the island allowed Cuban baseball enthusiasts to gain pride in the feats of their compatriots wherever they lived or played ball. Significantly, those on the island acknowledged the role of baseball in the émigré communities and its association with the nationalist cause. Aurelio Miranda, a founding member of the Habana baseball club, waxed poetic in proclaiming baseball would aid the nation-building process. "I always believed that baseball not only promised to promote the physical development of our youth and provide them a virtuous recreation . . . but that it would also serve other purposes—to form, for example, robust citizens adept at struggle."[9] That struggle aimed to make a Cuban society free of colonial domination; in the interim, they built communities in Key West, Tampa, New York, and elsewhere.

To Make Their World New

Life in Key West improved for the previously arrived Cuban émigrés
with each successive wave of arrivals. Walking its streets, they could
hear Spanish interspersed with English, smell the familiar aroma of
Cuban cuisine and cigars wafting through the air, and participate in
discussions of the latest developments in Cuba. With Havana a short
trip by steamship, in times of political tranquillity Cubans in Key West
would routinely make the ninety-mile trip south to spend their week-
ends visiting family and friends after purchasing goods unavailable
back home. This proximity contributed to Key West's becoming a favored destination. By 1885, the Cuban-born population in Key West
totaled 4,517, nearly a third of its 13,945 residents, but that number
did not include the children of Cuban émigrés like Alex Pompez who
were part of the first generation born in Key West.[10]

As their numbers grew, so did their possibilities. Cuban émigrés
established mutual aid societies and social clubs such as the Convención Cubano and Club San Carlos, which sustained community members in times of economic hardship and aided the recently arrived in
their period of adjustment. Although typically social in their orientation,
these organizations at times took a decidedly political tone, hosting
speakers who informed members of the latest developments within the
insurgency or labor activists who sought to organize the workers among
them. These clubs provided émigrés a space to envision a Cuba free of
Spanish colonial authority as well as to address their situation in the
United States.

Countless Cubans here constantly affixed their sights southward
and planned for how to achieve a free, democratic Cuba. Political dissi-
dents keyed in on this locale due to its geographical proximity to Cuba
and also its well-organized community of émigrés. By the 1890s, Key
West replaced New York City as the center of the leadership of the insurgency stateside. A large veteran military contingent called Key West
home, including seventeen generals from the Ten Years' War, two of
whom—Carlos Roloff and Serafin Sanchez—would lead the 1895 expedition that launched the third War for Independence in Cuba.[11]

The significance that nationalist leaders gave Key West's émigré
community was no clearer than when the Cuban Apostle himself, José

Martí, visited. Exiled from Cuba by the Spanish colonial government, Martí moved to New York City in 1881 and dedicated himself to organizing Cubans to overthrow the shackles of colonialism in their native land. His writings enlivened the dream of *Cuba Libre* and inspired a new generation of Cubans to join the cause; his essay "Nuestra América," published in January 1891, provided inspiration for insurgents old and new. His biggest challenge at this point was convincing the cadre of revolutionary leaders and veterans of the two previous wars for Cuban independence that his plan and organization was worth aligning themselves with in yet another push for war and independence. He understood that while he already had secured support from the communities in New York City and Tampa, the support of Key West Cubans was crucial to a project as ambitious as his: organizing the Partido Revolucionario Cubano (PRC, or Cuban Revolutionary Party) as the main organization mobilizing the Cuban independence movement. Cubans here had a political cachet and possessed the wealth to underwrite this project that would make reality his vision of a new Cuba free of Spain and that was "with all and for the good of all." The problem was that Cubans in Key West had already formed over sixty pro-independence groups.[12]

Following his welcoming reception at the dock in late December 1891, Martí met privately with some local leaders the first several days of his visit even though he was suffering from a cold and had been ordered by his doctor to take bed rest. On the night of January 3, Martí made his first public presentation at the Club San Carlos. Introduced by José Francisco Lamadriz, Martí continued trying to bridge the differences among the existing Key West groups that supported Cuban independence. He met with group leaders at the Hotel Duval and outlined the PRC's platform, hoping to sway to his new organization the Key West leaders already sympathetic to the cause of Cuban independence but who possessed their own ideas about how best to achieve that aim. On the last night of this historic first visit, the locals gathered at the Club San Carlos to fete Martí. Children recited poetry. Local dignitaries took their turn speaking to the gathering, including Serafin Bello, Génaro Hernández, and José Pompez. When those gathered finally put the PRC platform to a vote, the motion carried.[13]

Martí's visit aligned an important contingent of supporters from the Key West colony with his camp. In April, Key West supporters agreed to formally create a chapter of the Partido Revolucionario Cubano; its formation came just three months after the first chapter's creation in New York City. Those gathered elected officers and a board of directors. Indicative of his standing within the community and among the nationalist supporters, José Pompez was elected to the chapter's board of directors.

The intervening years in Key West had been quite good for him. A lawyer by training, he also possessed an entrepreneurial streak, operating a cigar factory that generated enough money to sustain a comfortable life and donate to Martí's cause. He had married Loretta Mendoza and the couple gave birth to their son Alejandro on May 3, 1890, and other children followed: Armando, Leonora, and José. Additionally, he had gained further prominence in the community, becoming part of an inner circle of Martí's confidants in Key West, included among those Martí wrote to and about in his private letters and in his published writings as the Cuban revolutionary leader sought to maintain the support of his vital Key West connections. These days were not all filled with joy, however. A February 1892 letter penned by Martí to the leaders of Key West PRC chapter noted that Pompez was grieving. Martí expounded on the tragedy that had caused Pompez's grief in an issue of *Patria* (the official PRC publication): "And now to the eloquent Pompez, the shrewd and builder Pompez, young and noble Cuban from Key West, has died the most recently born of the honorable man."[14] Grief at the loss of a child is handled in different ways; Pompez opted to pursue public service. Just months after his child had been buried, he successfully ran on the Republican ticket for a seat as a Monroe County representative in the Florida House of Representatives.

Pompez's election to the statehouse was emblematic of the high level of organization, political acumen, and nationalist loyalty among Cubans in Key West. Cubans had elected their own to local and state office for several reasons. First, located over six hundred miles away from the state capital in Tallahassee, Key West was literally and figuratively a world away. Second, the composition of the local population— about a third locally born "Conchs," another third Cuban émigrés, and a quarter Bahamians—made Key West unique among Florida's major cities: the sheer number of eligible Cuban voters made them a vital voting bloc. Four years earlier, rather than merely voting along party lines, Cubans had elected two of their own as Monroe County representatives to the statehouse. Third, Cubans prominent in the cigar industry in Monroe County and in Florida in general made wealthy Cuban cigar-factory owners valuable allies. Finally, Cubans came in a range of skin colors and, moreover, those who supported the Cuban revolutionary movement embraced a nonracial national identity that Martí espoused. These economic, political, and social factors complicated the efforts of "Redeemers," who sought to impose a hard Jim Crow color line that separated black and white based on skin color alone.[15]

The rookie legislator's participation in the 1893 Florida legislative session began on April 4 with taking the oath of office. Much of the first day was spent listening to the Speaker of the House welcome the legislators and partaking in procedural votes to fill various House posts such as chief clerk and chaplain. Assigned to the Public Health Committee, Pompez introduced bills and resolutions that included one on the qualifications of jurors and another on child labor. On April 10, he offered a resolution for the appointment of a committee "to inquire into the matter of fees collected by the Board of Health authorities of the port of Key West." The House adopted the resolution and named him one of the special committee's three members. The committee report he delivered called for equal treatment of arrivals at the ports in Key West, Tampa, and Jacksonville. (Fumigation rooms were still in use at Key West's port, where primarily Cubans entered, yet their use had stopped at the other ports.) The House formally adopted the report's findings and recommendations. On May 3, the House brought out of committee a child labor bill that Pompez proposed that aimed "to prevent minors under thirteen years of age from being employed in factories." With a few minor amendments the bill passed, 42–10. The next day the House leadership "indefinitely excused" him: he had traveled the longest way to get to Tallahassee and it was time to return to Key West to attend to his own affairs.[16]

Tampa Bound

On the heels of his time in the Florida House, José Pompez received an enticing offer to relocate his cigar operations and family to the Tampa area. About a decade earlier, in October 1885, Tampa area business

developers had successfully recruited cigar baron Vicente Martínez
Ybor to move his Key West–based operations north. Cigar factory
owners were hard-pressed to turn down cheap land and a guarantee of
labor peace—although the means through which labor peace was secured later raised eyebrows. The package the Tampa Board of Trade
offered was too good to pass up for Ybor: a subsidized purchase of forty
acres just northeast of Tampa proper. Due to its location, Ybor enjoyed
relatively free rein to build what equated to a company town and later
became incorporated as Ybor City. Hoping to avoid the labor strife
that afflicted his operations in Key West, Ybor offered cigar workers
what he deemed good wages and living conditions, including housing
employees could purchase at cost. The Cubans who moved to Ybor
City, and later West Tampa, would continue the practice of using baseball to maintain intimate ties to the island and to demonstrate their
ardent support for the liberation of Cuba. Incorporated in 1886, Ybor
City soon featured baseball diamonds in addition to its cigar factories,
worker cottages, and social club buildings. Ybor residents formed baseball clubs that ventured out of the neighborhood to challenge other
teams. On October 26, 1888, *The Tampa Morning Tribune* reported
the "first colored baseball game" had taken place the previous Monday
afternoon in Ybor City. The two Cuban teams made clear their identity
and politics through their names, Cuba and Porvenir (the Future). Their
contest occurred approximately a month after Ybor City hosted the
Layton baseball team on what the *Tribune* described as a "newly made
diamond one block in the rear of Pons [cigar] factory."[17]

José Pompez's cigar operation was never on par with Ybor's, but it
nonetheless attracted the attention of the West Tampa Development
Company. Desirous of developing land west of Tampa and Ybor City,
the company offered him two building lots in the West Tampa area
first surveyed in April 1892. The affordable price for the building lots
and their central location in West Tampa made the offer doubly attractive. Affordable housing made moving to West Tampa attractive for
cigar workers: hundreds of cottages, some costing as little as $400, that
could be purchased with a 20 percent down payment and on a monthly
installment were constructed. But life in West Tampa was rudimentary, not at all like life in Havana, New York City, or even Key West. In
Pompez's case, he completed the purchase of the West Tampa prop-

erty just off of Main Street for $1,000 in May 1894. His cigar factory was built there while local builder John Drew constructed a new house for his family, one of five luxurious residences Drew built that year, each costing more than three times the average for a worker's cottage.[18] Once settled in his new home, Pompez put his political acumen to work toward drafting the charter for the fledgling town. He worked with a group that completed the papers for incorporation. Official recognition of West Tampa came on May 18, 1895. West Tampa's population at its incorporation totaled 2,335; it would grow into the fifth largest city in Florida with 10,000 residents in less than twenty years. A month after incorporation, West Tampa held its municipal elections, in which Pompez won the city clerk position.[19]

In June 1896, José Pompez successfully won reelection; he held the position until his death later that year on November 12. Staunchly committed to Martí, the PRC, and the ongoing War for Independence in Cuba, he bequeathed his estate to the insurgency. This last powerful gesture left his widow Loretta having to lean on the local Cuban community in Tampa and her parents in Key West for support.[20] The loss of his father created a considerable void in young Alex's life; the legacy set by his father's example in life and death cast a shadow that would loom over him. His father's election to the Florida statehouse was notable for its timing, occurring as members of the Democratic Party perpetrated extreme acts of racial terror and intimidation to suppress black participation in the electoral process.

Pompez's father had been a product of a particular generation; exiled from their native lands for their belief in democracy and freedom, they engaged in a sustained anticolonial struggle. They did not stop living because Spanish colonial rulers compelled them to leave the island for their pursuit of a free Cuba. This drove men like José Pompez to remake themselves while they engaged in a cause larger than themselves. The donation of his estate to the Cuban insurgent movement demonstrated a commitment to a greater cause than just the individual and family.

Further indicative of the place that *Cuba Libre* had in the hearts of the generations of Cuban émigrés, the liberal mixing of politics and baseball increased as the nationalist insurgency gained support in the early 1890s. Many local institutions in Cuban communities served as vital centers for raising funds for the insurgent Cuban army—what they called Ejército Mambí. Games organized by supporters of the insurgency occasionally featured political speeches by José Martí, Antonio Maceo, and other nationalist leaders. One Cuban exile, Emilia de Córdoba, made this mixture explicit, and is credited with initiating the practice of using baseball games to raise funds for the insurgent movement. Such games also provided cover for recruiting men willing to take up arms or fill other roles for the cause.[21] Key West native Agustín "Tinti" Molina was such a man; his actions highlighted how embedded baseball was within the insurgency and nationalist Cuban culture. In early January 1895, Cuban insurgent leaders in Florida devised a plan to communicate to fellow leaders on the island the signal to launch their military offensive and initiate the revolution. The plan required smuggling the message rolled up in a cigar from West Tampa to Cuba. According to lore, leaders selected Molina as the smuggler in this covert operation. A skilled ballplayer who would later play professionally in the States and in Cuba, Molina traveled to the island under the pretext of playing several games for the Matanzas team in the Cuban League. Once his purpose was accomplished, he returned stateside; his next visit to Cuba would occur as part of an expedition of armed insurgents in the War for Independence.[22]

Involvement in subversive activities against Spanish colonial rulers typically resulted in drastic punishment for those arrested. Emilio Sabourín learned this in 1895. An established figure in Cuban baseball, Sabourín belonged to the Habana Base Ball Club and had participated in the first officially recognized game on the island in 1874. Arrested for involvement in the theft of ammunition from a Spanish government storage facility in Cuba and for funneling profits from Cuban League operations to the independence movement, colonial authorities sentenced him to twelve years behind bars. Imprisoned in a dank Spanish prison in Ceuta, on the northern coast of Morocco, he died less than three years later.[23] Luis Someillan did not suffer such a grim outcome, but he was likewise tried and imprisoned for crimes against the Spanish colonial government. An amateur player in his youth, Someillan was partly educated in the States and became a naturalized U.S. citizen. In the 1890s, he operated a tobacco concern in Havana that exported to cigar makers in Key West. In January 1896, he and other suspects were arrested in Havana for insurrectionary activities. He did not meet a sympathetic judicial tribunal. Early in January 1897 he was tried, convicted, and ultimately sentenced to life in prison on the Isle of Pines; he was released on November 23, 1897.[24]

The link between baseball and insurgency became even more visible once the war began in earnest in 1895 as thousands enlisted in the insurgent army; others provided material support. In Ybor City, a local periodical *La Pelota* covered both sport and politics and forwarded all proceeds to the Partido Revolucionario Cubano.[25] The lineups of teams in Tampa, Key West, and Cuban communities elsewhere contained many names of individuals who later willingly exchanged their bats and gloves for guns and bullets to fight the Spanish. They and others further embedded baseball into Cuban national culture, reaffirming the bond linking Cubans on the island with émigrés living in Key West, Tampa, Philadelphia, and New York City. Moreover, it made baseball little different than music and literature produced by Cubans during this time, cultural forms and practices that served as a connective membrane whereby they maintained their "Cuban-ness" and demonstrated their commitment to one day return to their island free of Spanish colonial rulers.

Seasons of Change

For Alex and the West Tampa Cuban community, the death of José Pompez was yet another in a series of losses—losses that followed good news. Less than six months after celebrating his reelection as city clerk, José Pompez was being interred. A day after the Florida state government officially recognized the charter for the city of West Tampa word arrived from the Cuban battlefront: José Martí had fallen in the Battle of Dos Ríos in Oriente Province. The Apostle was lost; the War for Independence would drag into a third year with seemingly little headway. In April 1898, U.S. troops would intervene, transforming the war into its own "Spanish-American War" and quickly dispatching the Spanish military forces. A truly independent Cuba would not come into being for quite some time, however. The U.S. military occupied Cuba until 1902, leaving only after the Cuban constitutional assembly included the Platt Amendment into its new constitution. The terms of the Platt Amendment called into question whether Cuba was truly an independent nation, stipulating that Cuba could not enter into peace treaties with another country, that the United States could intervene militarily in Cuban affairs on its own behest, and that the Cuban president could call for U.S. military assistance when the need arose.

The social changes that transpired in Tampa over the next decade made life more difficult for those who were black, brown, or Cuban—or any combination of the three. On the one hand, growing up in Tampa exposed a young Alex to the world of cigars, baseball, gambling, community-level organizing, and politics. On the other hand, he and other Cubans experienced a sea change when it came to social relations as the color line gained even greater significance for U.S.-born blacks and foreign-born Cubans and their progeny living in Tampa. Where exactly Cubans stood collectively along the color line was not a settled question. Prior to 1900s, an individual's location along the color line was open to negotiation if you were Cuban, especially if you were lighter-skinned, came from some means, or retained significant aspects of Cuban culture that others saw as foreign. This created opportunities for Cubans often unavailable to U.S.-born blacks. The local baseball scene underscored this difference. By 1894 Afro-Cubans in Tampa had organized a traveling baseball club that faced black baseball teams in the region as well as participated in interracial contests against local Italian teams or other white Tampa-area squads. Yet, in reality, just about every Cuban baseball game was already an interracial affair. Cubans drew little distinction when it came to color and playing baseball; it was when they ventured beyond the friendly confines of Ybor City or West Tampa that the color line really came into play.[26] Jim Crow laws made life difficult for all those who were not accepted as white, which contributed to a growing rift between light-skinned Cubans and Afro-Cubans. Equally significant, the patriotic struggle that had once bonded Cubans together no longer existed after the United States had routed the Spanish. Beliefs in racial difference—which had been "deliberately obscured" in the push for national independence—percolated to the surface. Thereafter it was not just a matter of where you stood but also who was willing to stand by you when it came to race and the color line.[27]

Thousands of émigrés left Tampa and returned to Cuba in the years following the end of Spanish rule. Many returned hopeful of rebuilding their homeland ravaged most recently by three years of warfare. Those who stayed in Tampa turned their attention to more immediate concerns. The Supreme Court's decision in *Plessy v. Ferguson* (1896) had given legal sanction to the practice of "separate but equal." Whites in the South could now freely enact Jim Crow laws to segregate public institutions; private organizations and institutions could continue to racially discriminate without fear of legal reprisal. The *Plessy* decision legalized practices already under way in Florida. A year before the *Plessy* rendering, the Florida legislature passed a law barring integrated public schools: offenders could be fined up to $100. The new law affected Alex Pompez and other Cuban children in West Tampa who were just entering school. Two weeks after the Florida law went into effect, Fernando Figueredo, superintendent of West Tampa schools and head of the local PRC chapter, applied for public funding for the school Cubans operated out of Céspedes Hall. However, the school was viewed as violating state law, since it did not rigidly distinguish color within its student body. Figueredo was forced to withdraw the funding request and operate the school privately as an integrated institution.[28]

Fractures within Tampa's Cuban community became more readily apparent as Jim Crow further encroached on their daily lives. Social clubs once united in the struggle for Cuban independence split along racial lines. In October 1900, lighter-skinned Cubans left El Club Nacional Cubano, producing speculation, then as now, about the motivation for their departure. Formed the previous October, the club had welcomed Cubans of all colors; but less than a year later the group splintered. Were the lighter-skinned Cubans attempting to draw an important distinction with Cubans who clearly had African ancestry for Floridians concerned with distinguishing between white and black? Was their departure an open declaration of an underlying racial belief they had suppressed while working together to liberate Cuba? Whatever the reason, the effect was the same: Afro-Cubans were left on their own to navigate the color line and Jim Crow in Tampa.[29]

Within the year, Tampa's Afro-Cubans formed Sociedad de Libre Pensadores de Martí-Maceo, later called La Union Martí-Maceo, which evolved into a crucial institution for the Afro-Cuban community.

Martí-Maceo addressed matters of insurance, health care, and labor benefits for its members, who were mostly cigar workers. It also served as a key point of distinction from African Americans: U.S.-born blacks were ineligible for membership. Medical benefits offered members treatment in Cuba if certain medical services were unavailable in Tampa. Given the ubiquity of segregation in Tampa, this gave Afro-Cubans the option of avoiding the use of Tampa's segregated black hospital, the Clara Frye Hospital, and instead traveling to Cuba for medical treatment. Such benefits bolstered membership, which grew to over three hundred by 1910.[30]

Interestingly, the formation of a baseball team, the Cuban Giants, was among the first actions taken by Martí-Maceo. Although the club was short-lived, baseball flourished throughout Tampa, exposing locals to the increasing significance of the racial divide in Tampa's baseball circuit and beyond. As one Afro-Cuban resident remembered, "Every single factory had a team at one time, but no colored, just white. Now, if you were white and you was a good ball player, they would sign you up in the cigar factory in order to play. But a Negro, no."[31]

Opportunities would open for Afro-Cubans in semiprofessional and professional baseball in the decades that followed, especially as efforts to formally organize black baseball into national Negro leagues succeeded. Increased exchange between black baseball clubs in the States and touring Cuban baseball teams from the Island bolstered those organizational efforts. In these years, Tampa and other Florida towns became stopping points for Cuban teams conducting tours of the United States. This gave the Pompez family and other Tampa residents the opportunity to witness the All Cubans team and other clubs.[32] Exchange within the budding professional circuit exposed Cuban players to the formidable barriers that prevented their entry into the major leagues. They, like most Cubans born in stateside communities, would perform primarily in the black professional circuit; perceptions of their racial roots would impact the routes that they could travel within U.S. professional baseball.

The Route to Harlem

Dealing with the loss of her husband and now tending to her children alone, Loretta Pompez moved her family to Key West to live with her parents, Tomás and Cecilia Mendoza. The move provided the stability any loving mother desires for her young children, and she had four in tow: her youngest son, José; her lone daughter, Leonora; Armando; and her eldest, Alex. Her father, who had become a naturalized U.S. citizen in 1868, still worked as a cigar maker and owned the home where Loretta as well as her sisters Juana and Tomasa all resided.[33] In 1902 she decided to try out family life in Havana, as the Cuban Republic had finally came into being. Spending part of his teen years in Havana, Alex would later claim, "infected [me] with baseball's atmosphere that was ingrained in the Republic."[34] His destiny in baseball would not be on the field. Nor would Havana keep his interest for too long; no place did during his teen years.

From 1902 to 1910 Alex moved regularly between Havana, his grandparents' home in Key West, and Tampa. A May 28, 1904, trip on the steamer SS *Mascotte* took him from Havana to Key West. Listed on the ship's manifest of passengers as sixteen—an indication the fourteen-year-old was not above manipulating his age—he had already begun working as a cigar maker. The manifest also captured the racial confusion that he would deal with throughout his adult life: rather than list him as Cuban, the manifest had his race as African. Four years later he traveled aboard another ship to Tampa. This time he returned with his brother Armando, and the two found work as cigar makers and lived as boarders in Ybor City.[35]

The Cuba that Alex had left behind had made only halting progress in fulfilling Martí's vision of a nation "with all and for the good of all." Economic opportunities were unevenly available on the island. Years of pent-up frustration with the leaders of the Cuban Republic failing to deliver a "rightful share" contributed to Afro-Cuban veterans along with leading political and social figures organizing the Partido Independiente de Color (Independent Party of Color, or PIC) in 1908. Since it identified race as an organizing principle, some Cubans viewed this political party as a radical departure from the social compact about race, nation, and politics. Within the year the Cuban government banned the organization of political parties along lines of race or class. Tensions increased over the ensuing year, and a "race war" would erupt in May 1912. Over the three months that followed, Cuban military forces and armed groups of white vigilantes slaughtered an estimated five thousand to six thousand Afro-Cubans.[36] The campaign of racial terror white Cubans exacted on Afro-Cubans, regardless of any actual affiliation with the PIC, demonstrated that Cuba was not quite the place for Pompez or others who might organize or participate in organizations as both black and Cuban.

Violence against labor organizers and others who refused to "know their place" that accompanied the rise of Jim Crow increased in the first decades of the twentieth century. Tampa's cigar industry had always stood apart from the rest of the local economy and had seemed impervious to the evolving racial order. The experts in its cigar manufacturing sector, Cubans had proven indispensable to the industry and were thus able to institute a wage scale for cigar workers that "depended on skill rather than color."[37] The industry was nonetheless riddled with recurring labor strife. This occurred partly because the labor force ranked among the best-informed groups of workers anywhere. Implementing a practice cigar makers imported from Cuba, the workers at the cigar factory hired a *lector* (reader) who read the latest newspapers, political tracts, and classical literary texts while they worked, thus keeping them abreast of the latest labor struggles in Florida and beyond.[38]

An underlying tension within labor relations lingered in Tampa after the enticement of Vicente Martínez Ybor's cigar factory to the city. Local business leaders, politicians, and police officials had promised labor peace, by whatever means necessary. A vigilante-style repression quelled a cigar worker strike in 1901 as fifteen union leaders were kidnapped under cover of darkness and taken to Honduras; this was the fulfillment of the promised labor peace. In this instance, the vigilantes were led by prominent white political and business figures, including D. B. McKay, owner of the *The Tampa Daily Times*. The vigilantes thus succeeded in breaking the strike organized by La Resistencia (the resistance), a locally organized labor union that was pushing for a closed shop. That same year the whites-only primary was declared legal in the state, enabling the white Democratic Party to take control of Florida state politics.[39] Efforts to suppress the black vote would take on a new dimension in 1908. A group of white political figures formed the White Municipal League, whose central purpose was to "prevent the future operation of the Negro vote as a balance of power in municipal elections." On the morning of the 1910 municipal election, *The Tampa Morning Tribune* reported that candidates no longer had to "go down into the dives of the 'Scrub' [the black community] to hobnob with the festive colored brother on his own ground, to 'fight the devil with fire' by resorting to money, used in the most shameful way, as a means of securing the bulk of the Negro vote."[40]

A July 1910 strike brought matters to a head once again. Composed of some of Tampa and West Tampa's most prominent white citizens, vigilante committees unleashed another violent barrage that forced cigar makers back to work without any concessions. The message could not have been clearer: there would be no collective bargaining, as the local authorities would serve as "neutral arbiters." While some cigar workers returned to the cigar factories dejected, others opted to leave the area for New York or return to Cuba. The lynching of several Italians involved in the unionization efforts proved a tipping point. In the area's racial politics, Italians and Cubans were Latin "cousins," and some white locals viewed both groups as little better than "Negroes." If Italians were subject to lynch law in Tampa, then a mulatto Cuban who opposed segregation surely would be similarly subject to southern-style vigilante justice.[41]

Segregation had become ubiquitous throughout northern and central Florida. Even before José Pompez moved his family to West Tampa, African Americans already had their own neighborhood, the Scrub, separate from Tampa's white residents. The Scrub lay between Tampa's commercial center and Ybor City; West Tampa was developed two miles farther west of Ybor City. Although not as rigid, the living situation for Cubans developed its own form of segregation that was no less powerful than what U.S.-born blacks encountered. While Ybor City's master plan for housing lacked a provision for a "Negro section," a section where black Cubans predominated would nonetheless emerge by the 1910s.

Born in Ybor City in 1919, Evelio Grillo vividly recalled the circumstances of growing up in Tampa as someone who was black, Cuban, and American. Grillo and other darker-skinned Cubans attended "black" schools, worshipped at different churches, and joined different mutual aid societies than their lighter-skinned compatriots. Ethnic boundaries between African Americans and black Cubans in Tampa were "deliberately sharpened" despite increased interactions. Cubans learned where the lines existed from both personal experience and the collective knowledge passed down by relatives and neighbors. That is to say that race entered into life differently for Afro-Cubans and U.S.-born blacks, but it did so just the same. Racial discrimination in Ybor was subtle, as in Cuba, consisting of "behaviors and attitudes that likely would have escaped the notice of white southerners in Tampa."[42]

Historical generations, social class, and family background separated Pompez and Grillo, affecting the possibilities they envisioned as individuals. The ideology of the Cuban independence movement instilled the idea of collaboration across racial lines toward building a new and better society in the Tampa of Pompez's youth. A generation later Grillo grew up in a Tampa where Jim Crow segregation had gained legal standing, lighter-skinned Cubans had for the most part deserted institutions they once shared with their darker-skinned compatriots, and the state's Republican Party had abandoned black Floridians and their campaign for civil rights.[43] Increased racial violence accompanied limited opportunities for blacks. "Our choices became clear," Grillo wrote in his memoir, "to swim in black American society or drown in the Latin ghettos of New York City, never to be an integral part of American life."[44] Pompez's upbringing, cultural capital, and political generation combined for him to imagine and pursue possibilities in New York City that Grillo considered untenable a generation later.

Pompez had initially found stability during this return to Tampa, even joining La Union Martí-Maceo as a dues-paying member in 1910. However, when a general strike among cigar workers brought the industry to a halt with little prospect for a favorable resolution, he sensed the time was right for him to leave not just Tampa but the state as well. No longer a teenager, and with conditions in Tampa worsening, he decided to join the wave of black migrants who headed north to New York City. He soon entered a Harlem in its initial stages of flourishing into a black cultural mecca. Living the formative years of his youth in Tampa, Key West, and Havana had greatly informed his identity and outlook while also inculcating in him a passion for baseball. It is little surprise that when he migrated to New York City as an adult, he quickly immersed himself in the masculine world of cigar makers, baseball, and gambling.

Unlike Evelio Grillo, a fellow black Cuban and native son of Tampa, the twenty-year-old Pompez was willing to see if he could avoid "drowning" in the "Latin ghettos" of New York and make it. He again found employment as a cigar maker, earning $20 a week. Shortly after, he opened a cigar store and initiated his participation in the numbers.[45] He also established a relationship with Nathaniel "Nat" Strong, the leading booking agent in the New York metropolitan area for baseball and other sports. The opportunities seemed boundless for him to mix his love for baseball with a business acumen he somehow had inherited from his father. Tampa and its virulent race relations felt worlds away. Harlem presented him with the chance to remake himself from mere cigar maker to entrepreneur, numbers king, and sports mogul. There he could become more than the son of a patriot: he could himself become El Cubano—"the Cuban"—a Harlem numbers king.

2

MAKING HARLEM HOME

We, as a committee of law-abiding citizens of the United States of Spanish extraction, wish to make a vigorous protest against malicious and libelous attacks made on our group in a signed article by Edgar M. Gray [*sic*] published last week and called "The Spanish Menace in Harlem."

We feel that the Negro press is striving to bring about amity among all races *and particularly the darker races* with the native American Negro. But publications of such articles as the one mentioned above only creates disharmony between native American Negroes and Spanish speaking people in this country. The charges made against us comes [*sic*] from a man who has some grievance against an individual of the Spanish race and it was hate that aroused this outburst.

We do not care to answer individually the many vile and malicious charges made against us but would say that we, like the American Negroes, ask that the whole Spanish group in New York be not judged by the conduct of a few individuals.

(signed)
Alexander Pompez,
Chairman.

Harlem residents who purchased the January 28, 1928, edition of the *New York Age* found Pompez's letter on its front page. Written on behalf of "Spanish-speaking people," the public letter was a response to "Spanish Menace in Harlem" by Edgar M. Grey, a West Indian journalist whose article had appeared in another Harlem paper, *The American and West Indian News*. That article "made the blanket charge that this particular group of citizens were un-American in their practices and in a large degree responsible for immoral conditions in Harlem."[1] A multipronged response to sway public opinion in Harlem ensued. The local community formed a committee and selected Pompez as its chair. In the days following the publication of Grey's article, Pompez—along with several other prominent Latinos—visited the *New York Age*'s offices in Harlem. Committee members decided to submit a public letter of protest to the paper; publisher Fred Moore, a longtime associate of Pompez, ensured it would get published.

Pompez underwent a significant evolution in his first two decades in Harlem. From a young cigar maker who arrived with little more than his name, he evolved into someone members of Harlem's Spanish-speaking community turned to for leadership in a moment of public crisis. How exactly did he earn the respect of fellow Latinos in Harlem? How was he successful in transforming himself into someone to know, someone with the social capital to have their collective grievance heard? And how did he make Harlem the home that neither Tampa nor Key West would be for him? The answers to these questions lie partly in how Harlem was a place of liberation for him. Over the next four decades he contributed to the making of black Harlem's cultural milieu through his wide-ranging activities, which included operating a highly successful numbers bank, owning black baseball teams and restaurants, and promoting boxing matches and other sporting events. The manner in which he operated his enterprises received occasional criticism for seeking to minimize what others saw as important distinctions between blacks and whites, "Negroes" and "Latins," U.S. and foreign-born. Yet his approach created commercial opportunities for him that others in either the numbers scene or the professional baseball world did not fully explore.

Living in Harlem provided a chance to try to escape the shadow cast by his father and those of his generation—of selfless sacrifice for *la causa* of *Cuba Libre*. Yes, Cuba was now free; yet the racial climate in Cuba in the first decade of the Republic had proven inhospitable for those organizing along the lines of race. Tampa was little better in the early decades of the twentieth century. Campaigns of racial violence and intimidation there likewise sought to put blacks in "their place," and as the Jim Crow regime hardened the color line's impact, it became less and less significant whether or not one was a black Cuban. This, combined with the repression of labor activism among cigar workers, prompted a steady stream of Afro-Cubans migrating to New York.

Going north to Harlem offered an escape for hundreds of thousands of blacks fleeing the entrenchment of Jim Crow segregation in the South and in search of better economic prospects. The number of foreign-born blacks grew dramatically as the overall black population in New York City—and more specifically Harlem—surged. At the start of the twentieth century New York City's black population totaled 60,000, including 5,000 who were foreign-born. By 1930 its black population skyrocketed to 328,000, with the majority residing in Manhattan (224,000) and nearly a fifth of these being foreign-born (40,000).[2] The flow into Harlem was indeed multidirectional. Here immigrants from the Spanish- and English-speaking Caribbean, such as Arturo "Arthur" Schomburg and Countee Cullen, respectively, came across migrants from the U.S. South like James Baldwin as well as native black New Yorkers. Their reasons for heading north to Harlem differed. Collectively, their movement and settlement made Harlem a nodal point in the African diaspora where black people from throughout the Americas confronted questions about the meaning of blackness, community, and national identification in new ways.

Setting Up Shop

New York truly represented a new beginning for Pompez. When he arrived in 1910, the heart of Harlem's black life was centered in the 130s. That decade saw Harlem welcome black luminaries such as W.E.B. Du-Bois, James Weldon Johnson, Madame C. J. Walker, Claude McKay, and Marcus Garvey, among others from throughout the Americas.[3] A steady stream of Cubans also migrated from Ybor City. The hub of the community they built was just north of Central Park, from 110th Street to 115th Street between Lenox and Lexington avenues. There Afro-Cubans remade their lives away from southern-style segregation, yet here they encountered the peculiar northern form of de facto segregation.

In Pompez's case, he was young, unattached, and no longer under the ominous shadow of Jim Crow and its legal or extralegal enforcers, such as the Night Riders who stole away black or outside "agitators." Cigar making was his skill; his easy, self-assured manner inspired the confidence of others; his ambition opened doors. The timing of his arrival enabled him to enter the numbers game and the formal Negro baseball leagues on the ground floor. The two enterprises were cottage industries for black Harlem and would become inextricably linked, as numbers money would largely underwrite the two longest-lasting Negro-league franchises to play in New York City: the New York Black Yankees and Pompez's own Cuban Stars (later renamed the New York Cubans).

The numbers game emerged as a major economic institution in Harlem in the 1920s. The exact date of its introduction to New York City remains open to debate, but the process of its spread and the general actors involved are rather well established. Nearly all accounts credit Caribbean Latinos and West Indian immigrants for popularizing the numbers. A Dominican named Carlos Duran, known locally as Dominique, is celebrated in one version for introducing the game in 1913. Perhaps more significant, Dominique brought blacks and Latinos into the fold, with a veritable who's who of Harlem's numbers barons either trained by or associated with Dominique: Casper Holstein, Stephanie St. Clair, Ellsworth "Bumpy" Johnson, and Pompez.[4] Credited as "the man who really invented the numbers game" by the *Baltimore Afro-American*, El Catalán (Floretino Hernández) stood among the earliest to convert a *bolita* operations to the numbers, operating in Harlem's "Spanish quarters," below 116th Street on the East Side. Hernández's customers were skeptical. Insisting that their chances of winning had been reduced, they left and his business floundered. Yet others who previously ran *bolita* followed El Catalán's lead and started their own numbers banks. With Dominique and El Catalán at the forefront, the heavy involvement of Latinos in the rise of the numbers led to its popular name as the "Cuban" or "Spanish" lottery.[5]

Familiarity with the numbers game and its antecedent *bolita* came from Pompez's having grown up in the Tampa area. Although gambling was illegal in the Tampa of his youth, *bolita* was so pervasive in Ybor City that some described it as Ybor's second industry. The game's payoff fueled its popularity: a winning nickel bet would yield $8. A key distinction between *bolita* and the numbers stood in the drawing of a winning number. In *bolita*, a selected individual would stick his hand in a bag filled with balls numbered from 1 to 100 and grab one ball; then someone else would cut the bag, allowing the other balls to scatter onto the ground. Numbers bankers developed a more sophisticated means of determining a winner, using printed results from the Clearing House exchange or results from horse races at a predetermined racetrack. The local *bolita* operation provided a rudimentary template for the structure of a numbers operation: wagers made at barbershops, beauty salons, saloons, candy shops, and grocery stores; a central banking center for collating wagers and money collected; organization of jobs, from the local collector to the banker.[6]

Pompez arrived just in time for the introduction of the numbers game to Harlem; his participation in the business continued the connection between cigars, the numbers, and baseball. He opened a cigar store on Seventh Avenue and his numbers operations grew steadily, from collecting $600 in daily wagers in the early days to taking in between $7,000 and $9,000 daily in 1932.[7] During this span he evolved into one of a group of Harlem numbers kings who collectively controlled the majority of bets and territory.

Numbers bankers and their subordinates were expected to abide by an unwritten code of conduct to secure the public trust in their individual operations and in the overall enterprise. Bankers had to be viewed as trustworthy; bettors had to be confident bankers would not welsh on the payouts. Operated similar to the modern pick-three lottery, bettors picked a number from 000 to 999, wagering from as little as a penny up to several dollars. (Some bankers were unwilling to take bets larger than a dollar because they were fearful of a large payout.) Winning numbers paid off at a rate of 600 to 1; a nickel wager could mean $30, which could cover a month's rent and other living expenses. The remaining money went to cover the bank's operating costs: employee salaries, "protection" to police and city officials, and profit. Numbers banks typically accepted bets six days a week, operating just over three hundred days a year.[8]

The numbers shaped the pace of a day in Harlem: from the closing of bets at 10:00 a.m., to the publication of the results in the Clearing

House in the afternoon papers, to the paying out of winnings in the early evening hours. Writer Winthrop Lane captured the powerful hold the numbers had on the daily rhythms, describing a woman scouring the day's newspaper while riding the subway after a day's work. "Turning the pages hastily, she seems to be hunting for a particular place. . . . Finding an item, she gazes closely at it for a moment, and then throws the paper onto the seat beside her. She has a dejected look." The woman's hasty search for the closing number posted by the Clearing House illuminates one way numbers bankers sought to inspire confidence that their game was not fixed: numbers barons could not fix the closing numbers of that institution. Determining the winning number from posted results in the Clearing House involved its own intricacy. Lane explained how the system worked: "Suppose the exchanges were $793,482,450 and balances $86,453,624. She is then interested in the number 936, because that is made up of the seventh and eighth digits, reading from the right, of the first, and the seventh digit of the second."[9]

The numbers provided partial or full employment to scores of Harlemites. At its peak in the mid-1930s, nearly thirty thousand were employed, according to the *Amsterdam News*.[10] A variety of jobs existed within a numbers operation: Runners carried messages between the bank and other employees. Slip collectors took in the bets written on "policy slips": the slips had the number being played, the amount wagered, and the bettor's initials. The "bag man" collected the money wagered. Banks avoided having the same person collect slips and money to avoid an immediate connection if stopped by police. Lookouts patrolled the territory, watching for police or for enforcers from other banks. Enforcers (the "muscle") ensured that employees did not cut into the money collected or being paid out and protected their employer's territory from encroachment by other numbers bankers. A trusted few worked directly in the banks, counting the money taken in and doling out the winnings. Then there were the most trusted individuals, who served as "lieutenants" (controllers) and were often a sounding board for the banker.[11]

Getting into the Game

In addition to opening his cigar store, Pompez found work with Nat
Strong in his booking agency. The president of Inter-City Baseball
Association, Strong enjoyed an advantageous position that came partly
from his friendship with New York Giants owner Andrew Freedman
and other political movers in Tammany Hall. The practical knowledge
and political connections of the established sports promoter made him
the best possible tutor for Pompez. Strong taught the young Cuban-
American the details involved in sports promotion, soliciting potential
opponents for teams using the agency, securing venues, and scheduling
games. The two thus struck a mutually beneficial relationship, one that
allowed Pompez to partake in his lifelong love, baseball. Each possessed something the other needed.[12] Pompez offered Strong better
access to Latino markets in New York and the Caribbean that Strong
had yet to cultivate successfully. His Spanish-language skills allowed
him to handle dealings with Cuban teams seeking bookings through
Strong's agency during their tours of the States. It also permitted Pompez to expand the scheduling portfolio of Strong's teams to include
locations outside the continental United States. This part of their relationship drew dividends when Strong's Brooklyn Royal Giants toured
Puerto Rico for the first time after the 1916 season.[13]

Strong established his dominant position within the New York
baseball scene early in the twentieth century. From the 1920s onward,
he wielded almost dictatorial control over booking the open dates at
New York's major-league venues: Yankee Stadium, Ebbets Field, and the
Polo Grounds. Assured of receiving a cut from all Negro-league events
held at these venues, Strong was resented by most operating black baseball teams and semiprofessional clubs. He was not a disinterested party
in booking games. The Irish-American operated both the white semiprofessional Brooklyn Bushwicks and the black Brooklyn Royal Giants.
He would often hear complaints from his competitors that he saved
the best dates for his teams while charging excessive fees to serve as
booking agent. This fueled mistrust toward Strong throughout black
baseball circles. Owners and the press questioned the extent of his
commitment to helping black baseball flourish in the East and whether
he actually was using his privileged position and booking agency in a

quest for singular control of the eastern baseball scene. For the aspiring sports promoter recently arrived from Tampa, however, Strong offered a pathway into the business of baseball and sports promotion—and a way to use profits from his numbers operations in more legitimate ventures.

The Cuban Stars team that visited Puerto Rico in 1916 and later toured the States represented Pompez's first professional assemblage. Just like other black baseball operators, he relied on Strong's agency to secure bookings at New York's best semiprofessional venues: Brooklyn's Dexter Park, the Bronx's Catholic Protectory, and Manhattan's Dyckman Oval. In contrast to most black baseball entrepreneurs, Pompez exercised independence from Strong's booking agency for part of the year. When his Cuban Stars toured the Caribbean in the winters, Pompez relied on his cultural background and the skills he had acquired working for Strong to secure bookings. From its inception he envisioned his baseball operation as one that cultivated the Americas, Spanish- and English-speaking, as its main market, one from which he could both acquire talent and attract consumers. That he himself was bilingual and multicultural made such an approach both manageable and successful; it would distinguish him from the other Negro-league owners and lead to his longevity in black baseball.

Pompez's new entry increased competition for booking exhibitions for the other Cuban teams conducting regular tours in the States. This was especially the case in smaller locales between the major cities in the Northeast and Midwest. Prior to Pompez's venture, Abel Linares had used Nat Strong's agency to book games in these smaller markets. The terms for such bookings were enticing for local teams: a $60 guarantee with the option of 50 percent of the entire gross gate and grandstand receipts; a $25 guarantee if rained out. The solicitations from Strong's agency emphasized the uniqueness of those Cuban Stars, noting that every Cuban player "is a genuine Cuban, and belongs to the Cuban National league."[14] But starting in 1916, Pompez gave semipro and local teams another Cuban option, thereby encroaching on Linares's "territory"—and under the same Cuban Stars name, no less.

Pompez linked the different points of his personal migrations through the slate he arranged for his Cuban Stars. From May until September, his team played against white, black, and integrated competition across the Northeast and Midwest, and then barnstormed winters throughout the Caribbean. This was true of the 1916 Cuban Stars, who returned to Puerto Rico that October. The Cuban Stars did not come alone, bringing along Nat Strong's Brooklyn Royal Giants to play the Puerto Ricans. The 1916 return visit to Puerto Rico initiated Pompez's practice of using locations in the Spanish-speaking Americas to build a transnational market for his baseball enterprise. These winter tours were vital to his acquiring of new talent for the Cuban Stars, particularly as he extended his reach beyond Cuba.

Cuban teams were popular drawing cards in the Northeast. Part of the reason for the attraction was a misperception: U.S. aficionados often interpreted Cuban success at the "American" game as validation of the U.S. intervention in Cuba in 1898 and of the U.S. military occupation afterward. The U.S. occupation did facilitate the greater flow of people, commerce, and ideas between Cuba and the States. In the years that followed, Abel Linares, Agustín Molina, and other Cuban baseball figures freely brought Cuban teams to play exhibition games in the States. Linares's early teams consisted of predominantly lighter-skinned Cubans, players such as Rafael Almeida, Armando Marsans, and Adolfo Luque, all three of whom later appeared in the majors. But Pompez's roster was composed primarily of players who were "ineligible" to play in the majors due to their skin color.

Pompez's first Cuban Stars squads conducted what historians call barnstorming tours. Unlike teams that participated in a formal league with their own home park, barnstormers had an itinerant schedule. Lacking a preset full-season schedule, barnstorming teams usually had scheduled games in major cities—in the case of the black baseball circuit in the 1910s, this meant New York, Philadelphia, and Chicago—but solicited additional bookings as they traveled from one metropolitan area to another. As a result, they spent the majority of their time on the road, playing in front of small crowds in towns scattered across the Midwest and Northeast.

Since his team was often treated as Cuban and not necessarily as a black team, Pompez occasionally found a minor-league team and even a big-league team willing to schedule exhibitions against them. Difficulties arose when his Cuban Stars appeared. The difference was obvious: Pompez's teams featured primarily Afro-Cubans. At times fans and opposing teams reacted negatively. Philadelphia acquired a reputation as a particularly difficult place. There his team endured "jeering and insulting names" and other "rough stuff" from white opponents. Decreasing competitiveness stoked their passions. "Colored teams are so strong now that it is impossible for white semi-pro clubs to beat us," he opined. "Fans are enraged at the continual spectacle of these clubs being licked."[15] Losing contests to teams filled with players viewed as their social inferiors at times unleashed the worse in some, revealing the various degrees of unease about interracial competition and the inability to assert athletic superiority.

Hostile reactions roiled him as much as his players: this Pompez learned not from afar, sitting behind a desk at the team's baseball headquarters in Harlem, but rather through direct observation. Operating in a hands-on manner from his team's earliest days, the Cuban Stars owner actually managed the team on game day, completing the batting lineup and deciding when to make pitching changes.[16] Given his positions, he had to keep his emotions in check about the diamond.

Pompez's relations with his players had a peculiar tenor. In 1916 the twenty-six-year-old owner was less than five years older than the majority of his fourteen players and younger than two of them. Running the team involved an intricate balancing act: from applying a firm hand as the owner, to offering as manager a sympathetic ear for the social issues and cultural dynamics his players confronted, to being vigilant about the blurring of lines between employer and friend. For his baseball operations to achieve on-field success and commercial profitability—or at least viability—Pompez would have to learn to be more than a sympathetic friend to the young men under his charge.

"The Spanish Menace in Harlem"

Unease with the growing presence of Latinos also occurred away from the baseball diamond. In addition to the Little Ybor section that Cubans formed on the southern edge of Harlem, there was the emergence of the much larger "Spanish" Harlem. Those living in Harlem were sometimes unsettled by the different reception Spanish-speaking people received from landlords and local businesses compared with what U.S.-born blacks received. A few, like Edgar Grey, believed something more insidious was transpiring: the corruption and degradation of Harlem by the continuing waves of Latinos calling Harlem home.

A growing influx of Spanish-speaking immigrants from the Caribbean, mainly Puerto Ricans after World War I, combined with discriminatory rental practices to spur the formation of Spanish Harlem. Certain landlords rented their units only to "Spanish" applicants, complained Harlem resident Edward Ryan to the *Amsterdam News* in September 1927. This disturbing trend Ryan witnessed firsthand while apartment hunting in Harlem. "From 112th to 118th streets are to be found several vacancies," Ryan wrote, "but when you apply you are told 'only for Spanish.' It does not matter what the complexion of the prospective tenant is, so long as he speaks the lingo it's all right." Ryan's letter to the editor cited the divisiveness the discriminatory practice caused: "It puts the same race of people against each other merely on the grounds of a difference in language."[17] Much to his chagrin, the effort to ward off English-speaking blacks succeeded. By 1935 the area from Fifth Avenue east to the Harlem River from 116th Street south to 100th Street had become home to over 150,000 Latinos, predominantly Puerto Rican, and came to be affectionately called El Barrio.[18] The prominence of the foreign-born element with their distinctive tongue prompted concerns about the ability of blacks and Latinos to live side by side and whether darker-skinned Latinos could assimilate into Harlem's black community.

This concern dogged Pompez in his social and business interactions inside and outside of Harlem, on and away from the playing field. Publication of "The Spanish Menace in Harlem" in January 1928 was a telling incident. Written under the byline of Edgar M. Grey, the incendiary article blamed Latino residents for Harlem's deteriorating conditions and those of New York City as a whole. The column spurred "Spanish-speaking citizens" to defend their community; selecting Pompez as its chairman, the group launched a counteroffensive to the charge they were "un-American in their practices and in a large degree responsible for immoral conditions in Harlem." The group's public letter outlined their grievances as "law-abiding citizens of the United States of Spanish extraction" and people of "the darker races." The letter appealed to "native American Negroes" to find common cause in fighting racial hatred that could divide Harlem's communities and therefore to dismiss the slanderous Grey column. Committee members called on the editors of *The American and West Indian News* to have Grey disavow the article's claims and publicly apologize. Instead, the paper's editors denied his authorship of the article, claiming their internal investigation had found that Grey had been "out of the city at the time his paper went to press and did not know of the article until the paper had been printed" and that someone else had penned the article under his byline.[19]

This was not the first time Grey had been embroiled in a controversy within Harlem's political circles. In early August 1919, the Sierra Leone native, most likely of West Indian parents, was officially expelled from Marcus Garvey's Universal Negro Improvement Association (UNIA) as the director and assistant secretary of the Black Star Line company. Grey, it turns out, had voluntarily gone to the district attorney to have Garvey investigated for misappropriation of Black Star Line funds. When Garvey caught wind of this act of disloyalty, he moved to have Grey expelled and thereby discredited among his followers. Expelled from the UNIA ranks, Grey scuttled from job to job within Harlem, working for a time as a chiropractor and as a postal clerk, among other jobs, before settling in journalism. In 1923, after testifying in Garvey's trial for mail fraud, Grey started publishing articles in the *Amsterdam News*, and after three years was elevated to a contributing editor. From the *Amsterdam News* position he helped launch *The American and West Indian News*, a short-lived publication. Grey's work experience before arriving in New York in 1911 had allowed him to witness up close the culture and people of Puerto Rico and the Dominican Republic. He spent 1906 working as an interpreter for the U.S. government in Puerto Rico; he followed this stint working three years as the English secretary to Don Juan Moncastro, who Grey claimed was president of the Dominican Republic.[20]

The committee's published letter provides the clearest articulation of the racial project Pompez aligned himself with while he operated in the numbers. The position articulated in the letter was akin to the nonracial Cuban national ideology his father and other followers of José Martí had embraced: one that called for individuals to find common cause against oppressive ideas and forces that might foster division. For

Martí, it was necessary to envision a Cuban national identity that was "more than white, more than black." For Pompez and the committee, this meant identifying as a member of a language and cultural community who were "members of the darker races" and more than just Cuban or Puerto Rican. This articulation of "Spanish" identity was not an embracing of North American whiteness but rather a recognition of the ways that cultural differences distinguished Latinos from African Americans, West Indians, and others in Harlem's heterogeneous community. Identification of those of "Spanish extraction" in the Americas as among "the darker races" resonates with the ideas of the African American scholar W.E.B. DuBois, later a neighbor of Pompez at 409 Edgecombe in Sugar Hill.

Pompez and his fellow committee members found strong support in *New York Age* publisher Fred Moore. Deciding to repudiate Edgar Grey was not a hard choice for Moore: he and Grey had tangled over several years in a battle over the question of naturalization of West Indians.[21] Not coincidentally, the *New York Age* published "Porto Ricans as Citizens" on its editorial page in the January 28 issue, which included Pompez's letter on its front page. The editorial gave a different, affirmative view of New York City's Spanish-speaking residents and chided the other "local race journal" for publishing an article "so sweeping and rabid in its language as to defeat its purpose." The *Age* accused *The American and West Indian News* of using broad strokes in characterizing Cubans, Puerto Ricans, and other Spanish-speaking residents as "product[s] of the most debased environment" and of enacting the "same sort of intolerance that Negroes are protesting against on the part of the white press."[22]

The front-page publication of his committee's letter demonstrates the value of the connections Pompez had established within Harlem's circles. Extending from the baseball diamond and the numbers world to its social elite, elected officials, and political fixers, these connections gave him access to a prominent black weekly that allowed him to communicate with a wide swath of those walking Harlem's streets. That he ran a numbers racket was no secret, but this did not preclude him from partaking in social gatherings that included W.E.B. DuBois, noted author James Weldon Johnson, journalist Lester Walton (later U.S. ambassador to Liberia), and Reverend Adam Clayton Powell, Sr. These men were among the two hundred invited guests at the golden wedding anniversary celebration of *New York Age* publisher Fred Moore and his wife, Ida, in April 1929. The celebration offered an example of how at particular moments Harlem's social and political worlds gathered in ways that disrupted clear demarcation between respectable society and the underworld. Indeed, invited guests included not only black Harlem's intellectual and social elite but also Mayor Jimmy Walker, senior law enforcement officials, and sitting city judges along with several of Harlem numbers kings, including Pompez, Casper Holstein, and Henry Miro.

The "Spanish Menace" article unveiled the discomfort some had with the prominent role Latinos like Pompez had in the numbers and its influence on everyday life in Harlem. Yet their commercial and social activities contributed to Harlem's cultural vitality and quickened its development into a black cultural mecca. Running a numbers bank made Pompez a wealthy man and financed his foray into professional baseball and other ventures in the sporting world; it would also place all of his business enterprises in jeopardy.

Numbers bankers were always on their guard for law enforcement officials. They worried every time police officers walking the beat peered into the storefront windows of their cigar store, candy store, or whatever business they were using as a front to collect wagers. Officers would step into the stores to make idle chatter, all the while evaluating the scene, gathering intelligence for their superiors. Some visited because they knew exactly what was going on; they stopped by to remind those minding the store that turning a blind eye cost money and payday was nigh. Keeping the police off their backs took money, but not necessarily paid to the officer walking the beat. Bankers had to aim higher, trying to build relations with precinct captains and officials in command with the power to ensure their spot was not an active target. Yet this was always a fragile combination: the numbers man, the police official, and cash to look away so that the numbers game could continue apace.

Numbers barons grew well acquainted with the balancing act of navigating the legal system and dealing with law enforcement. On January 24, 1923, Pompez and two of his numbers workers, Manolo Valdes and Joseph Miranda, all got "pinched" for policy violations. The arrest no doubt reminded Pompez that he was operating on the other side of the line. But bankers like him had developed an intricate system to minimize the damage by separating different components of their operations. Those who collected the policy slips were not the same who gathered the money wagered. The banking center of their numbers operations was regularly moved. This was sound strategy, making it difficult for police to narrow their sights on one location and sweep in to gather all the betting slips and money, and creating what decades later would be termed "plausible deniability." But on that January night of his arrest, as he called on his lawyers to arrange bail and minimize the damage, Pompez knew he would have to reorganize his workers, adjust his security plans, and retrace his steps to avoid the hassle of getting arrested again. Of course, this did not mean leaving the numbers business, just being smarter about how he handled his affairs.[23]

A new collaborative business venture that required Pompez's attention had come to fruition just days prior to his arrest. Four days before police took him into custody, he was meeting with other black baseball entrepreneurs at the Christian Street YMCA in Philadelphia to formulate a plan to create the Eastern Colored League (ECL).[24] Three years had passed since Andrew "Rube" Foster had organized the Negro National League (NNL), the first successful black professional baseball league. It was high time for black baseball operators in the East to stop their incessant fighting and organize. That, of course, would require team owners to subordinate their individual outlook to a collective mentality. These baseball owners had to get their act together for black baseball in the East to be viewed as being on par with the NNL in the view of the black press and fans.

Money earned running numbers was part of the foundation upon which the formal Negro leagues were constructed. Black baseball was not unique in this regard: numerous businesses in Harlem and other black urban centers were financed in part through numbers money. Numbers bankers filled a financial void, especially because "when banks would not lend black people money to grow through education and small businesses, the numbers people often filled the gap."[25] Certainly not all money went to support legitimate businesses. Numbers barons also bankrolled the start-ups of other aspiring numbers bankers. Such was the relationship between Pompez and William Augustus "Gus" Greenlee. According to William "Judy" Johnson, a Negro-league stand-out in the 1930s, the Harlem gambling impresario taught Greenlee his trade and provided start-up capital for him to launch his own numbers operation, which quickly reigned in Pittsburgh.[26]

Both Pompez and Greenlee would figure prominently in their local communities' sporting culture. Participation in the underground entrepreneurial sector reflected a strategic approach that Pompez and others like him embraced to cope with the reality of the color line and racial segregation within and beyond the sporting world. His formative years exposed him to the realities of race and segregation. Facing the dilemma of an ambiguous racial location in the United States as both black and Latino, Pompez chose to pursue alliances inside and outside of Harlem that allowed blacks and Latinos to counter the power of segregation on their lives. In his everyday interactions in and about Harlem, he negotiated what others perceived as hard-and-fast ideas of difference. "A tall American-born Negro of Cuban parentage," he moved within and throughout Harlem's "black" and "Spanish" worlds.[27] These worlds did not have impermeable boundaries. Like the bibliophile Arthur Schomburg, the musician Mario Bauzá, and other black Latinos, Pompez lived in both, contributing to the cultural and intellectual vitality of Harlem as its Renaissance was flourishing. Harlem evolved into his home, for it offered him possibilities that he could not pursue in the same way or to the same degree anywhere else. The social and economic realities of what he had witnessed in Tampa, Havana, and now Harlem had taught him an important lesson: to succeed in the numbers business and in black baseball, he could not leave either part of his identity behind but instead had to use both to guide his steps.

Familiarity with baseball's popularity among Latinos and throughout the Spanish-speaking Caribbean served Pompez well after he arrived in Harlem and launched his Cuban Stars. His travels between the United States and Cuba to attend to his business affairs, visit family, or reconnect with friends also gave him the opportunity to scope out up-and-coming baseball talent. Building a winning franchise would require creativity in the search for fresh talent—especially since Abel Linares and his right-hand man, Tinti Molina, enjoyed the advantage of over fifteen years of experience working both in the United States and in the Cuban circuit. As a relative newcomer, Pompez might be viewed by Cubans on the island as encroaching on their market. Equally significant, his travels throughout the Americas refreshed his awareness of the cultural adjustment Latinos faced in their dealing with the evolving set of racial practices in the States. This would be his advantage over Linares and Molina: he knew the U.S. scene much better than they did and therefore could attend to Latino players' needs better and more directly. That would be his challenge and his purpose in making Cubans stars in the Negro leagues.

3

LAUNCHING THE CUBAN STARS

We must have a League and then we can refuse to play any club which cannot guarantee us protection against the conduct of the fans and players. But now we are handicapped and must accept games wherever and whenever we can get them.
                    —Pompez in The Pittsburgh Courier, *July 28, 1928*

The need for a Negro league in the East was never clearer than when the Eastern Colored League collapsed, leaving its former members on their own to schedule games with semiprofessional and independent white teams. Leagues offered protection, both financial and social. League teams could count on a league schedule to provide a baseline of revenue and games where the crowds were truly interested in black baseball. Independent ball meant vulnerability: no fixed league schedule meant venturing into hostile territory in search of a payday. A league allowed owners to operate from a position of power, as Pompez stated in *The Pittsburgh Courier,* and the prospect of playing independent ball represented a significant step backward. Harm inflicted on one league team by an independent club could draw collective punishment: the entire league could refuse to schedule any exhibitions with the offenders. That prospect kept most white semipro and independent teams in check, careful that neither they nor their fans damaged their relationship with official Negro-league teams. Black team owners well understood that racial behaviors were governed as much by attention to the financial bottom line as by a sense of moral rectitude about equality.

The 1920s brought about a new era for Latinos in the Negro leagues as Cuban teams went from barnstorming to participation in league play. Better-paying opportunities for Latin American players increased with the formal creation of the Negro leagues. Prior to Pompez's entry, opportunities for Cubans in black baseball came solely through Abel Linares's Midwest-based Cuban Stars, a charter member of the original Negro National League. Linares enjoyed an insider's advantage in scouting and signing Cuban players to take north to the States as an owner of the Habana club in the Cuban league. He exercised an almost exclusive hold over Cuban talent in the U.S. professional circuit until 1908, when teams from organized baseball and independent ball started to pluck lighter-skinned players off his team. The Boston Braves, New York Giants, and Cincinnati Reds as well as minor-league teams signed Rafael Almeida, Adolfo Luque, and Armando Marsans, among other players, away from his squad. Another sign his hold was deteriorating came in 1914 when J. L. Wilkinson's All Nations team lured the Afro-Cuban pitching star José Méndez away. The NNL's formation further increased competition for Cuban talent. The Kansas City Monarchs, the Detroit Stars, and Rube Foster's Chicago American Giants all signed talented Cubans originally introduced to the black baseball circuit by Linares. As a result, the Cuban Stars who joined the NNL in 1920 entered without the services of the pitching ace Méndez, the slugger Cristóbal Torriente, or the outstanding catcher José Rodríguez. Wider availability of Cuban players to all teams in the black circuit contributed to Linares's Cuban Stars remaining a second-division team for its entire existence.

Pompez posed the most enduring challenge to Linares as the two battled constantly to sign the most talented Cuban ballplayers. A roster spot on either of their Cuban Stars teams translated into nearly year-round employment: the U.S. baseball season typically stretched from early May into October and the Cuban league played December through early February. As competition for Cuban talent intensified, Pompez abandoned the practice of filling his club's roster exclusively with Cuban stars from the Cuban League. Instead he ventured to wherever baseball was played in Latin America to acquire talent and thus diversified the Latino talent base in the U.S. black baseball circuit. Although they employed different approaches, together Linares and Pompez introduced the majority of talented Latinos to the Negro leagues.

The lack of a permanent home base and ballpark posed another significant obstacle for Linares in establishing a loyal following and general stability in the States. Managed by Tinti Molina and operated out of Chicago, Linares's team rented John Schorling's South Side Park in 1920 but remained at the mercy of the scheduling priority given to the Leland Giants, who called South Side home. His team's Chicago base placed him at a distinct disadvantage compared with Pompez's New York City–based team. Chicago in the 1910s lacked a sizable Cuban community or Latino fan base; the first significant wave of Spanish-speaking immigrants arrived in Chicago during World War I and was primarily from Mexico. Conversely, a significant Caribbean Latino population had established itself in New York City, and Harlem more specifically, during this same decade. Tens of thousands of Puerto Ricans came after passage of the 1917 Jones Act, which had granted them U.S. citizenship. New York City also had a small but well-established Cuban community, which, along with the Puerto Rican community, was fanatical about baseball.

Headquartered in Harlem with an office on 114th Street, Pompez's Cuban Stars would participate in the eastern-based independent circuit from 1916 through the demise of organized black baseball there in 1932. During this span his Cuban Stars also lacked a regular home. Dyckman Oval would be the nearest thing to a home park, but Pompez lacked control over booking games there and was therefore competing with other clubs for dates. Located on 204th Street, bordered by Nagle Avenue, Academy Street, and Tenth Avenue, Dyckman Oval was arguably the best appointed venue in Manhattan for semipro and black baseball teams to perform, with its covered grandstand and, after Prohibition, beer garden. In addition to baseball games, Dyckman hosted boxing bouts during the summer and football games in the fall. Season openers at the Oval always brought out dignitaries. Such was the case in May 1921 when New York City mayor John Hylan ventured up to Dyckman to throw the first pitch before a game between the Cuban Stars and the semipro Tesreau Bears.[1] However, as the 1920s opened, questions lingered whether Ed Bolden, Nat Strong, Pompez, and the other big operators could forge an agreement and create a functional league in the East. Finally, in 1923 the Eastern Colored League (ECL) was formed; it lasted five tumultuous seasons.

From All Cuban to Cuban Stars

Rube Foster, then a standout pitcher from Texas, found inspiration in his participation in the Cuban League in 1906. A member of the Fe team that winter, everywhere Foster looked, he saw Cuban men running the operation and throngs of enthusiastic fans of all shades in the stands. No color line divided Cuban professional baseball; its amateur ranks were another matter. Upon returning to the States, Foster endeavored to organize black professional teams that played in Chicago, Detroit, St. Louis, and Kansas City, among others in the Midwest, into a national league. In 1906 he incorporated his effort under the name International League of Colored Baseball Clubs; among the charter clubs was Linares's Cuban Stars. Time and again as each venture floundered, Foster continued to include a Cuban team as part of his planned circuit. He finally realized his ambition in 1920; the Negro National League initiated operations under his motto "We Are the Ship, All Else the Sea."

Black baseball entered a new era with the successful organization of the Negro National League and the Eastern Colored League in 1923. Independent professional ball was much less prestigious and more economically precarious: its pace of travel was exhausting, park conditions uneven, the racial attitudes of fans who filled the stands unpredictable. Independent baseball lacked an arbiter to handle disputes over rights to players, teams welshing on payment, or the quality of umpires. By contrast, league play ensured a modicum of organizational stability with its set schedule, guarantee of revenue sharing among its members, and a centralized leadership to adjudicate disputes. A formal league also promoted a level of respect for contractual agreements between owners and players. Submission of team rosters to the league office worked similarly to the reserve list system in the majors, except Negro-league player contracts lacked a reserve clause, which actually limited Negro-league owners' commitment to their players but also did not prevent players from contract jumping between leagues.

Nat Strong stood as the biggest obstacle to launching formal league play in the East. His unwillingness to enter his Brooklyn Royal Giants in an eastern-based circuit prevented others from falling into line. His control of bookings at venues throughout the New York metropolitan area gave black baseball team operators pause about speaking publicly against him. They did not want to risk losing out on prime bookings at the best parks, especially since few of them possessed their own proper ballpark. Ed Bolden and his Hilldale Darby Daisies enjoyed good relations with those who booked games in Philadelphia. Thomas Jackson likewise had access to a ballpark in Atlantic City due to his relationship with local baseball power brokers. The same could not be said of James Keenan and his Lincoln Giants, who operated out of the Bronx, or of Charles Spedden's Black Sox in Baltimore. Nor did Pompez have a ballpark that his Cuban Stars called home. These six black baseball magnates gathered nonetheless in the winter of 1922 attempting to forge an agreement and organize a new league.

Meeting in the days before Christmas, the magnates decided to form the Eastern Colored League (ECL). "Realizing that harmony is the paramount issue of any organization," the six entrepreneurs "hit upon a unique solution for the government of the Association," the *New York Age* reported.[2] Thus, they created a commission system with each team having a commissioner on the governing board instead of electing a president unaffiliated with a member team. This decision would be the source of much bickering as the six self-interested parties attempted to formulate policy and render decisions on disputes between clubs.

Shortly after ringing in the New Year, important news came out of New York City courts for all those who aspired to host contests at Dyckman Oval. The city had been awarded the title to Dyckman Oval in a decision rendered by Supreme Court Justice Isidor Wasservogel. According to *The New York Times*, the city sought immediate possession, "because of the income accruing from its use for baseball games."[3] The decision had seemingly stripped off a layer of whom ECL owners had to work with to arrange games at the oval.

Reconvened at Philadelphia's Christian Street YMCA ten days after the pronouncement about Dyckman, ECL owners turned their attention to two urgent matters: a league schedule and umpires. Presided over by Bolden, the owners decided to launch their new league on April 28 and to create a schedule that balanced every franchise's ability to stage home games on holidays as well as an equal number of home and away games. Considerable attention was given to the umpire question. Although owners expressed the need to hire "competent, unbiased umpires," they ultimately decided home teams would hire the umpiring crew.

Whatever progress had been made in Philadelphia quickly moved to the back of Pompez's mind. Upon his return to Harlem, he was arrested on January 24 for "policy" violation, having been caught dealing in the numbers games. Hauled before the Magistrates' Court in the Twelfth District, he was released on $1,000 bail, as were his workers Manolo Valdes and Joseph Miranda.[4] The arrest made it a convenient time to get out of town, so Pompez headed to Cuba to scout some talent and finalize his roster for the 1923 season. Therefore, he was the only owner absent when the ECL owners met in Philadelphia for the last preseason gathering before the launch of its inaugural campaign. The *New York Age* stated that a scouting trip to Cuba was the reason for his absence.[5] Indeed, while the owners conducted their gathering, he was aboard the SS *Cuba* en route from Havana with his new crop of players. His 1923 Cuban Stars showcased the expanding base of his scouting and his keen eye for talent. In addition to returning players Alejandro Oms, Pelayo Chacón, and Bernardo Baró, the arriving team included the pitcher Oscar Levis, the first Panamanian to perform in the circuit, and a seventeen-year-old rookie, Martín Dihigo, whose ascent into black baseball stardom began that season.

The tall, sinewy rookie worked his way into the Cuban Stars starting lineup, playing different positions until he earned the first-base job by mid-June. He impressed those who followed the ECL circuit with his powerful hitting as the Cuban Stars battled for the ECL pennant throughout the season. Away from the baseball diamond, Dihigo had his first exposure to the workings of the U.S. racial system with its southern Jim Crow laws and northern practices of discrimination. Drawing a $100 a month salary was fine, but the varied reception of whites bewildered the young Cuban. He recounted the initial shock to a Cuban interviewer: "I began to experience firsthand the hatred of 'gringos,' going through lots of hardships and vexations." Travels with the Cuban Stars through the ECL circuit and playing exhibition games in remote towns throughout the Northeast and the Midwest exposed him to segregated restaurants, hotels, and other facilities where he was denied equal treatment or access for being black and a foreigner. This pricked

his awareness that he was subjected to "all types of double discrimination, for being black and for being of Latino origin." "Those gringos
were such cretins that in many hotels, if they, by chance, admitted us,
they would go to the extreme of denying us water to bathe. The food, the
mess hall, the waiter, it was all the same," he later wrote in an autobiog-
raphy published in Cuba.[6] In spite of such travails, he excelled on the
field, as did his Cuban Stars teammates.

Led by the heavy-hitting Dihigo and Alejandro Oms, the Cuban
Stars offered its ECL foes stronger competition than Linares's squad
did for its NNL peers. In its first league season, Pompez's Cuban Stars
compiled a winning season and finished in second place—feats Linares's club never accomplished. This Pompez accomplished through an
ever-expanding search for talent in the Caribbean. His quest at times
sparked criticism from the black press in New York. In March 1925,
New York Age columnist John Clark described the wide search the
Cuban Stars owner conducted. "Ere the ides of March roll around,
Alex Pompez, suave mentor of the Cuban entry in the Eastern outfit,
has planned to board a rattler for the 'Keys' of Florida and thence by
bark to his native Queen of the Antilles in search of new talents to bol-
ster up the invading Stars." Clark noted that Pompez's itinerary included
stops in Puerto Rico, the Dominican Republic, and the lesser-known
baseball haunts of Saint Kitts and Saint Thomas. "Alex's problem is no
small one," the sportswriter remarked, "due to the fact that only a limited number of efficient pastimers are turned out on these verdant
isles." What upset Clark, however, was that "the invading manager flatly
refuses to use any of the boys who are natives of the 'States.'"[7] His
complaint captures part of the tension that existed in the project of
building a black league that included a Cuban team. At one level, the
writer chided Pompez for being too aggressive in scouring the Caribbean playing fields for Latino talent versus signing homegrown African American talent. On another, he positioned the Cuban-American
as a foreigner, an "invading" leader at the helm of a foreign force.

Fellow ECL commissioners saw Pompez as deeply committed to
the enterprise of black baseball, however. This was evident at the end
of the 1924 season when ECL and NNL owners attempted to organize the first Negro League World Series. After failing to organize a
showcase series between the league champions the previous year, the

owners selected two representatives from each league to negotiate: Rube Foster and Dr. Howard Smith from the NNL; Charles Spedden and Alex Pompez from the ECL. Their task was to hammer out an agreement for a season-ending championship series, including a game schedule, host cities, and the split of the gate receipts. The selection of Pompez reflected the fellow ECL commissioners' belief that he could be a hard but fair negotiator for their circuit. The negotiations were not always smooth—at one point major-league commissioner Judge Kenesaw "Mountain" Landis offered to intervene—but in the end, they succeeded, without any intervention. Led by the pitching of José Mendez, the NNL's Kansas City Monarchs defeated the ECL's Hilldale Darby Daisies to secure the inaugural Negro League World Series.[8] Unfortunate for Pompez, his Cuban Stars suffered disappointing finishes—they were last in 1924 and fifth in the six-team league in 1925—such that his team would not appear in the circuit's World Series while the ECL was in existence.

Troublesome indications of the ECL's continued instability occurred repeatedly during its yearly operations. Team owners constantly threatened withdrawal over disagreements over scheduling, fulfillment of league games, player acquisitions, and umpiring. At their August 1926 meeting, owners discussed at length the failure of Jim Keenan's Lincoln Giants to play league games against either the Cuban Stars or the Brooklyn Royal Giants. The Cuban Stars stood atop the league standings at that point in the 1926 season, but the lack of games against Keenan's team called into question its standing and claim on the league's top berth. Although the *Baltimore Afro-American* reported that "factional differences have kept the Cuban Stars from meeting Jim Keenan's outfit," for his part Keenan insisted that the Cubans' inability to secure a home park to host their half of the scheduled league games was the stumbling block.[9] Indeed, Pompez continued to lack control of a ballpark he could call home; Keenan, of course, knew this. The Bacharach Giants' Hammond Daniels devised a solution, offering Pompez use of his Atlantic City ballpark while the Bacharachs were on the road August 10 through 12. The offer demonstrated how the commission system was supposed to work. That did not prevent some from questioning Ed Bolden's leadership. Pompez defended Bolden, reminding critics that all the commissioners made the schedule and not just Bolden: "The fault belongs to all of us if any of the teams fail to keep it."[10]

While the owners bickered, the Cuban Stars' on-field performance and off-field conduct pleased the team's owner. Martín Dihigo's rapid development excited Pompez. "Dihigo is the greatest player in organized baseball in the country," he effused in describing his versatile, power-hitting gem. "Dihigo is not only a great pitcher, who takes his regular turn in the box, but he plays any position on the team, [and] handles a baseball bat with as much ease as an ordinary man handles a cane." The team's conduct away from the diamond also brought satisfaction. "We have no squabbling and no trouble about discipline on our clubs," he boasted to the *Baltimore Afro-American*. After the team retreated to a hotel, "there is no standing around the bar," he added, "not a single member of the team drinks and there is only one, the center fielder, who smokes." He even bragged, prematurely, that the team had "no quarrels or arguments with the umpire."[11]

Bolstered by Dihigo's exploits at the plate, the Cuban Stars sat atop the ECL on August 28, percentage points ahead of the Bacharach Giants but having played only 36 league games to Bacharach's 49. Enthusiasm waned after a series played at Maryland Park and Bacharach Park when the Cuban Stars dropped three out of four contests and slipped out of first place. "We were robbed of several games at the seashore last week," Pompez complained. "The umpiring was as rank as that at Black Sox park today." Calls during both ends of a doubleheader against Baltimore drew the ire of the Cuban Stars. In the second game, an umpire ruled Dihigo out after the Cuban had apparently swiped second base. Dihigo protested too vehemently and was ejected. The hometown *Afro-American* judiciously described the ensuing fracas: "The Cubans, usually a quiet bunch, were riled and expressed their feelings in their own Spanish language, which although not understood, left little to the imagination."[12] Their protestations did not sway the arbiters. The Cuban Stars fumed as they loaded into their two seven-passenger Packard sedans. With their ECL pennant hopes fading, it was a joyless ride back north.

The thought that the Bacharach Giants were waiting out the Cubans no doubt crossed Pompez's mind. The Bacharachs were refusing to schedule games against his squad at Brooklyn's Dexter Park. Perhaps Hammond Daniels hoped the Cuban Stars would continue their bad spell and drop far enough behind that the two teams would not have to play the games hosted by the Cubans. Pompez wired Bolden, informing the ECL chair of Nat Strong's willingness to book the games postponed from Decoration Day (now Memorial Day). "The final decision is up to him," he told the *Afro-American*. "We don't want anything but what is fair . . . but I hate to the devil to be robbed, and this kind of business of trying to win the pennant by any means, while it may injure us temporarily, will work permanent harm to baseball."[13] In consideration of the postponed games the commissioners decided to extend the season from September 15 to 26. The outcomes of the Dexter Park makeup games ultimately would not impact the ECL final standings: the Cuban Stars' losing streak continued and the team dropped from contention.

Defending the Claim

Deft talent evaluation and a near-exclusive claim to Latino talent in the ECL drove the relative success of Pompez's Cuban Stars compared to Linares's NNL club. The labor and time invested in locating and developing talent in the Caribbean steeled his resolve that the Latino market should be the exclusive domain of Cuban team owners. The *New York Age* and *Amsterdam News* both reported the displeasure Pompez, Linares, and Tinti Molina expressed about losing their perceived exclusivity. Squabbles over the right to sign the Latino players Pedro San and Esteban Montalvo in 1926 and 1927 illuminate the logic Pompez used to defend this "exclusive" right.[14] At root was a territorial claim to an exclusive market on Latino talent. Other Negro-league team owners had the entire African American market in the United States from which to scout and acquire talent. The Caribbean and Latin America were Pompez's domain. Effective recruitment of Latino talent resulted from a network of scouts and contacts who alerted Pompez to emerging talent. Current players served as informal scouts, recommending players who might interest him for the upcoming season in the States. Sportswriters who covered local professional circuits in the Caribbean were another source of preliminary scouting. But the Cuban-American entrepreneur did not leave the work to his players and press contacts, traveling each winter to scout new talent himself.

Pompez knew all too well that signing and bringing over a new Latin American recruit required additional work, such as filing official paperwork for visas or residency for clearance to have the player legally enter the United States. At times bureaucratic hiccups occurred. That was precisely what happened when he attempted to bring Dominican pitcher Pedro San through Puerto Rico to join his Cuban Stars after discovering San during a spring of 1925 visit to the Dominican Republic. Immigration authorities in San Juan did not permit San to accompany the Cuban Stars to the U.S. mainland, requiring that he first establish residency on the island, which took a year. San fulfilled this requirement early in 1926, but Pompez encountered another obstacle to San's donning the Cuban Stars flannels and becoming the circuit's first Dominican. The ECL's newest entry, the Newark Stars, had placed a claim on San's services. The case was taken before the league commissioners at their March 1926 meeting. Newark's competing claim perturbed Pompez, who had waited a whole year to unveil his newest pitching find. He presented his fellow commissioners with a letter from San written in Spanish. Unwilling to take Pompez's word for its translation, the commissioners tabled the matter and sought out a neutral party to translate San's letter. The good news came two weeks later: the commissioners had awarded San to Pompez's Cuban Stars.[15]

Dueling claims on another Latino player, the power-hitting outfielder Esteban Montalvo, arose the following season, this time pitting Pompez against Jim Keenan. Whereas John Clark had criticized Pompez previously, citing his concern that U.S.-born blacks were being denied playing opportunities, the Montalvo case yielded a much harsher charge: that racial prejudice was motivating the Cuban Stars owner's quest to monopolize Latino talent in the East.

Cut loose by Linares's NNL team in 1925 and having sat out all of the 1926 NNL season, Esteban Montalvo was a free agent for 1927, or so claimed Jim Keenan in signing Montalvo for his Lincoln Giants that April.[16] Worried that a competing claim might arise, Keenan kept the outfielder out of action until he received clearance from the new ECL president, Isaac Nutter. In the position less for than five months, Nutter had ascended to the ECL's top post as a result of a new leadership structure instituted after the 1926 season. Suggested by former ECL commission chair Ed Bolden, the new structure addressed previously expressed concerns about Bolden's potential bias as a commissioner, chairman, and team executive. To shield the league from such accusations, the president's position was created with "power of absolute decision" on questions the league commissioners brought to his attention.[17] Nutter was nominated for the post by Pompez at the mid-January meeting in Detroit, and his election made the Howard University–educated lawyer the first nonowner to head the ECL.

The Detroit owners' meeting where Nutter was elected followed several tumultuous weeks. Two weeks earlier Keenan had tendered the resignation of his Lincoln Giants from the circuit. His action could have precipitated the breakup of the ECL, and it would have "had it not been for the work of Alexander Pompez," according to the *New York Age*. "Players and fans alike, especially in New York, should be grateful to Mr. Pompez for saving organized colored baseball in the East," the *Age* proclaimed in its January 22 issue. "Through his diplomacy [he] made both sides see the need of adjusting their differences for the good of the game." Keenan withdrew his resignation; his fellow owners reelected him ECL secretary-treasurer. Little did Pompez know that a mere four months after brokering peace among ECL owners, he would be the one mired in a battle with Keenan and it would be Pompez who was accused of causing dissension.

In closely following the battle over the right to sign Esteban Montalvo, the *New York Age* changed its tone about Pompez, sharply criticizing the Cuban Stars owner in the affair. Nutter initially ruled in Keenan's favor, making Montalvo eligible to play for the Lincoln Giants. The ruling incensed Pompez. He claimed that the other ECL owners had a standing agreement that gave him the right of first refusal to sign any Latino player in the eastern circuit. "There are enough American born ball players for the other teams in the League to select from without their signing up Cubans," he informed sportswriters who covered the circuit. An *Age* journalist chastised the Cubans owner, stating that his "objection . . . is based on racial prejudice, although he won't admit as much." According the *Age*, Pompez was after "a monopoly on all Cuban players" and remained "especially bitter against Julio Rojo, the Cuban catcher, for his willingness to play with teams other than those composed of Cubans."[18]

Dissatisfied with Nutter's ruling, Pompez attempted an end run, appealing to the league commissioners. The maneuver undermined the authority of the league's new president. But the commissioners nonetheless aligned themselves with Pompez in pushing Nutter to overturn his initial ruling. The reversal frustrated Keenan, who again threatened withdrawal. He vented his frustration in the June 29 edition of the *Amsterdam News*. His fellow ECL owners "should have been the last ones to fight him in this matter. If there was to be a fight it should have come from the West," he told the paper. The main culprits in this imbroglio were Pompez and Nat Strong, Keenan charged: the former set against Cubans players on any team that wasn't Cuban; the latter "long a rival of Keenan's in semi-professional baseball circles of New York." In the end, Montalvo appeared in only in a handful of games with the Lincoln Giants while they remained in the ECL; the power-hitting Cuban returned to Linares's NNL team the following season.[19]

A competitive desire to field the best possible team and not allow his fellow owners any advantage informed Pompez's position. The Latino executive argued for an exclusive market based on the scouting work he regularly performed in scouring the Spanish-speaking Americas to locate new talent—work that fellow ECL owners who did not speak Spanish could not accomplish. In part he feared that others would benefit from his unique position as a bilingual talent evaluator and team owner without his receiving proper compensation from fellow owners.

The Montalvo controversy occurred early in a season in which the Cuban Stars' ECL chances looked promising. At the April owners' meeting Pompez announced that he had secured a home ballpark, David Stadium in Newark, which allowed his club to put down stakes at the spacious International League ballpark. In the second straight year that an ECL team sought to call Newark home, the *Amsterdam News* viewed Pompez's effort more favorably than Wilbur Crelin's previous attempt for two reasons. First, Crelin's club had been a start-up, whereas the Cuban Stars were a veteran team with established players. Second, Pompez possessed far more experience as a baseball promoter who could stimulate fan interest than a neophyte like Crelin.[20]

Buoyed by his success in securing an actual home park, a confident Pompez visited the *Baltimore Afro-American* office to share his enthusiasm for the upcoming campaign. "We are better, faster and stronger . . . and will cop the pennant which we lost the last half of the season last year."[21] He also shared this optimistic outlook with the *New York Age*, informing its sportswriter that his 1927 edition "will be the best team he has brough[t] over."

Speculation had long circulated within the press and among the Cuban Stars' followers that the team suffered end-of-season fades due to its players performing year-round. The annual schedule these players followed left little time for their bodies to recuperate. In addition to participating in the ECL, the Cuban Stars players performed in the Cuban League during the winter and often barnstormed between seasons. In the past, Pompez had permitted them to play during winters especially, since it sustained the players financially. A player could earn anywhere from $175 to $350 a month in the Eastern Colored League, whose season typically lasted late into September. In the winter leagues, Pompez informed a *Baltimore Afro-American* sportswriter, that same player "can make from $400 to $450 a month in Cuba playing baseball."[22]

However, after the repeated end-of-season slides, Pompez no longer embraced the idea that their year-round schedule did not have a negative toll. "Each year," he told the *New York Age*, "I get the best results from my club during the first couple of months of baseball here in the States. And I attribute it to the fact that some of my players have burned themselves out with winter play." The impact was most clearly evident in pitching aces Oscar Levis and Juanelo Mirabal, who tossed the majority of the team's innings. Pompez's optimism for the Cuban Stars 1927 campaign came from having convinced Levis and Mirabal to skip winter ball. His hope was that a winter's rest would put them in "the best condition for the hard games on the league schedule," and that this would propel the Cuban Stars to claim the ECL pennant.[23]

For much of the 1927 season, Pompez's prediction seemed prescient. In early September the Cuban Stars stood atop the ECL standings; they maintained the lead until dropping a twin bill to Hilldale mid-month. The Cuban Stars rebounded, and looked poised to grasp the second-half flag to qualify to play first-half winner Bacharach Giants for the ECL pennant. However, Pompez worried. A series of washouts meant the Cubans needed to reschedule contests: the last thing he wanted was accusations that he did not put forward an honest effort to make up league games. Then, if the Cuban Stars captured the top berth in the second half, protests would fly that his team had not truly earned the flag. Avoiding such protests was his goal. This he impressed upon the *Amsterdam News* sportswriter Lloyd Thompson, who reported "Senor Pompez, the Cuban mentor, is making it known in no uncertain tones that the Stars are fulfilling their schedule as staked out by the league solons."[24]

Given his team's hectic schedule in the season's concluding month, Pompez signed several reinforcements, including eighteen-year-old Juan "Tetelo" Vargas, the second Dominican to enter the black circuit. Vargas's signing drew notice, as did the diverse composition of the Cuban Stars roster. A three-game series against the Baltimore Black Sox at Griffith Stadium in the nation's capital attracted not only typical black baseball fans but also Latin American dignitaries, including "the Santo Domingo Minister and the Cuban Counsel and staff."[25] Pompez hoped the new players and overall excitement would propel the team forward: they needed to win their last seven-league contest to clinch the second half. Unfortunately, the Cuban Stars experienced another September fade and stumbled to a third-place finish.

Hard Times

Much as they had in previous off-seasons, the ECL teetered on the brink of dissolution. Uncertainty filled the air as rumors swirled of teams ready to drop league play. Owners of both black leagues gathered in Philadelphia in mid-February 1923. Their agenda included tending to their interleague working agreement to eliminate the loophole at the center of the Montalvo controversy. The executives inserted a new clause in their agreement: "No club may sign a player who has played all or part of a season with a league club until all other league clubs have waived their rights to him."[26] For their part, ECL owners reelected Nutter to head their circuit.

That off-season took a decidedly sad turn for Pompez. In the weeks leading up to the Philadelphia meeting, he learned that Pablo Mesa, veteran outfielder of seven seasons with his Cuban Stars, had died of tuberculosis back in Cuba; he was just twenty-six years old. Then he received word that star centerfielder Alejandro Oms had been stricken with the same affliction. Though initial reports held little hope for Oms, he survived but would not return to peak athletic performance until the 1929 campaign. Competition for signing Latino players intensified that winter with the emergence of a new barnstorming team of Cubans, Syd Pollock's Havana Red Sox. Major-league organizations had also begun to home in on the players who had previously filled Pompez's roster. This he tried to impress upon his fellow owners at their joint gathering in February. The *Afro-American* detailed his plea that "since his teams were frequently raided by both white and colored teams and since many good players are signed in Cuba, even before they come to America, he [should] be allowed priority in signing Cuban players." After hearing Pompez's case, the team owners passed a motion that the two circuits agree "not to sign any more Cuban players until Mr. Pompez had completed his roster."[27] The agreement assured him that the Latin American baseball beat would be respected as his territory within black baseball. It also meant borrowing an idea from the numbers game: numbers barons purportedly respected particular streets of Harlem as exclusive territories of operations in order not only to maintain peace but also to enjoy mutual prosperity. Whether this approach would ultimately aid Pompez in building a contender remained to be seen.

League president Isaac Nutter called the ECL owners to an emergency meeting in mid-March: Ed Bolden and Nat Strong had bolted from the league to play independent baseball. The remaining ECL owners—Pompez; Keenan of the Lincoln Giants; George Rossiter of the Baltimore Black Sox; and Tom Jackson of the Bacharach Giants—convened in Atlantic City. They denounced Bolden and Strong, labeling their teams "outlaws" and instituting a scheduling boycott. Several ECL owners welcomed Strong's defection. To them, his departure was "one of the best things could have happened": he was an impediment, someone who had "blocked numerous progressive measures that were brought up for action."[28] The defections raised uncertainty about the league's viability. This gave Pompez pause; he considered whether to play independent ball or just sell the Cuban Stars. Nutter tried to talk him out of leaving. He decided to give the league another shot as the owners admitted two new franchises: the Philadelphia-based Eastern All Stars and the Brooklyn Stars. A joint meeting of ECL and NNL owners a month earlier had fueled hopes that the ECL's problems could be resolved with the owners agreeing to change the terms for the splitting of revenues for league games, dropping the $150 a game guarantee for 35 percent of the gate for the visiting team with a $50 rain guarantee.[29]

Bolden defended his decision to leave the ECL in a letter to the *Afro-American*. The Hilldale executive outlined his participation in the league's organization and the circuit's ongoing problems. "I organized the league, and am heartily in favor of organized baseball," he wrote. However, ECL owners had a propensity to allow their self-interest to defeat the collective good. Umpiring was a case in point. "I also inaugurated a system of rotating umpires," Bolden explained. "Selfish Commissioners with a sinister motive objected, and succeeded in making the league accept the old home umpire system." That decision fostered accusations of favoritism—umpires' calls favoring the home team to better ensure being rehired. Lack of "cooperation" doomed the circuit. "One Club becomes dissatisfied because it cannot have everything its own way, and jumps out of the league when it sees fit, and jumps back again when it feels like it," Bolden continued. The fact that each team did not have their own home park hampered the league's development and created inequities. "Some clubs come to your park, and during the season take away thousands of dollars, yet they never have a park to give you anything in return."[30] In offering this final point, Bolden made a direct swipe at Pompez: teams such as the Cuban Stars that lacked a home ballpark, the Philadelphia-based owner claimed, failed to engage in the reciprocal business of hosting a full slate of home games for the league, which unevenly affected the financial ledgers and risk incurred by each club.

Other pressing matters occupied Pompez's mind early in 1928 as he juggled the business of being a numbers banker, a Negro-league team owner, and a member of Harlem's Latino community. The numbers business continued to flourish. Political matters had crowded into his agenda with the publication of the "Spanish Menace in Harlem" article in late January. He also attempted to intercede in the ECL's messy affairs by calling an owners-only meeting. Into his Harlem office filed Keenan, Baltimore's Rossiter, and Isaac Washington, representing the Bacharach Giants. Bolden and Alex Mayo came from Philadelphia to hear and see whether Pompez could exhibit the diplomatic finesse to broker an accord. Little optimism came out of the meeting: no degree of finesse could persuade the battling owners to let go of their individual angst and advance the collective project. In fact, quite the opposite occurred: the owners agreed they would all opt for independent ball. After the meeting, the *Chicago Defender* declared the circuit dead. The *Baltimore Afro-American* and the *Amsterdam News* followed suit.[31]

A last-ditch effort to save the circuit took place a week later at a meeting called by Nutter in Philadelphia. Whatever confidence Pompez still had in the collective enterprise fizzled away. The biggest news to come out of the gathering was that the Cuban Stars were up for sale. Nutter announced that a potential sale had fallen through: Martín Dihigo's jump to Cum Posey's Homestead Grays for what Pompez described as "the largest salary ever paid a Negro ball player" had scared off the buyer, who claimed "the club wasn't worth what Pompez wanted without Dihigo."[32] Whether Pompez was in or out and its impact on the circuit was the talk of the black press. Nutter's assurances before the Philadelphia meeting that the Cuban Stars owner was definitely staying and the subsequent discovery that this might not actually be his intention weakened the owners' confidence in Nutter. For Pompez, staying in the league hinged on his ability to book games. For example, if he could not play Hilldale at Nat Strong's Dexter Park in Brooklyn, he was done with the league. While Nutter agreed to the Dexter Park stipulation, Bolden did not, instead opting for independent ball. The animosity between Bolden and Strong remained too intense for any such arrangement.

Restocking his depleted roster commanded Pompez's attention as the ECL opened its 1928 season. Dealing with the death of Pablo Mesa and a recovering Alejandro Oms meant a revamped outfield. Bernardo Baró returned to his right-field post and was eventually rejoined by Oms, while Agustín Bejerano attempted to fill the hole created by Mesa's death. Replacing Dihigo was an impossible task, talent-wise, given his prodigious hitting and his versatility; Dihigo had yet to assume regular pitching duties for Pompez's team. Dihigo had demonstrated his versatility in the field once again in 1927, spending much of the campaign playing shortstop after the team's regular starter, Pelayo Chacón, fell to injury. The cleanup spot in the batting order formerly occupied by Dihigo was eventually turned over to Oms, but Pompez found it much harder to find someone to man the shortstop spot. Chacón's pace of recovery from injuries placed doubt on his 1928 season. To fill Chacón's spot, Pompez first signed Ramón Herrera, a former major leaguer who had spent parts of 1925 and 1926 with the Boston Red Sox. When neither Herrera nor Angel Alfonso panned out at short, Pompez dipped into Puerto Rico for the first time, signing speedy shortstop Emilio "Millito" Navarro.

For the Negro leagues' first Puerto Rican, the early June call to join the Cuban Stars involved leaving the Caribbean for the first time. Upon Navarro's arrival in port in New York City after five days aboard the steamer *San Lorenzo*, one of Pompez's men, a former player Francisco "Canilla" Rivas, met the twenty-two-year-old. Informing him that the team awaited him in Philadelphia, Rivas took Navarro to Grand Central Terminal and, after purchasing a ticket for him, gave travel instructions. "The train makes various stops before arriving at Philadelphia. Every time that the train makes a stop, an announcer blows a whistle and states the place where the train is arriving," he told the Puerto Rican, who was about to embark on his first train ride. "When you hear Philadelphia Terminal, exit the train because there the team manager and several players will be waiting for you." Despite the instructions, the trip worried the young ballplayer: "I did not have mastery over English, I had not even a cent, I did not know the city. What would happen if I mistakenly got off at the wrong stop?" Moreover, except for Pedro San, with whom Navarro had played in Puerto Rico the previous winter, none of the Cuban Stars knew him. The worry proved unwarranted. A group that included José María Fernández, Juanelo Mirabal, and Isidro Fabré welcomed him at the Philadelphia Terminal and escorted him to the ballpark. There, Pompez insisted that Navarro be put through a workout, but Fernández resisted, mindful of the newcomer's recent travels. However, Pompez and Fernández immediately liked what they saw, and Navarro was inserted into the leadoff slot for the next day's batting order.[33]

The swift-footed shortstop paced the revamped Cuban Stars offense and gained a fast following. Press accounts and box scores eschewed the use of his last name; like international soccer stars decades later, he went simply by "Millito."

The Cuban Stars owner had finally found a shortstop to his liking. Upon returning to Harlem, Pompez made sure all the arrangements had been taken care of for his new leadoff hitter. He also showed the diminutive Puerto Rican the city, perhaps recalling his own initial arrival. "[Pompez] took me downtown to show me the sights of the city," Navarro recalled. He was amazed by the clubs, the food, and the women. This was Harlem; this was New York City. But the owner could not protect Millito and his Cuban Stars teammates from the reality of segregation and oddities of racial thinking. A trip south to Richmond, Virginia, for Pompez's troupe included an unforgettable visit to a local restaurant. Seating themselves at a table, the group decided to speak in Spanish; they weren't served. A restaurant manager stopped by their table and inquired what language the men were speaking. Informed that it was Spanish, the manager responded, "Oh, you are West Indians." A Jim Crow lesson learned: spoken language could transform a group of questionable individuals from excludable black Americans to foreigners who could be served.[34]

The addition of Navarro could not salvage the season for the Cuban Stars, but his arrival continued Pompez's ever-widening acquisition of talent. After initially building a team entirely of Cuban talent, as Abel Linares had, Pompez successfully extended his reach into Panama, the Dominican Republic, and Puerto Rico by signing Oscar Levis, Pedro San, and Millito Navarro. In so doing, he had truly internationalized the Negro-league circuit, introducing the first Panamanian (Levis in 1921), the first Dominican (San in 1926), and the first Puerto Rican (Navarro in 1928).

ECL magnates continued to navigate rough waters into late May, when the Cuban Stars finally opted for independent ball. The *Amsterdam News* derided the decision: "If Alejandro Pompez of the Cubans felt that he was dealing a death blow to that association when he sent in his resignation to that body . . . he is doomed to disappointment." The league would go on without him, the paper declared. A battle over players loomed every time a franchise withdrew. The ECL charter stipulated that "players of all clubs surrendering franchises are the property of the league." The *Amsterdam News* predicted conflict as departing owners attempted to retain their players and the remaining ECL franchises tried to sign the "available" talent. "Not even the Cuban athletes are safe from the coming attack," the paper predicted. The Havana Red Sox were seeking admission into the ECL with an eye on players previously on Pompez's squad.[35] Fully aware of the ECL's shortcomings, Pompez nonetheless insisted that the organization was the key to protecting each team's players and moving forward into 1929. "We must have a League," he told *The Pittsburgh Courier* in July.[36] A league meant protection, individually and collectively. Yet this did not prevent him or other owners from quitting the ECL. In its place arose the American Negro League (ANL).

Troubles surfaced early for Pompez's Cuban Stars and the new venture. In late April, eight of his players failed to report to spring training camp in Jacksonville, Florida. Worse still, Pompez had already paid their transportation costs, and several among the absent had already accepted advance money. The names of the missing players were forwarded to the league, and the ANL owners suspended the eight: Pelayo Chacón, Alejandro Oms, Basilio Rosell, Millito Navarro, Tetelo Vargas, Eustaquio Pedroso, Ramón Bragaña, and Agustin Bejerano. Learning that Chacón had formed the Havana Cuban Stars with his other seven players upset Pompez. Just as unnerving, it was rumored that Nat Strong, his onetime mentor, had agreed to finance the new team. The ANL attempted to strike back. They advised booking agents that "no [ANL] club will play any team which plays any outfit using a suspended player or in any park when such a team plays."[37]

Once again Pompez had to work on restocking his team's roster. Replacing the suspended players meant filling more than half of the positions, as ANL team rosters were limited to fifteen players. A difficult task under normal circumstances was made even more challenging by the closeness of opening day. Then there were the new competitors for Latino talent: Strong's start-up team and Pollock's Havana Red Sox. Pompez moved to block the admission of Pollock's club into the ANL. An upset Pollock wrote a fiery letter to the *Amsterdam News* that decried the ANL as "a joke" for trying to ban his team. "Our record is clean, our business methods held in high esteem by managers throughout the country," he wrote. He labeled as hypocritical ANL policies that permitted its members to sign players away from independent teams but forbade such meddling from outsiders.[38] But Pollock's letter held little sway with the ANL leadership: they continued to ostracize his Red Sox. On the other hand, Pompez reconciled with most of his suspended players in late July. The league's discipline had forced them to come to terms and make "their peace with Alex," reported the *Amsterdam News*.[39] Their return could do little to save the season as the Cuban Stars remained mired in last place.

The early 1930s was a period of realignment in black baseball in the East. The ANL, even more short-lived than the ECL, disbanding after just one season. No league operated in 1930. Stalwarts like Bolden and Pompez would mostly play independent ball. Nat Strong seemingly hovered about like a vulture, ready to pick off players or schedule bookings for teams that reverted to independent ball. A few teams found this to be an opportune moment to enter black baseball. Such was the case with the New York Black Yankees, who would operate as Pompez's nearest geographic competitor in the black circuit starting in 1932.

A perennial also-ran that never garnered a first-place finish during its entire existence, the Black Yankees team could not have been more different from its namesake. Originally the Harlem Stars, it came under the control of James "Soldier Boy" Semler, a numbers magnate, although famed entertainer Bill "Bojangles" Robinson, who held a minority ownership interest, was the public face of the franchise. Equipped with old Yankees uniforms through an arrangement secured by Robinson, the Black Yankees initially aspired to hold their games at Yankee Stadium and the Polo Grounds. The team did not often grace those hallowed ballparks in its early days, and when it did, it usually was as part of four-team doubleheaders. The Black Yankees struggled to draw spectators and stay solvent. Semler turned to Nat Strong for an infusion of cash, and the team was beholden to Strong's booking agency thereafter. According to Semler, the change was one of necessity: "We needed cash and couldn't get it from any colored business men so we borrowed it from Strong."[40] Semler's predicament typified how certain whites were well positioned to capitalize on the economic disadvantages blacks encountered in the sporting world. It also shows the financial straits that black baseball owners found themselves in during the early years of the Great Depression and why several turned to numbers bankers to underwrite their ventures.

Black baseball came to a virtual standstill during the Depression. Though several leagues tried to fill the void after the ECL's collapse, the new Negro National League founded by Gus Greenlee in 1934 proved the most successful. Much had changed in black baseball in the interim. The largest figure to shape the black professional baseball world passed in the intervening years: Rube Foster late in 1930. Over the next decade the Negro leagues would reach their zenith, both financially and in popularity. None were as important yet as controversial in the climb to the summit as the numbers kings. Seriously undercapitalized like most black enterprises during the Depression, the Negro leagues survived largely due to the money invested by the numbers men, yet their direct involvement in rebuilding black baseball would later elicit questions about whether this enterprise was, like the numbers, a racket.

4

THE RISE AND FALL
OF A NUMBERS KING

They would have been steel tycoons, Wall Street brokers, auto moguls had they been white.   *—Richard Wright*

Numbers bankers lived on the edge—not just the edge of the law, but on the precipice of financial ruin. They worried constantly that just one number could bankrupt their operations. Bettors tended to be a superstitious lot: they had their dream books, charms, and unique methods of calculation—whatever they believed could inspire the right digits to wager and make the score. An assortment of numbers had popular appeal, given their superstitious significance. The desire to obtain the right number spawned the cottage industry of dream books, manuals that unlocked the mysteries of what our slumbering minds envision numerically. Problem arose when too many bettors played the same number and it hit. Numbers bankers had to scramble to gather enough cash to pay off the winners. Reputation was everything. If the clients got wind of a banker who had shirked bettors or had run off to the Caribbean with their winnings, that banker was done.

November 23, 1931, proved to be the day so many numbers bankers dreaded. The Clearing House posted its numbers. News spread to Harlem quicker than an express train headed uptown. Number 527 hit. It was the day before Thanksgiving, and hundreds of people had placed their nickel, dime, and quarter bets on 527. Any combination of the numbers 2, 5, and 7 had been seen as lucky for numbers bettors; explanations varied as to why. According to one, there were five letters in the name of Jesus, who arose after two days of being dead, and those two spiritual numbers added together equaled seven: placing these in order yielded the number 527.

Harlem numbers kings like Pompez, who regularly took $6,000 to $7,000 in daily action, had to scurry. After the wagers his bank had taken in that day, he was short $68,000. That was a lot of cash to gather from various locations, debtors, and commercial banks whose workers were about to head out for the Thanksgiving holiday. Everyone involved in the numbers knew that 527 had hit. And there were plenty who had played the number with Pompez's bank; they would have a lot for which to be thankful. At least $115 in wagers was placed on 527 in his bank alone: if the average wager was a quarter, then there were at least 560 people awaiting their winnings. For Pompez and the other numbers bankers, this was Black Wednesday.[1]

Dutch Schultz smelled blood in the water: few things made him happier than to sense a moment of weakness among those he sought to dominate. Schultz had been homing in on the Harlem's numbers scene since word that the repeal of Prohibition was nigh; the bootlegger needed a new revenue stream. Once he grew wise to the sheer volume of money that the numbers generated, he decided to muscle his way into the Harlem racket.[2] A violent campaign ensued that scared a few numbers kings into retirement, including Casper Holstein, who "retired" and returned to the Caribbean. Plainly put, Dutch successfully executed a hostile takeover, one that pushed nearly all of Harlem's African American, West Indian, and Latino numbers bankers out of prominent roles. Only a brave few, such as Madame St. Clair, refused. In their place stood the Dutchman, whose henchmen's brutal intimidation tactics introduced a level of violence previously unseen in Harlem's numbers, which radically transformed from a system based on working understandings between bankers about respecting territories to one based on violent competition and the policing of boundaries.[3]

Schultz had set his sights on Pompez's numbers business. The Cuban had held him off until now. Black Wednesday placed his reputation on the line: $68,000 was a lot of liquid capital to round up on a holiday weekend. Schultz's men came in to offer assistance. Dutch would provide the cash to cover the shortage if Pompez would just join him—now.

Solly Girsch came to Pompez's cigar store with a message: Meet the following evening at 8:00 p.m. at the Cayuga Club, on 118th Street between Seventh and Lenox. Girsch did most of the talking. The rub: Schultz wanted Pompez to pay for protection. Dutch had gotten Big Joe Ison to pay, and he had been brought to the meeting to attest to this fact, lest Pompez not believe it. The deal, Girsch explained, would involve Schultz providing the cash to pay off the bettors from Black Wednesday in exchange for a 60–40 split of Pompez's banking business. Schultz, of course, would take the 60 percent share. Pompez would be placed on salary: $250 weekly.

The numbers sounded right, but everyone in Harlem numbers knew there was more involved to partnering with Schultz. His entreaties to partner up were easy to turn down at one level: he never had equal partners, they always worked for him, and he got paid his share, then his men (the lawyers, political and legal connections, and muscle), then his partners in Harlem. And his violent reputation had preceded him.

Pompez attempted to stand tall and speak convincingly. "Well, you have got the wrong man, because I haven't got the business and I haven't got the money to pay any protection, and furthermore we don't need protection in this business, and I can't pay him anything at the present time." He continued calling in his debts and trying to pay back those who had won on that fateful Wednesday.

A week and half later, Girsch and an associate reappeared at the cigar store. "Well, you better be thinking this over," Girsch stated in a more threatening tone, "because it will be for your own benefit."

Pompez tried to relocate operations immediately, but it proved a wasted move. Bo Weinberg and Bernard "Lulu" Rosenkrantz came calling at the new location. What's the delay? they inquired. Pompez had given his word that he would turn over the bank, they insisted, another move to strong-arm the numbers king into their fold despite what he had said. There were no receipts to hand over to the combination, he informed them. The previous days had been spent paying his 527 bettors, winnowing the shortage to about $8,000. The men relayed the update; Schultz dispatched another of his men, George Weinberg, who appeared early the next morning at Pompez's door with the cash to cover the remaining shortage. Now the partners could start clean, with no outstanding debts to the bettors.[4]

The year 1931 had not been a good one from the start. The American Negro League disbanded, meaning no league play for the Cuban Stars. Then in May Pompez's younger sister, Leonora, and her husband, Pedro Rodríguez, died. Entrusted to handle her affairs and to take care of his three nephews, Pompez dispatched his longtime friend Joseph Miranda to the Bronx to purchase a family plot in the massive Woodlawn Cemetery to bury his sister and brother-in-law.[5] Still in mourning, he was hounded by unwelcome visitors to his Sugar Hill apartment, his cigar stores, and his Lenox Avenue offices. Then Black Wednesday occurred. Now he was being pressured to work for the Dutchman himself.

Being Made an Example Of

Dutch Schultz's takeover was a peculiar demonstration, as he commandeered what many had defined as a race enterprise in Harlem. Not only did Schultz actively practice intimidation and violent policing of debtors and his numbers runners, but his syndicate also enjoyed relative immunity from prosecution for his activities in Harlem. Dutch, it became obvious, had several well-placed Democratic Party officials and police officers on his payroll.[6] The violence that ensued on Harlem streets eventually motivated the district attorney to name Thomas Dewey as special prosecutor in 1935 and to launch an antiracketeering crackdown that included among its targets the numbers game.

Schultz was not a welcome guest on Harlem streets. Residents contrasted his operational approach with that of Pompez and Harlem's other deposed numbers kings. "Unlike Schultz, who tried to hog it all," Harlemites believed Pompez and Joe Ison, for example, "were willing to 'take some and leave some,' and did not go around 'Bustin' heads,' and are 'a credit to the game.'"[7]

The New Year arrived and Schultz's men reappeared at the cigar store. Weinberg informed Pompez that Schultz had called a bankers' meeting at Big Joe's place. Although he had yet to deliver his bank into Schultz's hands, Pompez knew that he had better attend. Upon entering Ison's house, he saw the familiar faces of his fellow numbers bankers who had once ruled Harlem streets: Marcial Flores, Henry Miro,

Elmer Maloney, and Ison. The purpose of the meeting was for the Harlem bankers to form a combination, Weinberg and Schultz's other men informed those gathered. The numbers could be controlled and the bankers could again operate by respecting each other's territory, collectors would not try to take business away from one another, and everyone would pay the same percentage and the amount of the hits and bets. Just like the old days, Schultz's men insisted to the numbers barons. The major difference was that they would all be working for Dutch.

The meeting worried Pompez. He told Dixie Davis, who actually represented both Pompez and Schultz at the time, "I want to make [up] my mind to come and join this combination because I am tired of fighting these people." Davis advised him that joining would be the wiser course of action, as there was no use fighting Schultz and his men any longer: they had the money, the connections, and the power. "The best thing you can do for your own good is turn in to this combination," Davis told him.

"Why don't you go and see the Dutchman and see what he says about it?" Weinberg advised. "He is not going to hurt you. He is not going to do anything to you, but just explain the situation." The appointment to see the Dutchman was set for Saturday the following week.[8]

Bo and Lulu appeared around 11:00 p.m. at Pompez's 409 Edgecombe apartment. The two offered to take him for a ride around Central Park and have a talk. Pompez knew the wiser course was to go: Schultz could be messed with for only so long before he or his men roughed Pompez up or got trigger-happy. But, fortunately for Pompez, Schultz and his men needed him. Pompez was a conduit to a diverse clientele, a market share that Schultz desired. Those who bet with his bank were not just English-speaking but also included recently arrived and native-born Latinos. Pompez was the biggest of Harlem's Latino numbers kings, and Schultz needed El Cubano as a face man, someone whom the locals trusted and with whom they would continue to do business.

When they finally arrived at Dixie Davis's apartment, Davis and George Weinberg were already there, but not Schultz. Pompez had already made the acquaintance of everyone in the room through the previous invitations to form a combination. George had established the habit of showing up at wherever Pompez moved his banking operations. His escorts tonight, Bo and Lulu, had stopped by his apartment and his cigar store on numerous occasions. He had yet to personally meet the Dutchman. They waited. Finally, at about two in the morning, Dutch appeared.

Bo Weinberg introduced the two. Pompez greeted Dutch, who was direct.

"What's the matter you didn't want to come to see me?" Schultz asked him. "Did you think you were to get a man with horns in his head?"

"No. I thought I was going to see a man just like any other man."

"Well, I am glad you come over. I want to see you come in here," Dutch said, motioning Pompez to enter the kitchen and sit at the table, where there were four chairs: one for the visitor, another for Dixie Davis, and the others for Bo and George Weinberg. Schultz would stand for this sit-down and run the meeting.

"I sent four men to see you about paying us protection. We are going in Harlem and everybody in Harlem is going to pay us protection," Schultz intoned.

"I am very sorry, but I cannot pay you protection because I have lost a lot of money in the game," Pompez replied. "I had a bad number, 527, and I lost a lot of money and I haven't got it, and I don't want to promise something I can't make good in the future."

"How about taking the business over?" Schultz asked, as if he were truly interested in a collaborative venture.

"What is your proposition in that matter?" Pompez inquired, knowing it was better to hear Schultz out than to be outright dismissive of any proposition Dutch was putting on the table.

"We will give you forty percent of the winners and give you a salary for living, $250 a week, and we will take the losses in case there is any losses." Schultz was simply repeating the standing offer.

"Well, I am sorry I cannot accept this proposition at the present time because I owe people money, that I was hit very hard and I still owe some people and I want to pay them before I come with you," Pompez replied, looking for a glimmer of a way out.

Schultz, closing whatever loophole the Harlem's numbers king's sought, declared: "All right, we will do this. From now on consider yourself my partner and if you have any big hits that you cannot make good come to us and we will give you the money to pay the people, so you can hold your business."

Pompez agreed. There was no way out.

"How long will it take you to pay these people?"

"About two or three weeks to see if I can overcome all these debts that I have," Pompez informed his new partner.

Worn out from his meeting with Dutch, Pompez hurried from the kitchen and out of Davis's apartment to head back to Harlem at about five in the morning. He had agreed to become the next in the line of Harlem's numbers barons to join Schultz's operation. Ison, Flores, and Miro had all joined, and now Schultz had gotten him, too.

But Pompez kept operating his bank on his own, and the two weeks passed without his turning over the bank. Bo and Lulu paid another visit to his cigar store. "What's the matter that you didn't go back?" Bo asked.

"I haven't finished paying my people, and I want to pay them before I go in with you all," Pompez replied. He knew full well the purpose of their visit, but if he entered into the combination with no significant debt, it might be easier to break from it later.

"All right; why don't you go and see the Dutchman and get him to explain the situation to you?" Weinberg said, extending a new invitation, which was more of a veiled threat this time. Dutch did not like repeating himself to anyone.

"All right, I will go and see him if it is necessary," Pompez answered, recognizing that time had run out and he could no longer give Schultz the runaround.

Weinberg and Lulu Rosenkrantz pulled up to his cigar store on West 145th Street to transport him to the next sit-down. The car was different this time, a bulletproof Cadillac sedan. The meeting place was also new, Davis's mother's house at 898 West End Avenue. However, Schultz's timing was the same: he appeared around 2:00 a.m. with four bodyguards.

"Well, I am glad you are over here tonight, because I want to see you," Schultz began as he walked Pompez into the kitchen. It was just the two of them to talk, *hombre a hombre*. No witnesses around the table to serve as intermediaries and to calm the situation if necessary.

Schultz showed that he meant business, taking out his gun from his waistband and laying it on the table between them.

"I hate a damned liar," Schultz opened. "You promised to turn in your business after two weeks after that and I heard—you didn't turn it in—I heard from Henry Miro that he says that you are going to fight us, that you are not going to turn that business to us, and I want you to know that you are dealing with a different type of people now, that you are not dealing with these spics in Harlem."

Schultz now spoke menacingly. "You are going to be the first nigger I am going to make an example in Harlem, and I don't care and I don't give a damn if you make a statement from here to the Battery to the police that I am going to hurt you. It won't do you any good."

"I am sorry that you should talk that way," Pompez replied while gathering his courage. "You are the first man to insult me for any reason whatever. I was promised to come here to do business with you and you go and insult me. If you feel that way, we don't do any business."

"That's what's the matter with all you Spanish-speaking people," Schultz fired back. "You got too much blood in your veins. But this is one time that you are going to turn in your business in to us. Like it or not."

"I haven't said to anybody that I am going to fight you," Pompez retorted, denying what others had apparently informed Schultz.

"I am going to prove that you did say so. I am going to call Henry Miro right now." Schultz called Dixie Davis into the room, commanding him to get Miro to the meeting immediately.

Davis sensed that matters were quickly deteriorating. He whispered to Pompez as he passed him on the way to phone Miro: "Now, listen. If you say that you are going to give this man a fight, tell me and stop me from calling him, because you may get yourself in a big trouble."

"I haven't told anybody I am going to fight this man, because it isn't possible for me to fight a big man like this," he told Davis, aware that matters could be going a lot better and that things could easily get worse.

Davis phoned Miro and informed him that Dutch needed to see him immediately. Despite being rustled out of bed, Miro promptly arrived and was ushered into the kitchen. "Didn't you tell me that Pompez say he was going to give us a fight and say 'I am not going to turn the business in'?" Schultz asked Miro. The Puerto Rican numbers man remained silent. Enraged, Schultz berated Miro for lying to him about Pompez. His silence earned him a scolding, but another lie—or perhaps the truth—could have cost Pompez dearly.

Dutch and Pompez hashed out another, revised schedule for the Cuban to turn in his business. Another two weeks' extension to repay his debts and turn the bank over—it was a rare instance of Schultz's exercising patience. Pompez again refused to take money from Schultz to cover his shortage. He would later admit that this was a tactical delay and that he was indeed trying to duck Schultz; he truly was not interested in partnering with the Dutchman.[9]

March arrived, and Pompez could delay no longer. He called Schultz and took his $7,000 to pay off the lingering debt. Pleased, Schultz dispatched George Weinberg to Pompez's cigar store with the cash. After the money was delivered, Pompez took Weinberg to the center of his banking operations at 150th Street and Broadway.

Gathering his workers around, he informed everyone of the decision. "Now, boys, I joined the combination. I am going in with the racketeers, and the only thing I want you to do is to keep it a secret because I don't want people to know that I am hooked up with this type of people." Pompez ended his announcement cryptically: "I don't want to keep fighting these people because I am afraid to lose my life."[10]

Pompez turned over the keys to Weinberg, whom Schultz entrusted with control of the everyday operations of Pompez's former bank. Its top individuals were also replaced with Schultz's own people. The arrangement was no partnership but clearly a demotion for Pompez.

The Fall and Rise of a Numbers King

Pompez was arguably the biggest catch in Schultz's campaign to rule over Harlem's numbers. Dutch demonstrated this by assigning George Weinberg, one of his higher-level white workers, to run the bank. In other banks that Schultz had taken over, he did not bother to place his trusted lieutenants but instead put three black men in charge of protecting his interests: William "Bub" Hewlett, Fritzi Grand, and Malcolm "Blue" Renier. The three ventured into other strong-arm businesses for themselves; their criminal activities would eventually result in the long-term incarceration of each.[11]

Pompez was now a pawn in Schultz's ongoing chess match with legal authorities. This no doubt frustrated the Cuban-American, who later learned that Dutch used money generated by Pompez's former bank to pay "protection" to Democratic officials and law enforcement.[12] Now basically a controller for Schultz's syndicate, as a result of Schultz's takeover, Pompez had been stripped of his social status and the elevated sense of masculinity that came with being a numbers king. In times past, he and other numbers barons had enjoyed a sense of power from their ability to get things done in Harlem by spurring local political figures into action. Schultz's entry into their world with the cooperation of Tammany Hall's Democratic machine neutralized whatever social capital Harlem's numbers kings had once enjoyed.

Although the numbers game was primarily a masculine domain, Madame St. Clair not only rose to the highest level in the racket but was also the most significant Harlem banker to successfully evade Schultz's clutches. When the male numbers bankers fled or joined Schultz, "Madame Queen" openly defied him, steadfastly keeping her operations independent. Unfazed by the gender dynamics, and perhaps taking advantage of them, St. Clair sparred verbally with Schultz in the papers.[13] In doing so, she expressed what many Harlemites suspected: that the white mobster had gained control of Harlem's numbers with the complicity of certain elected officials and law enforcement officers.[14]

Schultz's ability to operate in Harlem with relative impunity compared with the black and Latino numbers bankers who had operated there before him signaled how greatly race mattered, even in the sporting world. Segregation affected much of New York City's entertainment, affecting everyone from the performers to club owners and executives. Venues like the Cotton Club featured African Americans, West Indians, and Latinos as performers onstage but did not welcome them as part of the paying crowd. In baseball, perceptions of race and individual identity influenced where players got to play, in either the Negro leagues or the majors. Less evident was its impact on the front office and ownership. In this regard, both baseball and the numbers presented opportunities unavailable elsewhere for individuals like Pompez.

The numbers brought Pompez great wealth and allowed him to live in Harlem's most exclusive areas, from Strivers Row in the 1920s to the top of Sugar Hill at 409 Edgecombe in the 1930s and 1940s. Not all were pleased when Pompez and his kind moved into their Harlem neighborhood. Writing for the *Amsterdam News*, A. M. Wendell Malliet described the unease that occurred when the numbers barons "invaded" the exclusive neighborhoods of the black bourgeoisie. Residents of Sugar Hill, according to Malliet, "had moved into the 'ritzy' section in the hope that they would live and move in a class by themselves, free from the tumult and the shouting of the maddening crowd."[15] Among the policy barons specifically named in Malliet's article as having established both shop and residence in Sugar Hill were Pompez and Ison, at Edgecombe Avenue (321 and 409) and St. Nicholas Avenue (880 and 870).

Playing the numbers was not just about gambling for leisure but partly a response to the economic and social realities in which Harlemites lived. Harlem's residents encountered racial strife in all aspects of their everyday lives. Discriminatory hiring practices at the department stores they frequented on 125th Street meant that few if any of their own were hired to work there. The exorbitant rental rates they paid did not guarantee that landlords would maintain their housing. It was not the Jim Crow South, where laws forbade equal access and opportunity to blacks and shattered any illusions of social equality, but the impact of such social practices and of de facto segregation was nonetheless harsh.[16] Theirs was a world of dreams deferred, as the poet Langston Hughes wrote. As a result, Harlem streets were filled with sounds of protests, pickets, and parades, along with more informal actions to fight against inequality. Some, such as Newark Eagles owner Effa Manley, enlisted mainstream organizations such as the NAACP and formed protest campaigns such as the "Don't Buy Where You Can't Work" campaign. Others joined Marcus Garvey's UNIA or the Communist Party and pressed for a more radical agenda. These were the Depression years, and economic conditions and opportunities were even worse for most of Harlem's residents than for the rest of the city's working-class poor.

Where jobs were often scarce and prospects slim, many Harlemites turned to the numbers. By 1932, when Schultz's men took control,

Pompez's bank's daily gross averaged between $7,000 and $8,000, well over $2 million a year.[17] Newspaper accounts estimated his gross as substantially higher; his combined numbers banking operation with Big Joe Ison grossed approximately $5 million in 1935, reportedly Harlem's biggest numbers operation.[18] The heavy numbers betting in Harlem brought scrutiny from local ministers, police, and increasingly the district attorney's office.

An anti-vice crusade shifted from Prohibition to other aspects of the seedy underbelly of urban life, which meant vigilance was necessary for those in the numbers business. They were liable to become targets of law enforcement at any time for upsetting the wrong local politician or precinct captain. Almost a year to the day of Black Wednesday, police raided Pompez's bank operating under George Weinberg's supervision.[19] The arrests were quickly disposed of, as Schultz promised would be done for all those in his combination. Such occurrences reminded numbers bankers that it was not always clear who was or was not on the take within the law enforcement community or in political circles. Indeed, a numbers banker had to aim his bribes high enough in the hierarchy so that such problems went away. However, not all beat cops and especially not all those on the vice squad knew the deal.

Despite his well-aimed contributions, the heat kept coming after Schultz, busting into his banking centers, arresting his people. This annoyed Schultz, who spent thousands of dollars a month paying political officials and police to make sure these sweeps did not impact his operations; his men were not supposed to get arrested and dragged before the local magistrates. Each arrest cost money and time; they mucked up his operations.

In a sweep that made front-page news in the *Amsterdam News*, police successfully raided Schultz's operations. Police nabbed Pompez, the "one time all powerful czar in the numbers racket in Harlem," who had resisted "to the last" the efforts of Schultz, according to the paper. Cops also raided his "luxurious apartment" and business office, which yielded plenty of evidence: policy slips for $5,000 wagered in the numbers. The sweep sent Schultz a message; not only was Pompez locked up, but another fifteen stationery and candy stores that doubled as drop points were shut down. The Magistrates' Court also set a higher bail on Pompez ($2,500) than on the others and, following recently instituted guidelines, fined first offenders found guilty of carrying policy slips.[20] After the arrest, Schultz used back channels and Dixie Davis to get the charges dismissed.

Pompez had become a symbolic target of law enforcement, and Schultz weighed the benefits of continuing their partnership. The Harlem numbers man, too, expressed his dissatisfaction with his arrangement with Schultz. Pompez alleged that although his weekly salary was to be $250, he never got more than $75. More egregious, the combination owed him $36,000 in profits, by his estimation. Then, in March, Harry Schoenhaus and George Weinberg, high-ranking members of Schultz's outfit, refused to pay out on big hits that bettors scored on Pompez's bank, leaving unfulfilled the terms of their agreement from two years earlier.

Maintaining one's reputation was vital, and not paying out could mean ruin. Pompez inquired about the situation with Weinberg: "Well, I want you to know that we cannot pay you that money for this hit," Weinberg informed him. "You better do what you can and get the money from the shortage that you already have because we have no money to give because we spent all the money that we had in Dutch Schultz's [income tax evasion] case. We have no money."

"What about my share in this business?" Pompez asked.

"Well, if we ever get money together, we will pay you your money."

Weinberg's response did not raise Pompez's hopes about ever seeing what was owed him. His bank's money was being spent elsewhere, and now they want him to pay off the hits himself. Perhaps there was some solace in knowing that Schultz's outfit now owed him more than he owed them—that perhaps he could venture back on his own. Indeed, he would later claim that this was the moment "they quit me."[21]

Back in the Game

Pompez decided to proceed as if he were freed of his obligation to Schultz's combination and to start afresh, not just in "the business" but in his personal life as well. On July 8, 1934, he took marital vows for the second time, marrying Ruth Seldon. His first marriage, to a woman named Margarita, had ended in divorce. That marriage remains shrouded in mystery. The couple lived for a time at 11 West 131st Street, but no record exists in the files in New York Municipal Archives of their union taking place in New York County. There are a few scattered references elsewhere to Margarita and Pompez being married: a listing on his World War I registration card, completed on September 12, 1918—on which five years were added to his age—and a 1929 invitation for "Mr. and Mrs. Alexander Pompez" to the fiftieth wedding anniversary celebration of *New York Age* publisher Fred Moore and his wife in 1929. Black newspapers scarcely bothered to mention her, although their marriage seemingly lasted ten years. Neither the *New York Age* nor the *Amsterdam News*—which gave so much attention to the feats of Pompez's Cuban Stars and his numbers activities—mentioned Margarita during that span. Perhaps it was a marriage hampered by the realities of his constantly being on the road, traveling with his Cuban Stars. Or it may have been his numbers involvement, as a result of which he was in and out of trouble with the law. Whatever the case, Pompez's first marriage did not survive, and in an era when few got divorced and fewer remarried, Pompez did precisely that.

Pompez's second marriage was a successful one; ten years his junior, Ruth would be there for his biggest trials and triumphs. Marriage to the former Miss Seldon illustrated the social circles he traversed and how they blurred distinctions between the respectable class and the criminal world of black America. Ruth came from a respectable African American family from Virginia—not rich but a black middle-class family of strivers. Her sister was the mother of Edward Brooke, who later gained national stature as the first African American elected to the U.S. Senate since Reconstruction. Brooke's parents did not hide the fact that Ruth was married to a Harlem numbers man. In fact, they sent a teenage Edward along with his sister Helene to spend summer vacations at Aunt Ruth and Uncle Alex's 409 Edgecombe residence at the height of Pompez's reign. Senator Brooke later recalled watching "in fascination as Uncle Alex and Aunt Ruth counted thousands of dollars in small bills on their dining room table."[22]

Participation in the "underground" entrepreneurial sector was part of Pompez's strategic approach to coping with the limitations imposed by racial discrimination within the sporting world and everyday life. He made his personal wealth from his numbers bank operations and funneled earnings to finance his baseball operations. The numbers connection would be a key element to the revival of the Negro leagues. In the midst of the Depression, both the midwestern and eastern circuits ceased operations in 1933. Gus Greenlee was unequivocal about the numbers' importance within black baseball and the black community during this dire economic crisis, stating to *The Pittsburgh Courier* that "if it hadn't been for the numbers, my people would have been a lot worse off then they were."[23]

Furloughed for most of his time working for Schultz, Pompez reorganized his Cuban Stars team as the New York Cubans and sought admission into the Negro National League late in 1934.[24] Surprisingly, NNL owners debated several months before granting admission. While several factors played into this, what was not a significant source of contention in their debate was Pompez's involvement in the numbers. Numbers bankers either ran or bankrolled the Brooklyn Eagles (Abe Manley), the New York Black Yankees (James Semler), the Chicago American Giants (Robert Cole), and the Homestead Grays (Rufus Jackson), and his friend Gus Greenlee ran the league. These particular men were not universally seen as a scourge upon the black community in which they operated; rather, they were regarded with ambivalence and even acceptance. Black America had a complex view of the racial climate that affected the institutions of their community and of the role of the numbers kings within them. Literary giant Richard Wright acknowledged that numbers bankers often occupied a dual position within these communities, writing that "the numbers racketeers in the black community were black entrepreneurs and community leaders at the same time."[25] In fact, black baseball team owners were condemned only when they failed to operate a team in an earnest manner. For this reason Semler and Cole were "universally condemned" by Negro leaguers and their followers. In Semler's case, he drew scorn for trying "to get by on the drawing power of over-the-hill stars" and for putting a less-than-stellar team on the field.[26]

The debate that did occur at the NNL owners' meetings from November 1934 through January 1935 focused on whether Pompez had a viable ballpark under his control for league play. Both of New York City's major black papers, the *Amsterdam News* and the *New York Age*, advocated for the admission of his New York Cubans. Romeo Dougherty used his weekly *Amsterdam News* column to offer a clear-throated endorsement. At their November meeting, NNL owners cited the seating capacity of Dyckman Oval as a problem in rejecting Pompez's application. Dougherty chastised the owners, stating they "did not have the slightest inkling as to his plans for the use of Dyckman Oval" and that Pompez was "prepared to spend thousands of dollars building stands and making the Dyckman field something of which Negroes here would have been proud."[27]

Additionally, Dougherty pointed out that the majority of New York City's black community resided in Harlem, outnumbering that of Brooklyn 300,000 to 70,000. However, Harlem had no Negro-league team to call its own, while NNL owners had granted Abe and Effa Manley a franchise in Brooklyn, Nat Strong's backyard. Harlem's baseball fans and the community merited their own NNL franchise. Former player George "Chappie" Johnson wrote to the *Amsterdam News* in ardent support of Pompez. "I have known Mr. Pompez for years . . . [H]e is one of our greatest promoters and has spent a large amount of money to put colored baseball where it should be." For Johnson, Pompez was the right man for Harlem fans and Dyckman Oval the right spot.[28]

Gaining the support of Greenlee was not the major hurdle. Pompez's New York squad would not be encroaching on his territory. Greenlee's investment in the building of Greenlee Field had set an important example, creating a venue under his direct control. Securing the support of the other owners was contingent on their believing that Pompez could accomplish the same at Dyckman. The failure the Black Yankees had suffered in trying to make Dyckman their home no doubt weighed on deliberations. Outdated grandstands, poor advertising, and Semler's weak ownership doomed the Black Yankees' effort, according to Romeo Dougherty. Unlike Semler, Pompez had Dougherty convinced of his serious commitment to the renovation of Dyckman: "No Negro stood around with a gang of dough ready to do what Alex Pompez plans to do, hence this is a horse of an entirely different color that we are advocating for entrance into the League."[29] *New York Age* scribe Lewis Dial also expressed little doubt about Pompez's ability to renovate Dyckman Oval: "He is a well known sportsman around these parts, has an unquestionably good character and an abundance of funds to support his idea."[30] Pompez's personal background and his Latin American experience were unrivaled assets in black baseball, in Dougherty's mind. "Cubans, Puerto Ricans and a number of the other peoples from the former possessions of Spain are just as rabid as you are over the game," Dougherty observed in a December 1934 column. Letters from Cuban, Puerto Rican, and West Indian fans expressing their excitement at the prospect of Pompez's having a team in the NNL poured in to the *Amsterdam News* columnist. Indeed, no one else could draw on Harlem's growing Spanish-speaking population.[31]

Word came out as NNL owners prepared for their January 1935 meeting: Nat Strong, the most powerful presence in the city's semiprofessional and black baseball circuits, was gone. *Nat Strong Is Dead; Prominent in Sport* announced the *New York Times* on January 11; he had suffered a heart attack just days after having turned sixty-one. Credited with introducing night baseball in New York City by installing lights at Dexter Park in 1930, Strong was celebrated his obituary for having "devoted the greater part of his life to baseball.[32] His death signaled the passing of an era. Black baseball executives were no longer bound to work through his agency to secure bookings. The terms his booking agency had charged—typically 5 to 10 percent—had long angered them. Particularly irksome was Strong's offer of a flat guarantee ($500 to $600) to play lucrative Sunday night games at Dexter Park instead of offering "the common option of receiving a percentage of the profits."[33] Those days were over. Max Rosner and William Leuschner would take the helm of the Nat Strong, Inc., booking agency, which meant less obstinate, entrenched individuals running the operations.

News of Strong's death brought out mixed emotions while casting "a spell of gloom" over the regularly scheduled NNL owners' meeting that took place at the Harlem YMCA. "Although white he played an outstanding part in Negro baseball," the *New York Age* observed. "He made a fortune from booking games (mostly colored) . . . [and] had a stranglehold on the baseball booking business in this city." Many mourned for the man but few were saddened to witness the passing of his reign. "He was an unusually good friend to those he selected as his friends," Gus Greenlee wrote in a letter published in *The Pittsburgh*

Courier, "but a most vindictive enemy. Very little sentiment entered into his dealings. Just plain, hard business." Strong's staunch opposition to the establishment of a strong Negro league in the East was therefore understandable, Greenlee offered. "Organized baseball would destroy his institution which had taken a lifetime to build. And for his own protection, he fought the idea, every time it was presented or seemed to be expanding—with every weapon at his command."[34]

The owners gathered at the Harlem YMCA for their January 12 meeting to consider the way forward. Presided over by league commissioner Rollo Wilson, nine franchises sent representatives: Ed Bolden and Eddie Gottlieb (the Philadelphia Stars); H. G. Hall (the Chicago American Giants and the Nashville Elite Giants); Greenlee (the Pittsburgh Crawfords); Charles H. Tyler (the Newark Dodgers), Rufus Jackson (the Homestead Grays); Ben Taylor and Abe Manley (the Brooklyn Eagles); and Pompez (the New York Cubans). After taking care of preliminary matters, Wilson called on Pompez to present his plans. The prospective franchise holder informed the gathering he was ready to spend $35,000 to "make New York baseball conscious as far as Negro baseball is concerned." He had already consulted with engineers and an architect about Dyckman Oval's renovation "with an eye to improving the spot, enlarging the seating capacity to twelve thousand persons, improving the playing field and player accommodations." Dyckman's location made it the best venue for Harlem fans: it was just a ten-minute subway ride on the newly opened IRT line, very accessible to its three hundred thousand black residents. This time NNL owners unanimously approved his application: the New York Cubans were officially in the game.

Business completed, the owners reconvened that evening at Small's Paradise, at a dinner hosted by the Manleys. More than a hundred guests attended the dinner, including *New York Age* publisher Fred Moore, Eunice Carter (the first black woman assistant district attorney in New York), Reverend John R. Johnson, journalists, and "Harlem big shots."[35] The overall number was diminished, as many chose to attend a memorial service for Nat Strong held in New Rochelle.

Finally granted admission, Pompez opened a new office for the New York Cubans at 200 West 135th Street, hired Frank Forbes as the team's business manager, and, most significantly, finalized a lease with the New York City Parks Department for Dyckman Oval. Lacking a proper home field prior to 1935, his baseball teams had hosted "home" games in the Bronx (Catholic Oval and Protectory Oval), Brooklyn (Dexter Park), Manhattan (Dyckman and Olympic ovals), and Newark (Davids Stadium). Sixty thousand dollars spent on renovations brought installation of a floodlight system for night games and the addition of new box seats and a covered grandstand that expanded seating capacity to approximately twelve thousand. After observing its new stands and "up-to-date" renovations, the *Amsterdam News* reporter Romeo Dougherty wrote that Dyckman Oval made Dexter Park "look like a small town field." "There is no comfort that the fans can crave undone by Pompez Exhibition Co., Inc.," proclaimed the *New York Age* after the unveiling of the renovated Oval grounds, complete with a restaurant and beer garden.[36]

Dyckman Oval soon emerged as Harlem's sporting playground, hosting Negro-league baseball contests, black professional and college football games, and boxing and wrestling cards that featured African American and Latino athletes. The events booked at Dyckman beckoned Spanish-speaking sports fans as well as U.S.-born blacks. August would see a championship bout of Puerto Rican boxer Sixto Escobar at the Oval, his first fight stateside. More than ten thousand crowded into Dyckman to witness Escobar lose the National Boxing Association bantamweight title, "one of the largest gatherings in years to see a battle between little warriors in New York," the *Chicago Defender* noted. Later boxing action at the Oval included Cuban Kid Chocolate and Kid Gavilán and the local Puerto Rican favorite Pedro Montañez. The range of sporting events led Lewis Dial to proclaim, "Dyckman Oval is rapidly gaining the right to the title of Manhattan's amusement center . . . Every branch of sports from races to cricket have been exhibited at Pompez's beautiful miniature stadium."[37]

The Dyckman Oval scene was hopping, providing Harlem residents a haven at a time when they could not attend Harlem entertainment venues that were segregated, such as the Cotton Club. Jazz musicians, entertainers, local politicians, race leaders, and sporting figures such as Joe Louis and Jesse Owens in addition to the everyday fan visited the Oval. The celebrities in the Dyckman crowds even impressed the ballplayers. "Every time we played in New York at Dyckman's Oval,

Fats [Waller] was at the game," Philadelphia Stars outfielder Ted Page told historian Jim Bankes. "He used to play at the Lafayette Theater which was close to the Oval. When I say play, I mean play. That man could really tickle the ivories."[38]

Attendees at Dyckman Oval created what the British scholar Raymond Williams labeled a "structure of feeling," a unique cultural space that made Negro-league games distinct from major-league contests. An October 1935 *New York Age* editorial described a preference for the substantially different atmosphere at Negro-league games: "Fans who have seen the teams of the Negro National League play at Dyckman Oval say they prefer to see these boys in action to seeing many big leaguers because they play with more spirit and present a more colorful game." Enacted time and again, the "color" and "spirit" of the scene produced a sense of collectivity, pride, and affirmation in the accomplishment of building their own institutions and producing their own excellence outside of segregated institutions like the major leagues.[39]

The multiple functions of these gatherings at Dyckman—to entertain, unite, and even educate—were part of the design of Pompez's plan. The ballpark was also used as a site to raise money for charity. A July 16 night game between the Cubans and the Brooklyn Eagles was slated to benefit the United Children's Camp and allow "underprivileged children of Harlem" to attend summer camp. Low turnout at the game upset the *Amsterdam News* journalist Artie LaMar, who chastised Harlem fans for failing to show. "It can be said that Señor Pompez made a larger contribution to the affair than the average person will even stop to think about," LaMar wrote, "for it was the good señor's usual white following that made up the largest numbers of those present, which is another tally on the debit side of what those devoting their time and personal contributions fail to do because of lack of support from their own."[40]

The New York Cubans' ability to garner support from Harlem's sporting fans involved building on lines of affiliation and using Dyckman Oval's location to their advantage. Dyckman Oval lay north of Harlem in Upper Manhattan at 204th Street and Nagle Avenue, which could have complicated the team's ability to secure a stable fan base in Harlem. Local papers stressed its accessibility: fifteen minutes removed from Sugar Hill and a half hour from 110th Street; reachable by automobile just off the Harlem River Parkway; the last stop on the Eighth Avenue IND line. The Cubans team roster also sought to curry the favor of Harlem baseball fans through its strength and diversity. Among the first players Pompez lined up was the Cuban standout Martín Dihigo, a veteran of the old Cuban Stars who had spent the past four seasons in Venezuela. His responsibility would extend beyond the playing field in this return engagement; Pompez named him player-manager.[41] The rest of the roster featured an eclectic mixture of Latino and African American players. Former Black Yankees Clyde Spearman, Frank Blake, and Dave "Showboat" Thomas were signed by offering them a chance to escape professional life on the co-op plan for a regular salary. A gem was found in the hard-throwing right-handed pitcher Johnny "Schoolboy" Taylor. Just nineteen years old, the Connecticut native had a light complexion and had reportedly been scouted by at least two major-league teams, the New York Yankees and Philadelphia Athletics, until "it was found that he was colored."[42]

Work on Dyckman's renovations complete, the transformed venue was unveiled on May 26. Tickets for opening day at the refurbished ballpark cost fans eighty-five cents for a box seat, and fifty-five cents and forty cents for grandstand.[43] "It is a perfect baseball day," wrote the *Pittsburgh Courier* columnist Chester Washington from the press box. "The newly vamped stands and playing field is a thing of beauty." The stands were packed and included boxing champion Joe Louis and light-heavyweight contender John Henry Lewis as well as NNL commissioner Ferdinand Q. Morton and league chair Gus Greenlee. Pompez's legal troubles, his multiple arrests, and his having to testify before a corruption investigation did not deter Bernard Deutsch, president of the board of aldermen, from accepting the honor of throwing the ceremonial first pitch. The renovated Dyckman was a hit with the fans and the press in attendance, but for this day the New York Cubans were not: Cum Posey's Homestead Grays swept the twin bill.[44]

The Cubans muddled through much of the first half of NNL campaign, finishing fourth as Greenlee's Pittsburgh Crawfords claimed the first-place flag. Pompez's Cubans rebounded in the second half. The Cubans took series from the Crawfords, the Homestead Grays, and the Chicago American Giants during a Midwest swing that put them in position to overtake the front-running Philadelphia Stars for the second-half flag and the right to challenge the Crawfords for the NNL title. The Stars and Cubans faced off in an early-September weekend engagement at Dyckman. Five thousand "frenzied" fans attended the contests as the Cubans swept the Stars, 5–1 and 8–6, clinching the second-half title.[45]

A Season of Change

Superstitions affect the minds, play, and actions of not just baseball players but also of fans and owners. The rituals and superstitions are countless (e.g., not mentioning that a pitcher is throwing a no-hitter), and when one feels they have been either willingly or unwittingly broken, a deep sense of foreboding usually arises, as if the outcome would have come out right had one done something differently. Such thoughts must have played in Pompez's mind as the celebrants he awaited in the New York Cubans offices never arrived from Dyckman Oval that late September night.

From a pure talent perspective, the 1935 NNL pennant series between the Crawfords and Cubans ranks among the greatest championship series ever played in black baseball. Pittsburgh's lineup featured future Hall of Famers Josh Gibson, James "Cool Papa" Bell, and Oscar Charleston as well as standouts Sam Bankhead, Jimmy Crutchfield, and Leroy Matlock. Directed by future Hall of Famer Martín Dihigo, the Cubans featured a constellation of star Latinos—Ramón Bragaña, Horacio "Rabbit" Martínez, Alejandro Oms, Lázaro Salazar, and Lefty Tiant—and the talented African Americans Clyde Spearman, Paul Dixon, Schoolboy Taylor, and John Stanley. The series upset the expectations of those who felt the Crawfords would simply overwhelm the Cubans. Pompez's team took the first two games, 6–2 and 4–0. Pittsburgh shut the Cubans down in game three 3–0 as the series shifted to Pittsburgh. Back in the familiar surroundings of Greenlee Field, the Crawfords also took game four 3–2, but the Cubans snapped up a 6–1 victory in game five behind the starting pitching of Dihigo and home runs of Spearman and Salazar for a three-games-to-two series advantage.

Triumph for the Harlem-based squad—the "Latins from Manhattan," as the city's black papers had come to celebrate Pompez's team—seemed nigh; excitement surged. "Three Up and One More to Go in Series?" read an *Amsterdam News* caption accompanying a picture of Dihigo with several of his Cubans players. "New York has made more noise over the coming of the new baseball league than any other town," wrote columnist Romeo Dougherty, who implored Harlem fans to "at least show our appreciation by trying to tax the capacity of the Oval."[46] Game six, played under the lights in Philadelphia, brought the Cubans within outs of clinching the pennant. The Cubans held a 6–3 lead in the ninth inning. The ball was in the hands of Dihigo, who entered in relief to save the game and secure the NNL pennant. However, Oscar Charleston blasted a three-run homer off Dihigo, giving Pittsburgh a 7–6 victory and tying the series at three games apiece.

Things looked promising for the Cubans in the seventh and deciding game. They were back at Dyckman with pitching ace Schoolboy Taylor starting, and he was backed by several teammates at the ready to take the mound. Supported by home runs from Spearman and Dixon, Taylor pitched the Cubans into the eighth inning of the series finale with a lead. Sensing that Schoolboy Taylor had tired, Dihigo assumed mound responsibilities, trying again to win the pennant for the man who had brought him to the States as an eighteen-year-old rookie in 1923. The Cubans got through the eighth clinging to a slim lead. His team three outs away from clinching the series, Pompez left Dyckman Oval to complete final touches on the setup for the victory celebration back in Harlem. Finally, everyone could witness the triumph of a team he organized—validation that he was more than a numbers king who dabbled in baseball to clean his numbers money.

The ninth inning proved the Cubans' downfall once more. The power-laden Crawfords lineup, which had already blasted home runs by Josh Gibson and Oscar Charleston and three extra base hits by Chester Williams, rallied late again. Pittsburgh notched two runs against Dihigo to take the lead. The Cubans mounted a comeback of their own that fell short, dropping the decisive seventh game 8–7. Pittsburgh had completed an incredible comeback, fighting off elimination and winning the last two games to take the NNL pennant. Pompez had broken a cardinal rule of baseball superstition: don't set up the postgame celebration until the twenty-seventh out is recorded and the clinching victory sealed. Instead, the Crawfords were the ones feted in New York City for having won the championship.[47]

The 1935 NNL championship series showcased the choices black baseball aficionados encountered in determining which teams to root for in the Negro leagues. Owned by a Cuban-American, the New York Cubans roster combined Caribbean-born Latinos and U.S.-born blacks. Gus Greenlee's Pittsburgh Crawfords included only African Americans—from the field to ownership. The choice for black baseball fans in and about New York City: emphasize racial and national identi-fication with African Americans and align themselves with the Craw-fords; or place their allegiance with Pompez's squad, which reflected Harlem's diversity. This choice was only truly possible in the black base-ball circuit, which had welcomed Latino entrepreneurs into its execu-tive ranks from its earliest days and Latino players by the score.

Whether inspired by earlier tensions over the "Spanish" presence in Harlem, his ascent back atop Harlem's sporting world, or a bonding together of blacks and Latinos in the face of Schultz's hostile takeover, Pompez had changed his hiring practices when his ballclub joined the NNL in 1935. Unlike its previous incarnation as the Cuban Stars, the New York Cubans included not only Cuban natives but also southern-born African Americans such as Showboat Thomas and northern-born Schoolboy Taylor as well as Dominican Horacio Martínez. In the years to come the team would also include New York–born Puerto Ricans such as Carlos "Charlie" Rivera and island-born Puerto Ricans Fran-cisco "Pancho" Coímbre and Carlos Santiago, along with West Indians such as Pat Scantlebury (who came via Panama). Pompez acted more boldly than any of his fellow Negro-league team owners in terms of cultivating such a diverse roster. Ever since Rube Foster's original Ne-gro National League in 1920, black baseball teams had sprinkled one or two Latinos on a roster full of African American players, but Pom-pez's 1935 Cubans struck a closer balance between English-speaking black players and Spanish-speaking Latinos.

Not everyone received his more inclusive roster with enthusiasm. In short, doubters viewed his new approach as an experiment doomed to fail. A team with a mix of African American and Latino talent had yet to prove a winning combination in the circuit. Perhaps as a projection of their own anxiety, followers worried that Pompez's bold experiment would hamper on-field performance as players negotiated lines of cultural difference not normally dealt with in the dugout. A shaky start to the 1935 season seemed to confirm that opinion. In a mid-season column, *New York Age* sportswriter Lewis Dial observed that although the Cubans looked like a "real classy outfit . . . for some reason or other, they fail to jell . . . It is rumored among fans that the Cubans and the Americans don't seem to pull together."[48] His July 27 column proposed a reorganization of the New York Cubans and the Havana Cuban Stars, its farm team. "Pompez has so much material that he could make another club," Dial observed before proposing an alteration of the two clubs: one entirely Latino and the other disproportionately African American. Aware that African Americans and Caribbean Latinos had worked together in the winter leagues, Pompez opted against Dial's proposal. His inclination proved correct, as the Cubans rebounded to compose a winning season that propelled them within a game of claiming the NNL title.

Pompez's new approach to filling the team's roster fell in line with demographic changes taking place in Harlem. Residents came not just from the U.S. South but from throughout the English-speaking and Spanish-speaking Caribbean. This resulted in a heretofore unseen diversity of black folk in a U.S. urban center. Indeed, those who came to see the New York Cubans play at Dyckman Oval reflected Harlem's diversity. Spanish and English comingled in the air as Cuban, Puerto Rican, and Dominican fans sat among African Americans, Panamanians, and West Indians. Away from the Oval, they battled over leadership of local political parties; Puerto Ricans and other Spanish-speaking residents were sometimes portrayed as a social problem; native black New Yorkers scoffed at southern blacks and Afro-Caribbean immigrants for their lack of sophistication. In Harlem, concurrent arrivals of English-speaking and Spanish-speaking immigrants from the U.S. South as well as the Caribbean—Puerto Ricans would establish their largest community off of their native island here—transformed the area.[49]

Writing in *The New York Times*, Rose Feld captured the diversity of Harlem's population and the presumption that race was their bond. "Within this territory, covering almost a thousand acres, live a people as diversified in their social, economic, political and religious aspects as any cosmopolitan center in the world. The only thing that binds them and makes them one is race," Feld wrote. "But implicit in that bond are scores of differences," she continued. "Harlem is American, the way New York is American, a melting pot of Spaniards, Puerto Ricans, South Americans, West Indians, Mexicans, Africans, and Abyssinians." The journalist then observed: "To the outside they present a homogenous body, standing as a unit. To the insider, they separate into distinct individual groups, with individual differences, antagonisms, loyalties, and prejudices."[50] These individuals themselves engaged in an everyday process in which they redefined what it meant to black, collectively and personally, as they forged what scholars came to call the Harlem Renaissance, a creative space for blacks from throughout the diaspora for the making of art, music, and literature. Harlemites did more than share a geographical area. They and others occupied a creative space called Harlem—embraced by some in later years as Harlemworld. In this space, literary figures such as James Baldwin and Zora Neale Hurston, entertainers and artists like Harry Belafonte and Augusta Savage, historians and public intellectuals like John Henrik Clarke and Arturo "Arthur" Schomburg, and ballplayers like Rodolfo Fernández and Charlie Rivera redefined themselves as they learned what it meant to be black in America. It was the same becoming and reinvention that Alex Pompez experienced in his years in Harlem.

El Bambino Visits Dyckman

Still smarting from the NNL series loss to the Crawfords, Pompez lined up a last pair of games for his Cubans before they dispersed to play winter ball. His squad would face the most recognizable face in baseball, Babe Ruth. The recently retired slugger's visit to Dyckman Oval would prove a success in multiple ways. First, an "overflow" crowd—estimated in various publications as low as five thousand and as high as ten thousand—filed into Dyckman to see Ruth, who was paid $3,000 for the appearance. Second, the New York Cubans swept the doubleheader from the Ruth All-Stars, a team of white semipro, minor-league, and former major-league players. Finally, the exhibition gave Harlem fans a chance to personally witness the Sultan of Swat on their turf performing against some of black baseball's finest: Dihigo, Oms, Tiant, and Schoolboy Taylor.

The doubleheader was Ruth's first appearance in New York as a player since his retirement earlier that spring. Those who came to see Ruth knock one out of Dyckman during game action left disappointed. Lefty Tiant's assortment of pitches kept Ruth off balance just enough to ensure a 6–1 Cubans victory. Ruth mustered one hit (a double) and walked once in five appearances at the plate in the first game but did put on a hitting exhibition between the two contests, knocking eight balls out of Dyckman. The home run king did not appear in the second game, another victory for Taylor and the Cubans, 15–5.[51]

One mainstream sportswriter made the trip to Dyckman Oval to cover the contests, the *New York World-Telegram*'s Tom Meany. For him, the scene was a far cry from Ruth's glory days and even his opening-day home run with the Boston Braves earlier in the year. "The spectators seemed to sense they were watching something pathetic . . . There were neither newsreel nor still cameras in evidence and no telegraph keys clattered brassily in the press box, which had less than half a dozen occupants. No civic dignitaries, not even an alderman, could be observed in the crowd," Meany observed. "The white sportswriter's description of the scene missed the point," baseball historian Leigh Montville later wrote. "This wasn't pathetic; it was perfect. If this was to be Babe Ruth's last baseball game, or maybe one of his last, it couldn't have been at a better place. The ticket prices were inexpensive, $1.10 for box seats, 55 cents for grandstands . . . The stands were filled with just folks."[52] Indeed, Meany missed on several levels, his description demonstrating a level of racial chauvinism typical of the white press view of black baseball. There was in fact at least one still camera at Dyckman that day: an *Amsterdam News* photographer captured Ruth's turns at the plate as well as that of New York Cubans Dihigo and Frank Duncan; his photographs accompanied game coverage in the paper's October 5 edition. Furthermore, black baseball fans did rejoice watching Ruth and the triumph of the New York Cubans. The event inspired the noted black songwriter Andy Razaf—lyricist of "Ain't Misbehavin'" and "Honeysuckle Rose"—to commemorate

Ruth's visit in the form of song, which the *Amsterdam News* printed in full. Razaf definitely counted himself among the Dyckman faithful in rooting for Pompez's Cubans squad that day. His song celebrated the Cubans' triumph, claiming that the Babe "batted the best he could," but when he faced "Tiant's splendid pitching, his hitting was not so good."[53]

Razaf's celebratory lyrics shed light on the meaning Harlem fans attached to Ruth's visit, the Cubans' performance, and Pompez's role in the sporting life of Harlem. The showcase event had been organized for them—not for the major-league fan or white sportswriters to witness again the (faded) glory of the Sultan of Swat. It was a memorable day for Harlem, a day that proved yet again to the *Amsterdam News* sportswriter Joe Bostic "what has been known by us ebony scribes for lo these many years, viz: the so-called semi pro and minor league white ball tossers have absolutely no business in the same town with the top flight Negro teams, to say nothing of in the same ball yard at the same time." And it was a vivid example of Pompez's promotional flair, what he could get done for Harlem's own.[54]

Dutch Is Dead

Buzz over the culmination of the baseball season and Ruth's visit to Dyckman had barely dissipated when word circulated through the Harlem streets: Dutch is dead. Schultz had escaped the special prosecutor Tom Dewey's effort to imprison the mobster. In August, Schultz's legal team secured an acquittal in his tax evasion case. That acquittal worried Harlem residents that they were not yet free of the Dutchman. New York mayor Fiorello La Guardia attempted to circumvent Schultz, ordering the police to arrest him on sight if he stepped back into the city. Schultz decided to relocate the center of his operations to Newark. More worrisome for him, word swirled in the bootlegger's old haunts and elsewhere within the criminal underworld that Schultz had upset his fellow overlords. On the evening of October 23, rivals within the underworld syndicate executed their plan, ambushing Dutch Schultz, Lulu Rosenkrantz, and Abe Landau at Newark's Palace Chop House & Tavern. They got to Schultz before Dewey successfully dismantled his criminal enterprise. The gangland-style killing of Schultz and his top lieutenants meant that a fresh start was possible for the numbers kings Schultz had strong-armed into his combination. The brutal campaign Schultz had waged in his quest for singular control had introduced a level of violence that radically transformed the numbers business. The terrain once ruled by working understandings among bankers about respecting territory was much more dangerous. Semiautomatic weapons were now a principal instrument used to ensure respect.[55]

A revival of Harlem's numbers followed the elimination of Schultz. This did not escape the notice of Tom Dewey, who was appointed special prosecutor by the mayor in June. Dewey's effort to rid the city of racketeers had uncovered Schultz's collaboration with Jimmy Hines, a white political operative and Democratic Party leader. This came after the Seabury Commission investigation, an inquiry into the operations of the city's Magistrates' Court and police arrest practices that yielded information about the payment of bribes and the making of political contributions by racketeers for "police protection." That spurred new investigations under Dewey's expansive investigatory power, including one into bail bonds that would bring numbers kings Henry Miro, Wilfred Brunder, and Pompez before the panel.[56] Miro testified that although Schultz was not the originator, he had mastered the practice of the political payoff and was thus able to dominate Harlem's numbers racket. Brought before investigators in late February, Pompez demonstrated that he could finagle the truth convincingly, informing them that he had once operated a "small" numbers bank with George Weinberg but had "neither lost nor made money." His arrest and release "under mysterious circumstances in Special Sessions" in the days prior to his less-than-truthful statement to investigators made their acceptance of his statement strikingly curious.[57] Indeed, he had enjoyed the strongest resurgence among the old Harlem numbers bankers. That he had invested his earnings into renovating Dyckman and creating a new entertainment center for Harlemites certainly helped. However, the fact that he enjoyed so public a revival displeased Dewey. The special prosecutor would spend eighteen months organizing for his indictment and capture.

Pompez's numbers bank and baseball operations truly enjoyed a revival in 1935. Everyone from within the numbers who had once loomed as a threat to his ability to operate independently was either dead or in hiding. The elimination of Dutch Schultz and his "muscle" cleared the path to operate without fear of intimidation or wanton violence. In fact, Dewey now stood as the biggest hurdle to the flourishing of Pompez's sporting enterprises, with Dyckman Oval serving as their entertainment center and his New York Cubans competing among black baseball's elite.

A two-day meeting at the Harlem YMCA in the first weekend of March had given owners the opportunity to reorganize the NNL circuit. They approved two franchise transfers: the Eagles from Brooklyn to Newark, and the Elite Giants from Nashville to Baltimore. Meanwhile, the Chicago American Giants withdrew. The New York Cubans established an additional base of operation for their Saturday games: Hinchliffe Stadium in Paterson, New Jersey. Displaced from Hinchliffe, the Black Yankees would be a travel-only team for the 1936 season while playing independent ball. This, along with Pompez's signing of several former Black Yankees players, upset owner James Semler, who briefly filed a lawsuit against Pompez. The suit was dropped when the Black Yankees gained admission into the NNL for the second half of the 1936 season.[58]

The real heat on the Cubans owner came not from Semler but from the special prosecutor's office. On May 25, just two weeks into the season, Dewey secured an indictment based on the sworn testimony of individuals who claimed to work for Pompez as collectors. "Baseball Magnate Reported Indicted," *The Philadelphia Tribune* proclaimed on May 28. The paper reported the "Cuban-American" had not been seen in Harlem or the Dyckman Oval area for three weeks. His absence fueled speculation that he had been kidnapped. Asked about their boss's whereabouts, his New York Cubans employees simply answered he was out of town. Pompez's closest friends whispered that perhaps he had gotten advance warning and had simply fled in anticipation of a forthcoming indictment. Friends denied his continued involvement in the numbers, although some admitted to his having handled Henry Miro's numbers bank while the Puerto Rican served two years in an Atlanta prison for tax evasion. A few claimed that Pompez had "virtually retired" from the numbers and had "transferred his money and time to the promotion of sports at Dyckman Oval."[59] Whatever the case, the Cubans owner was on the run.

The indictment did not catch him unaware. On April 13, more than a month before the indictment was handed down, he had renewed his U.S. passport, just in case. By the time Dewey's men came to arrest him, the numbers king was already headed out of the country. He fled to Cherbourg, France, via Canada; his return voyage to the States would not begin until August 8. He had prepared all winter to make that hasty departure, having both Roy Sparrow and Frank Forbes attend Negro-league owners meetings to prepare the duo to run his baseball operation in his absence.[60] When he returned from France in the fall, Pompez's continuing legal problems prompted his fellow NNL owners to inquire about the status of his franchise for the 1937 campaign. They sought assurance at their November meeting in Philadelphia. "I am 100 per cent for the league and will be in it as long as it exists," Pompez stated before proceeding to knock the source of the rumor. "I don't see why John Clark should take it upon himself to send out for publication the statement that I had not been heard from concerning the league for 1937."[61]

Pompez could give all the assurances to his fellow owners about his intention, but he could not control what special prosecutor Dewey had planned for him.

5

WITNESS FOR THE STATE

He became the only guy who ever snitched on the mob and lived to tell about it. —*Leon Day, Negro-league pitcher*

On Thursday, January 14, 1937, police arrived at Pompez's third-floor apartment at 409 Edgecombe intending to place him under arrest; Dewey had secured yet another indictment. Made cautious by the surprise visits by Schultz's men and now by the frequent appearances of police detectives, Pompez had transformed the exclusive Sugar Hill apartment into a "virtually impregnable fortress." The security safeguards he had installed, according to an Associated Negro Press wire story, ensured that "no white man or suspicious stranger can get past the lobby without being identified and approved by the phone from the Pompez apartment."[1] The safeguards thwarted this attempt to arrest him, and the police left empty-handed. They next tried to nab him at his baseball office off Lenox Avenue. As Pompez and his right-hand man, the retired pitcher Juanelo Mirabal, approached the building's elevator, they noticed its operator acting oddly, signaling with his head and eyes angled upward that danger loomed upstairs. Pompez had the elevator stopped before it reached his office floor. He and Mirabal climbed out a fire escape and disappeared into the Harlem masses. Capture averted.

The special prosecutor had thought he had sprung the perfect plan to capture Pompez and halt his banking operations in sending agents to both his residence and his business offices. The efforts of Dewey's team of police detectives, plainclothes officers, and special prosecutor's office agents were not in vain. The sweep conducted by his team netted seventy arrests and confiscated $34,000 in cash. The big catches this day were Masjoe Ison (Big Joe's younger brother) and Moe Weintraub, a white lawyer for the combination. While others were held as material witnesses and given low bail, Ison and Weintraub faced charges for conspiring to conduct a lottery. High bail was set for the pair: Ison's at $50,000, Weintraub's at $20,000. Deputy special prosecutor Eunice Carter, a black woman who also resided at 409 Edgecombe, had proven indispensable in gathering the information about the workings of Harlem numbers operations to execute the raid. The failure to capture Pompez, the principal figure of this investigation, made Dewey even more determined.[2]

Harlemites disputed some of the claims that came out of Dewey's camp about Pompez's operations and the impact of the sweep. Too many policy sweeps were for show, some complained, unleashing a wave of enforcement, arrests, and good press for a few days for politicians and law enforcement. But then the police retreated; the politicians, confident that the public had witnessed their good works, laid off; and the numbers game returned to business as usual. A few cynically countered that the Ison-Pompez combination was not the biggest in the city—that the pair were not really that big a deal.[3]

A network of friends, business colleagues, and professional associates came in handy as Pompez went on the run. With the police looking for him, he could not stroll into Penn Station with his wife, Ruth, in broad daylight and buy two tickets: she would stay behind at their Edgecombe apartment with enough money squirreled away to await his return. After hiding in Europe the previous year, he had to create a new path of escape first out of the city and then out of the country, as Dewey and his men had put out an all-points-bulletin on him. Word had long been out that the last time Pompez had escaped, he traveled north to Canada and then across the Atlantic via ship to avoid arrest. This time he decided to head south, stopping first in Philadelphia, where the Negro leaguer Dick Seay hid him as the numbers king arranged his next moves. In the interim, newspapers reported that Big Joe Ison had been arrested and that Dewey wanted him to turn state's evidence.

Pompez secured a Cuban passport and a tourist visa for Mexico under an alias, Antonio Moreno—the name of a Mexican movie actor but common enough that it would not raise immediate suspicions with border agents. Traveling first to Tucson, he crossed over into Mexico and headed down to Mexico City; his modes of transportation south to the Mexican capital city included bus, automobile, and private plane. Finally, after weeks of hiding and travel, he arrived in Mexico City, where his contacts had secured a comfortable villa in the tony Lomas Heights section for him to bide his time.[4] Pompez expected that his time in the Mexican capital would pass more easily than the months spent in France the previous year: he could find more of the cultural comforts with which he was familiar. He spoke Spanish fluently and had associates within Mexican professional baseball nearby.

Holed up in a Mexico City villa under his alias, Pompez waited for the situation back home to cool down. It didn't. Dewey had initiated an international manhunt to reel him back to New York. Rumors swirled; he was everywhere, yet nowhere Dewey could place his hands on him. A February 6 article in the *Amsterdam News* stated "authoritatively" that Pompez was in Cuba. Gossip had him elsewhere in the States; he had been spotted in France, in Mexico. But Dewey would do more than try to wait Pompez out this time. He sent his men to the March meeting of NNL executives to question Roy Sparrow about his boss's whereabouts.[5] Pompez had left Sparrow and Frank Forbes to tend to the New York Cubans franchise once again, promising his NNL owners that his Cubans would play the 1937 season.[6] As the end of March neared, that prospect dimmed. New York Cubans players had begun to sign elsewhere. Martín Dihigo was the first to depart, signing to play in the Dominican Republic in its newly organized summer league. Forbes and Sparrow attempted to contact Pompez in Mexico City to seek his advice on how to proceed after the team manager had departed. They quickly abandoned their effort after learning that "most of the players who usually come to New York would follow Dihigo." On April 17 the *New York Age* announced what Forbes and Sparrow had come to realize: "There'll be no New York Cubans this season."[7]

Unbeknownst to Pompez and his New York Cubans surrogates, Dewey had had the police tap phones in the numbers kingpin's New York home and at his business offices. The desperate calls Sparrow and

Forbes had made to their boss in Mexico City had clued legal authorities in to his approximate whereabouts. Although in hiding and fully aware that authorities were still searching for him, Pompez allowed his passion for baseball to overrule his survival instinct. He made a fateful call back to Roy Sparrow at the New York Cubans team office at Dyckman Oval to confer about preparations for the upcoming baseball season. New York City police listened to their long-distance conversations over a period of two weeks, using the information to pinpoint Pompez's exact location in Mexico.[8]

Mexico City was perhaps too comfortable, too familiar, for Pompez. He departed from the tight security of his rented villa and headed into town on several occasions—this, despite the fact that he knew the international dragnet was drawing closer. He had narrowly evaded the authorities late Saturday night, March 27: local police spotted him and began pursuit, forcing him to jump into his bulletproof sedan, which sped off into the downtown traffic amid gunfire. But that was not his first close call in Mexico. In the port city of Tampico, he and his men had outraced authorities to a local airfield so the numbers baron could be whisked away on a private plane. After their narrow escape that March night, Pompez and his men drove around the capital a few hours, hoping to shake whatever tail the police might have stuck on them when they fled downtown.

As Pompez headed back to the villa in Lomas Heights in the predawn hours, the *federales* surrounded his vehicle, threatening to open fire on him and his armed bodyguards. What would he do? Have his guards shoot their way out? Surrender and battle it out in the Mexican courts? He had spent much of 1936 on the lam. In Mexico just over two months, he really did not want to go back to New York City to face Dewey and his law enforcement team or, perhaps worse, answer to Schultz's mob associates. But he was cornered. He ordered his bodyguards to lay down their arms. His escape from New York, the *Amsterdam News* suggested, "has the makings of a blood-curdling detective story. Private airplanes; bullet-proof vests; high-powered, bullet-proof cars; ragged clothes; a bodyguard made up of a dozen desperadoes— all were used by the fleeing policy king to effect an escape from United States and Mexican law."[9] But at last the "gray-haired, statuesque racketeer-sportsman" was under arrest; the international manhunt had been successful. Pompez had acted on his survival instinct, which had gotten him out of Schultz's syndicate without retribution in 1934 and enabled him to survive and even thrive in the rough-and-tumble worlds of the numbers and black baseball. Now he had a new challenge to face.

Fighting Extradition

The arrest of Pompez the numbers kingpin was a breaking story. Newspapers dispatched reporters to Mexico City to detail his capture. *The New York Times*, the *Chicago Tribune*, the *Washington Post*, and other prominent daily papers that had previously followed his narrow escapes from Dewey used wire service reports to provide readers with the latest details. This was even bigger news in the black press, especially New York's *Amsterdam News* and *New York Age*, which had long tracked Pompez's activities on and off the baseball diamond.

Immediately after Pompez's arrest, U.S. officials initiated extradition proceedings. Seeking confirmation that Mexican law enforcement had the right man in custody and wanting to avoid the embarrassment of having Pompez slip through his hands again, Dewey arranged for a photograph of Pompez to be telegraphed to Mexican authorities. Pompez was strident: he retained counsel.[10]

"I'm going to fight extradition!" he yelled to reporters gathered outside the Mexico City jail. His declaration revealed a fighting spirit that continued despite his capture. The heat brought on by New York's special prosecutor had prompted him to flee the United States multiple times over the past twenty-four months. He had hidden in Canada, France, and Mexico, respectively, waiting for Tom Dewey to cool on the idea of prosecuting him and throwing him into prison. Now he was shouting out a jail cell window to the press, the prize catch of Mexican federal police and Dewey. He lacked the power to move state governments to do what he wanted, just a team of lawyers able to delay but not avoid the inevitable. He had been in jail before, only to be quickly bailed out and have his case either "mysteriously" thrown out or receive a fine that he could easily pay. But that was before; now he was in jail in a foreign country, and at some point he was going to be extradited.

Pompez's legal representation would play the hand given them by the Mexican federal legal system, a time-limited strategy of filing an appeal to stay the writ of extradition in each state court. At some point his appeals would be exhausted and he would be returned to stand trial. Thus far he had escaped significant damage to his reputation on Harlem streets and in the world of numbers. He had testified (i.e., tested his lies) in a manner that did not implicate himself or others in anything more serious than simply "policy" game violations. His ability to evade capture multiple times had frustrated Dewey and his men. Now Dewey had an emissary accompanied by New York City police detectives en route to Mexico City to retrieve their prisoner. What was the special prosecutor's grand design? Only bits of information about Dewey's antiracketeering probes had been accessible to Pompez as he hid in Mexico City. A lot depended on who exactly was the prime target of Dewey's investigation; whether it was the politicians or the underworld figures who had collaborated with Schultz; and to what degree Dewey felt he could secure not just indictments but convictions.

As he sat there, a prisoner awaiting extradition, Pompez no doubt wondered about Dewey's ultimate motive in seeking to extradite him back to New York. Did the special prosecutor have bigger plans than simply shutting down the numbers baron's lucrative operations and incarcerating him? Was he simply a pawn in Dewey's chess match with Tammany Hall's Democratic machine? For Alex Pompez, the choice might quickly become sing or Sing Sing. The sight of him at the witness stand delivering state's evidence would surely displease Schultz's mob associates as well as his Tammany Hall collaborators. What would be their form of retribution?

In those lonely days, Pompez assuredly contemplated how his fortune had turned so dramatically for the worse. The numbers crowd had proven as loyal as ever when he had resumed operating independent of Dutch Schultz in 1934; the money poured in. That vaulted him back atop Harlem's sporting world. Negro National League team owners admitted his New York Cubans into the eastern-based circuit and he unveiled a renovated Dyckman Oval the following April; the *New York Age* had hailed it as Harlem's entertainment center. Each achievement attested to his savvy in managing his illicit numbers enterprise while maintaining goodwill on Harlem streets. Political entanglements could be handled, he had learned. The right contributions to the appropriate club or campaign usually took care of political concerns and could disappear court cases or other legal indiscretions. But sitting in a Mexico City jail with Dewey's men coming to claim their prize catch—this was different.

Pompez's connections in Mexico did not run up all the way to its president but did include Jorge Pasquel, oil tycoon and driving force behind the formation of the Mexican League, which would launch a challenge to the major leagues for America's best baseball talent in the 1940s. Pasquel could aid him in dealing with minor everyday matters: food, access to friends, and decent facilities. However, over the next six months a deft legal team would figure most prominently, keeping him out of the legal clutches of the City of New York.

Pompez was no common prisoner. The foreign press milled about the Mexico City jail, seeking access to the Cuban-American in detention. Mexican authorities declared no press interviews pending completion of extradition proceedings. However, Pompez needed an audience to hear his side. Foreign journalists shouted their questions from outside the jail, conducting an impromptu press conference. Dewey's prize detainee alternated between speaking in "perfect English and Spanish" and seemed to have a ready explanation for every question the reporters yelled.[11]

Why did he travel under an assumed name?

"Because when I learned they were investigating gambling I was afraid to give my real name."

Why travel to Mexico?

He was trying to sell the same lighting system he had installed in Dyckman Oval to baseball officials in Mexico City, he informed reporters. He hoped to promote night baseball games that October.[12]

He then commenced denying involvement in the kidnapping of a ten-year-old boy, Charles Mattson, in Tacoma, Washington. Upon his arrest, Mexican authorities had announced that their prisoner was a suspect in the Mattson kidnapping, insisting that they had found proof Pompez had been in Tacoma the day of the boy's abduction. The Mattson case had developed national intrigue in the United States when the boy was found dead days later, prompting President Franklin Roosevelt to issue an official statement pleading for assistance in the capture of the perpetrators.

"I've never been to Tacoma: What state is it in?"

Emphatically denying any connection with the kidnapping, Pompez admitted to having been a prominent figure in New York's numbers racket but claimed he had left it two years earlier and others were just using his name. "I've got a police record in New York as a gambler, so Dewey wants me, but my only interest now is baseball. I own the Dyckman Oval in New York," he assured the reporters.

Mexican officials retracted their claim that Pompez was a suspect in the Mattson case; however, they declared that his tourist visa had expired on January 30. Having overstayed his visa, he was "liable to expulsion as an alien illegally in Mexico," police authorities announced. Pompez refuted that claim, insisting his tourist visa was good for six months: he was there legally.[13]

Meanwhile, Pompez's lawyers filed a writ of habeas corpus in the fight against extradition. *The New York Times*, which had a journalist following the case from Mexico City, reported that Pompez's legal team was arguing that participation in the numbers game did not qualify as an extraditable offense: such games were not illegal in Mexico. New York City police were "trying to make a big-time criminal out of me," he told reporters, adding that Dewey "wants to make a fuss over me" because he was planning to run for governor of New York.

"If they get me before that Dewey grand jury I'm licked before I start," Pompez insisted. "They ain't got nothing on me but gambling and that ain't a crime here in Mexico."

The Cuban-American felt he was once again being transformed into a pawn in someone else's chess match. Dewey's determination to have Pompez in custody was partly because of the Cuban-American's position within Dutch Schultz's outfit: if Pompez had been a prize catch for Schultz, he was all the more important a catch for Dewey following the murder of Schultz and his most trusted associates. Pompez offered an inside view on the workings of Schultz's operation; he was not merely a paid mouthpiece like Schultz's lawyer Richard "Dixie" Davis. Pompez possessed no such loyalty to Schultz or those who had collaborated with the Dutchman. In fact, *The Pittsburgh Courier* reported, Pompez was the "most likely to produce the evidence which might lead to the disbarment of J. Richard Davis."[14]

Given the facts of the numbers case against him, *The New York Times* and other newspapers expected Pompez's extradition from

Mexico to occur quickly. On April 7 the *Times* published reports that Pompez was likely to be en route to New York "within a few hours" after a Mexican state court turned down his petition for a "permanent writ of habeas corpus." Confident that he was about to get his man, Dewey had dispatched Charles P. Grimes, an assistant to the special prosecutor, to Mexico City along with two New York City police detectives to retrieve their prisoner. Grimes informed journalists that Dewey had not authorized him to make "any statement that the numbers boss would get special consideration to return to New York to testify." Grimes would return days later empty-handed, however. On April 7, Judge Arturo Martínez granted an injunction request from Pompez's lawyers "temporarily restraining Mexican authorities from returning him to the United States." Judge Martínez scheduled a hearing for Saturday, April 10, to determine whether to make the injunction permanent. He and other judges would later reach the same conclusion: no permanent injunction. However, each temporary injunction provided at least seventy-two hours extension of his time in Mexico in jail but out of Dewey's hands. After receiving two such injunctions, *The New York Times* noted that there were "twenty-seven State courts to which to appeal. Both courts that gave temporary injunctions refused permanent ones."[15]

Dewey raised the legal ante, securing additional indictments against Pompez on two counts of extortion. One indictment charged that in late December 1932 he had collaborated with Dutch Schultz and others in extorting money from numbers bankers by "compelling them to join [Schultz's] organization." The other indictment alleged he had committed extortion in reducing the percentage controllers received from 30 to 25 percent in May 1933. Certified copies of the indictments signed by New York governor Lehman were forwarded to the State Department. A formal demand for the extradition of Pompez was then made to the Mexican government; the additional indictments Dewey secured added validity to Pompez's claim that numbers violations alone were not extraditable offenses.[16]

A month had passed since Pompez's initial capture when U.S. Embassy officials made another formal request for Pompez's extradition, this time on the extortion charge. A week later, on May 6, the case was presented to the Criminal Division of the First Federal District Court.[17]

When the judge agreed to execute the extradition order, Pompez's defense team filed an appeal to the Mexican Supreme Court. Dewey continued to wait, announcing to the press that he would send detectives and a special assistant to Mexico to retrieve his prisoner once the numbers baron had "exhausted his legal resources for delay."[18]

Pompez's legal wrangling was no longer front-page news in *The New York Times*, but black newspapers continued to follow it closely. The people of Harlem were deeply interested in his case; for them, it was front-page news. On May 29 *The Chicago Defender* announced that New York City had retaken possession of Dyckman Oval. "And so the plot to get Dyckman Oval out of Pompez's hands finally succeeded . . . White capital will take over and build a bigger park, which will be named Ridgewood Grove." In late July, Harlemites also followed developments in the prosecution of Dixie Davis, whom the *Amsterdam News* called the "mouthpiece of the numbers racketeers" and who had been indicted as a coconspirator with Pompez. Further background on the case came through an interview with an unnamed police officer published in the July 24 issue of the *Amsterdam News.* "The recognized czar" of Harlem's numbers racket before his escape to Mexico, Pompez, the police source claimed, had turned the bank over to another "Negro banker" who continued running it in the open. The *Amsterdam News* published another front-page story the next week that detailed the connections between Harlem numbers and city political figures, citing "a person high up in the policy racket" as its source. "Pompez will never be brought back to New York to face trial for banking numbers," the informant declared. "If he is returned here and talks before the Grand Jury he'll involve one of the biggest local politicians in the city . . . And this particular big shot politician, whose power reaches all the way to Washington, is going to see that he doesn't take the rap—in spite of the fact that he has been the real overlord of Harlem rackets for a long time. If Pompez is extradited he'll talk. And this particular politician can't stand any of that." Dewey continued to build his case against Pompez and his coconspirators, calling in six numbers bankers for interviews that week. The article noted, presciently, that Dewey had been advised that "although ordered extradited, Pompez will probably be able to remain in Mexico another four months, pending appeal from last week's decision."[19]

Summer turned into early fall and Dewey pressed on, turning up the heat on Harlem's numbers bankers. He brought them into his office an "average of three times a week," one numbers banker declared to the *Amsterdam News*. The reason for the constant invites to the special prosecutor's office, the numbers figure declared, was that "Dewey is trying to force the bankers to tell him their connection with a certain politician, who, it is claimed, is the intrepid prosecutor's real quarry. The politician is rated one of the biggest bosses in the city, with power that transcends even that of Dewey."[20]

Pompez had bought time—months—in the Mexico City prison. He made new acquaintances while he remained behind bars. Mexican oil tycoon Jorge Pasquel paid him several visits. The introduction was handled by Pompez's former New York Cubans manager, Martín Dihigo, who had performed that summer in the Dominican league before heading to Mexico to play. From behind bars Pompez talked baseball with Pasquel, who was embarking on a new venture, operating the Mexican League as a summer baseball league. Key to that endeavor would be the raiding of Negro-league rosters; Pasquel would offer salaries that few Negro leaguers could imagine earning in the States, in addition to a racially integrated league and accommodations. Dihigo, Josh Gibson, Ray Dandridge, and dozens of other top-flight Negro leaguers would play in Pasquel's league. Not surprisingly, a number of Pompez's New York Cuban players would find their way to the Mexican League in 1937 and in the years that followed.[21]

October Surprise

Dewey's ambition was not merely to reel in Pompez. Having experienced both the power of the city's government and its corrosive elements, Dewey eyed political office. Specifically, he had thrown his name into the political hopper as a fusion candidate for district attorney of New York County, hoping to replace Democrat William C. Dodge. Critics had accused Dodge of having permitted Dutch Schultz to run amok in Harlem and of resisting calls for special investigations of police practices and political corruption. In fact, Dewey's appointment as special prosecutor had come only after Dodge had rejected multiple calls for a special prosecution post and personally turned down the invitation to serve in that capacity. And although he had decided against seeking reelection, Dodge threw his support behind Tammany Hall's Democratic candidate, Harold Hastings.

The next move Dewey the political candidate executed would come to be known decades later in political circles as an "October surprise," a revelation or news event in the late days of an election cycle that spurs an individual to victory. After months of having failed to lure Pompez back with either a carrot or a stick, at long last Dewey convinced the numbers king to come back home to the city. It was exactly what Dewey needed in his election battle to defeat Harold Hastings.

After Mexican government officials signed the extradition papers on Tuesday, October 26, Pompez boarded a train for the United States accompanied by Mexican police. Later that night he reentered the States in Laredo, Texas, and was placed in the custody of two New York City police detectives. After nine months in Mexico, the majority of which he had spent in a Mexico City jail, Alex Pompez was heading home to New York. He had reportedly spent $115,000 for airplane and automobile excursions, special guards, and high-priced lawyers to stay out of Dewey's hands, and here he was, riding in cars, trains, and planes straight to Dewey.[22]

Time in prison had wrecked Pompez's physical and mental well-being. The debonair numbers king was worn from his months in a cell. His six-foot-tall frame had withered from the more than 200 pounds he had weighed when he left in January to less than 175 as he departed. "I have decided to give up," he told a journalist. "I am sick with a throat ailment, rheumatism, and my nerves are shot." Yet he remained resolute. "My crime was a misdemeanor. But they accused me of a felony. I am willing to face the rap and go back to New York as soon as they come for me." His decision to give up the fight against extradition and return to New York shook the policy racket in Harlem and beyond "to its very roots." A few familiar faces awaited him. Two weeks earlier Big Joe Ison had returned from Nice, France. (His younger brother Masjoe had remained in New York City's custody for months.) Big Joe was given a low $1,000 bail and released because Dewey had gotten him to turn state's evidence in the case against Pompez, Dixie Davis, George Weinberg, and the other alleged coconspirators.[23]

Dewey was positioning his pieces to take on Tammany Hall and now had the two biggest numbers bankers lined up on his side. "It is hard to get testimony voluntarily," Dewey told the press. "We have to go out, get the evidence, accuse the victims, and wring their stories from them." Those inside the numbers racket tended to fear reprisals from within the racket more than they feared the special prosecutor's office. Some would rather be imprisoned for a three-year stretch and come out alive than voluntarily testify against the mob that ruled the numbers world, one black newspaper observed.[24]

Pompez's train arrived in New York shortly after eight on Saturday morning, October 30; Election Day was the following Tuesday, November 2. The journey home was long. Harlem's numbers king "appeared only a shadow of himself" when he arrived in New York City's Grand Central Terminal, the *Amsterdam News* reported. "The startling Pompez shift from a defiant gangland baron into a meek timid man frightened for his very life, has caused Harlem to gasp," wrote another black newspaper, describing the reaction to his physical appearance.[25]

The police detectives shuttled the shackled Pompez straightaway from Grand Central to Dewey's office in the Woolworth Building. The two met for two hours, captor and captive, weary from the chase, anxious about what was yet to come. At three o'clock in the afternoon Pompez was taken to court and arraigned on extortion charges before Judge Ferdinand Pecora. The two indictment charges were read. Through his attorney I. T. Flatto, Pompez pled not guilty and reserved the right to change that plea within ten days. Judge Pecora announced bail: $1,000. Those in the courtroom were surprised—except Dewey, of course; bail was just what he had requested. The Harlem numbers king had turned state's evidence.

Pleased at netting his biggest numbers baron yet, Dewey answered reporters' questions following the arraignment. "Is it a reasonable inference that Pompez will name higher-ups other than those already named in the indictments?" asked one reporter. "That is a fair inference," Dewey responded.[26]

The special prosecutor was not going take any chances; he immediately assigned two police detectives to provide round-the-clock protection. Pompez worried constantly. This time he had to tell the truth; unlike when he had come before the investigators three years earlier, his freedom depended on telling the truth. In addition, he had heard the whispers, rumors, that some mobsters were out to "bump him off," now that he had returned and had agreed to testify. Those rumors had stalked him for months. He had not hidden and then fought extradition all those months just to avoid Dewey. According to the *Amsterdam News*, Dewey had persuaded one of Pompez's associates from the New York Cubans to travel to Mexico City to convince the numbers baron to return. The stumbling block: an order from the "policy mob" to remain where he was and that Pompez "would be bumped off if he returned."

After posting bail, Pompez left the courtroom with two NYPD detectives turned "bodyguards." The men secretly stopped in Harlem so Pompez could reunite ever so briefly with his wife, Ruth; for the first time in nine months they could embrace and reassure each other. At Grand Central, she stood on the platform watching her husband depart once more, this time on a northbound express train to Saranac Lake in upstate New York for "safe keeping."[27]

A Wicked Game

His most recent prized catch nestled in an undisclosed location in the Adirondacks, Dewey readied himself for Election Day. His hopes rested in an electorate tired of Tammany Hall's hold on the district attorney's office—that twenty straight years of the Democratic machine controlling the post that decided whom to prosecute was enough. Confident yet cautious, he embarked on a busy schedule the last two days before the vote. There was glad-handing to be done; press appearances to make; a few more speeches to deliver. The news of Pompez's return had rippled through Harlem circles. The timing of the prodigal numbers king's return was suspicious—or so thought District Attorney Dodge, who spoke with *The New York Times* a day before the election. "Mr. Dewey preened himself upon bringing back witnesses from as far off as Mexico . . . Tom, did you choose to bring Pompez back on the eve of election, amid camera flashlights and newspapers huzzahs?"[28] Dodge knew that Dewey had scored a coup by getting Pompez to turn state's evidence and that this would no doubt prove useful in parts of New York County tired of Tammany Hall's antics, especially those who had protected Schultz.

Dewey took on the entrenched Tammany machine at the polls and was elected district attorney by more than a hundred-thousand-vote margin. He had gathered his evidence, convened grand juries, secured indictments, and squirreled his witnesses across the state for another day. Sworn in on December 31, he and his team of assistant special prosecutors could move into their new offices and take on Tammany in the courts; as district attorney, he now decided whom to prosecute within New York County.

After two months in the wintry Adirondack hideaway, Pompez arrived to court in January to testify before Judge Pecora. The grand jury that Dewey convened targeted the other side of the Schultz collaboration within the numbers racket: his sights were on Tammany Hall fixer Jimmy Hines. The testimony he sought from Pompez was that of an insider familiar with how Schultz had arranged protection of his operations. The newly elected district attorney desired the same of Dixie Davis—who, unlike Pompez, had not fled the country, opting to hide out in Philadelphia. Dewey sent Assistant District Attorney Charles Grimes, accompanied by a pair of New York police detectives and a police sergeant, to take Davis into custody. Upon arriving in Philadelphia, Grimes telephoned the police department and met up with three Philadelphia police officers at City Hall before proceeding to the Sylvania Garden apartment building, one of two addresses where they suspected Davis was in hiding. The team pulled a ruse to enter the building, ringing the house telephone of a neighboring tenant and saying that there had been a bad accident. The electric lock on the apartment building's front door clicked open. The team worked their way to apartment 15-A. Dixie Davis was flummoxed when they burst in, then relief came over him: he had initially thought Schultz's former mob associates had sent a crew to kill him. Their mission accomplished, Grimes and the officers headed back to New York with two captives under their belt: the former Schultz enforcer George Weinberg and Davis. The two were held in a Philadelphia jail pending extradition, their bail set at $300,000.[29]

Davis returned to New York City on February 11, having given up opposition to extradition. But the disbarred Dixie wasn't talking. Dewey proceeded with trial preparations, given the Dutchman's former legal mouthpiece's lack of cooperation. At the preliminary arraignment on extortion charges, the judge weighed the lack of cooperation in setting bail for Davis: $200,000. Davis was going nowhere any time soon; a few weeks later, his tongue loosened, he got his bail reduced to $75,000 in a Brooklyn Supreme Court hearing.[30]

Trials can be quite revelatory, as rumors can be transformed into truths: who snitched; about what; how the police learned about the new "secret" banking center days after the move. Such matters often see the light of day in open court. For Pompez, the trials of Jimmy Hines would confirm things that he had suspected: that certain friends were not really friends at all, and that Schultz had truly masterminded a way to make Harlem pay under his ruthless rule. Wounded egos, crushed pride, and revelations of dead bodies emerged from testimony at the Hines trials as a trail of people walked up to the witness stand, took the oath, and admitted what they knew.

The testimony of Dixie Davis was particularly enlightening. Part of Schultz's inner circle, he had witnessed firsthand and often heard directly from the Dutchman about his misdeeds. His practicum in how to fix criminal cases came through his involvement with Pompez, Dixie informed the court. It turned out that Pompez's men were arrested frequently because Henry Miro was informing the police about his competitor's operations. Cruel irony: the man who had turned over his bank to Pompez while he served his three-year sentence in an Atlanta prison would return to Harlem and snitch on Pompez. Then there was Davis, playing both sides against the middle: he represented both Miro and Pompez. Dixie never let on to Pompez who was informing on his operations. Instead, he continued charging the Cuban-American numbers king for resolving his and his employees' legal problems. "Pompez had a long string of arrests," Davis wrote in a 1939 *Collier's* article that unveiled his deception. "I charged him a $15 or $25 legal fee for each case, and what the traffic would bear for the fix, varying the amount from $200 to $500 so he wouldn't get wise. It was over a month before he caught on."[31]

The manipulations of Dixie Davis—Pompez's lawyer—and the passing of information to the police of Henry Miro—Pompez's friend—reveal part of the inner workings of the numbers world. Miro's actions, writes the historian Rufus Schatzberg, illustrate how criminals "used the police to their advantage" while trying to enhance their own illicit operation. Such situations were handled differently within the Harlem numbers and in the white mob, Schatzberg argues. "If these were two white policy operations in the same situation it is most likely the informing incident would be followed by a violent confrontation." Rumors were often the igniter in such situations. However, this did not occur between Miro and Pompez, regardless of the degree of suspicion or actual knowledge Pompez had about Miro informing on him to the authorities. The two numbers kings followed the old code established in Harlem when the numbers was called the "policy" game; they eschewed physical violence to advance their operations.[32] Schultz's takeover in Harlem broke with the code: Dutch used violence as an important means of ensuring discipline. No one was safe. Davis witnessed this when a manic Schultz shot and killed a "trusted" lieutenant who Dutch suspected was skimming from one of his rackets. For Schultz, no one should buck his control or attempt to exploit his trust. Running to inform the police would not be tolerated. That nonsense had to be stopped. As the kingpin of Harlem numbers, he had managed to secure protection from the police. All it took were regular payments to the Monongahela Club and its head, Jimmy Hines.[33]

Permitted to return home to Harlem after testifying, the once reigning Harlem numbers king was back on Sugar Hill. He spent most of his days sequestered in his Edgecombe apartment except for a daily stroll through Harlem streets under police protection lest someone try to assassinate him. The walks and the time cloistered gave Pompez the opportunity to contemplate the deceit and manipulations that had come to light. Davis and Miro had both played him. In a couple of months he could exact a measure of revenge against Davis, who had thus far refused to turn state's evidence. Dewey's people instructed Pompez to prepare to testify; Davis was scheduled to go to trial on Monday, May 16. The Cuban-American numbers king, the *Amsterdam News* reported, was "anxious to spill the beans about the numbers racket."[34] He would not get his chance to testify against Davis. After the arrest of Jimmy Hines on May 25, Dixie decided to join Pompez in turning state's evidence. He, too, would testify and reveal the corruption in Tammany Hall and how Harlem's numbers money underwrote political campaigns as well as paid for police protection.

Accusations that Pompez was going to "squeal" circulated in black newspapers and within the numbers world. He attempted to defend himself, although there was truth behind the charge. He "flatly denied making any move that would implicate Jimmy Hines, Dixie Davis or any of those arrested along with him," the *Chicago Defender* announced on June 4. His hometown *Amsterdam News* raised the question nonetheless, publishing a photo of Pompez accompanied by the caption "Squealer?"[35] Harlemites actively debated who exactly the district attorney aimed to take down with his antiracketeering campaign. The "official attitude" toward Pompez and other "colored" numbers bankers, the Baltimore *Afro-American* stated in April 1938, was driven by the perception that they "never used their money for promotion of more deadly rackets as did Schultz; and that it will do no good to go too hard on colored bankers who had no choice but to become involved in the Shultz [*sic*] mob—no choice but death."[36] A similar assessment came from within black baseball. Homestead Grays owner Cum Posey wrote of his fellow NNL owner in his *Pittsburgh Courier* column: "Any person who had the honor of knowing Pompez personally is well aware that he is in no way a hardened criminal and does not look at life through the eyes of a criminal." Drawing a direct contrast between Pompez and New York's most notorious gangster, Posey insisted: "We venture that Pompez has been a many times bigger benefactor in the life of Harlem than he has been a nuisance. To put him in the same class as Dutch Schultz, Luciano and other cold blooded gangsters, is not fair to Pompez or others, who have been lucky enough to get a few dollars together, without a single individual receiving bodily harm."[37]

In making their assessment of numbers bankers, Harlemites took into account how race and power affected their lives every day as well as the level of commitment numbers bankers demonstrated to the development of their community. Favorable perceptions sometimes elevated numbers bankers to the status of "race" men or women for their philanthropic activities or their business practices that circulated much-needed capital within Harlem during times of economic slowdown and when stores along 125th Street resisted hiring blacks. The philanthropy of Casper Holstein, which included underwriting the Urban League's *Opportunity* magazine annual literary contest, made him into a revered figure in Harlem.[38] Pompez understood that reputation stood as the most significant factor to longevity in the numbers game: once lost, it was nearly impossible to recover. Unscrupulous numbers bankers who ran off with winnings quickly fell out of favor with Harlemites; their actions inspired the notion that the numbers was nothing more than a racket. Pompez worked hard to maintain his reputation as a square shooter, always paying all his bettors, even after "Black Wednesday." But it was more than just paying off that mattered. He was a "credit to the game," because he also reinvested his money in Harlem. His diverse businesses hired from among Harlem's own, resulting in jobs for African Americans, West Indians, and Latinos. Conversely, many Harlemites raged against well-placed Democratic city officials, local judges, and police officials who shielded Dutch Schultz's syndicate from the full brunt of the law. "While the average Negro in Harlem is in sympathy with Jimmy Hines and probably wants to see him beat the rap," A. M. Wendell Malliet wrote, "the feeling is one of 'getting even' now." Harlem residents recalled the days when "Negroes" from Cuba, Puerto Rico, and the West Indies ran the numbers game and provided "a good living for many thousand people." But Schultz and his gun-wielding coterie "booted" them out and "turned a supposedly innocent pastime among a poor people into an organized racket."[39]

Jimmy Hines, in contrast to Schultz, grew up in Harlem, but from an earlier era. His Harlem was an upwardly mobile working-class neighborhood of primarily white Americans of European ancestry. That Harlem underwent a dramatic transformation initiated during World War I and accelerating throughout the Great Depression. Harlem's new residents came from all over the Americas: the U.S. South, the West Indies, and the Spanish-speaking Caribbean. Uneasy around these new arrivals, most white residents fled. By the end of the 1930s, Harlem had evolved into the social and cultural center of black America. But for Hines, Harlem remained a seat of power as the entrenched Democratic political machine still operated in the 11th Assembly District out of the Monongahela Club on 116th Street. After serving in the war, he returned to Harlem and became a political operative in Tammany's Democratic machine. Over the next ten years he maneuvered his way into a prominent position, even challenging the longtime political boss Charles Murphy for control. Although not Murphy's successor when the old boss died in 1924, Hines had wrestled control of Tammany by the end of 1929, operating behind the scenes as a power broker and political fixer. His ability to raise funds to grease the political

machine drove his ascent into power; Schultz would be one of his largest contributors in the early 1930s.[40]

In 1932, Hines and Schultz came to an agreement by which Schultz
would buy protection from the police and judges. Keeping police from
snooping into his banking operations and other illegal activities required
money, Hines reminded him. Schultz agreed to pay Hines a salary that
over the next six years varied between $500 and $1,000 weekly for ensuring the protection. The arrangement illustrated how the two enjoyed an access to power that was largely unattainable to those from
whom much of that money came. That was what Dewey hoped to expose in his quest to bring Hines to justice.[41]

State's Evidence

The corruptive influence of Tammany had been a regular subject of
debate in political circles and among the general public. The Tammany
machine had long operated in legal and not-so-legal ways to ensure its
continuation in power. Historically, political machine officials called
on criminals to enforce voter discipline on Election Day. However,
what had transpired in the 1920s and 1930s when Dutch Schultz and
other criminal racketeers operated their illicit enterprises was something different, historian Mary Stolberg argues. "No one disputed that
criminals and Tammany Hall leaders had been partners since the beginning of the nineteenth century; but the relationship, according to
reformers, had grown more menacing," Stolberg observes. "Reformers
believed that the old system had broken down during Prohibition,
when wealthier gangsters came to control politicians, not vice versa."[42]
Jimmy Hines and Dutch Schultz embodied that change.

The Hines trials could propel Tom Dewey's political career to
new heights. Dewey did not entrust this important trial to one of his
assistant district attorneys but chose to handle the in-court duties himself. Successful prosecution of Hines hinged on a delicate balancing act
to avoid the perception that a cohort of criminals testifying as state's
evidence was being treated too lightly just to snag the politician. After
all, part of Dewey's final preparations in taking on the leader of the
Tammany Hall machine was not pursuing felony charges against Alex

Pompez and Big Joe Ison but allowing them to enter guilty pleas to misdemeanor charges of policy violations in the days preceding the August 15 start of the 1938 trial of Jimmy Hines. The two would receive a leniency recommendation from the district attorney in exchange for their testimony.[43]

In his opening statement, Dewey charged Hines with conspiracy to operate the numbers game, alleging that his willingness to accept proceeds from Dutch Schultz's illicit enterprise in exchange for protection from police and consideration from the courts made the Tammany political fixer complicit in the entire operation. Hines was not a silent partner in this operation, the district attorney argued. For evidence of this active participation, Dewey called on his group of witnesses testifying for the state.[44]

The time had come for Pompez to testify about how he became Schultz's "partner," the devastation of two Black Wednesdays, and Dutch's relentless effort to reel him into the syndicate. No one else had been the subject of Schultz's "venomous tongue," or been threatened at gunpoint by Dutch during negotiations, or maneuvered his way out of Schultz's hold and lived to offer the account in court. Time back in Harlem had enabled him to recuperate from the haggard countenance he bore upon returning from Mexico. The dapper, gray-haired witness cut quite the striking figure as he entered the courtroom and "seemed to dominate the whole court room as he testified in a soft accent first to losing his wealth—more than $70,000—on number 527, then to losing the policy bank to Schultz," *The New York Times* recounted.[45] His testimony was powerful and damning, especially if one accepted Dewey's premise that Hines had acted as Schultz's partner and not just been a beneficiary. Pompez never once glanced at the defense table, where Hines sat. The two had come from different worlds of possibilities and had ended up in the same courtroom: Pompez, the black Cuban-American, testifying for the prosecution; Hines, the white American, on trial charged with extortion, the symbol of the corruption wrought by Dutch Schultz and Tammany-style machine politics. Like everyone else in the courtroom, Hines hung on Pompez's every word, straining to hear his testimony and catch something that might be refuted by his defense lawyer Lloyd Stryker.[46]

Black Wednesday happened twice to him, Pompez responded to

a Dewey query. The first time took place in 1931, when number 527 hit. "My business was about seven or eight thousand dollars," he offered, but his loss for that day was $68,000. "Did you have a reserve fund in your bank to meet the loss with?" Dewey asked. "I paid everything I had in the world. . . . I paid every nickel I had in the world to the people that hit me," he replied.[47] A year later a different type of Black Wednesday occurred: police raided his numbers banking center and sixteen of his workers were caught sorting slips. Although the charges were ultimately discharged by a magistrate in Washington Heights Court, it was a costly day: a day's revenue confiscated as evidence, money paid to make the charges disappear, and lawyer fees to Davis to take care of matters.[48] The timbre of his voice changed when questions turned to his first meeting with Dutch. "The dead gangster seemed to live vividly in his memory," remarked *The New York Times.* He described the kitchen sit-down, Schultz's anger, and his not-so-subtle "parking" of his gun on the table between them. Barely into Pompez's testimony that Friday afternoon, Justice Pecora adjourned the court until Monday morning. The Harlem numbers king had already made an impression: the *Times* described his testimony as "the most important as affecting the issues in the case, and the most compelling as a personality."[49]

Questioned by Assistant District Attorney Charles Grimes when he returned to the witness stand on Monday, August 22, Pompez described encounters with Dan Smith, a former policeman who worked on Schultz's security detail and often served as a bodyguard for Dutch's moneyman Harry Schoenhaus. Grimes aimed to make clear the connection between Smith, Schultz's money, and Hines. Pompez detailed visits of Smith and Schoenhaus to his 409 Edgecombe apartment to collect the money from his numbers bank or cash reserves. A question by Grimes about what Smith did on these occasions prompted Hines's defense team to object vociferously. Their contention was that in a conspiracy case "the entire law of the inadmissibility of hearsay evidence [is] not abrogated." Justice Pecora sustained the defense's objection, to the dismay of Dewey and the prosecutorial team; an angry district attorney erupted, accusing the judge of favoring the defense.[50]

The courtroom listened raptly to the Cuban-American numbers baron's description of the dangers he encountered while in Schultz's outfit. Abe Landau threatened to "bump me off" in 1933, Pompez testified. Landau suspected Pompez was trying to double-cross Schultz's syndicate and that he had masterminded a work slowdown by controllers after Dutch had unilaterally reduced their percentage from 30 to 25 percent. His insistence that the reduction was a bad idea made them suspicious of Pompez. "I gave them an example concerning [the president of] Cuba," Pompez stated, who "did not pay employees of the government, but he pays the army, because without any army he could not be a President. So I told him the same with us over here; if we cut the percentage and we have no controllers or collectors, we cannot be bankers." The unenlightened response from Schultz and his men was that this was in Cuba. "We are here in New York, and we will take care of them." Violence was their solution. Don't worry about losing employees, Landau told Pompez: "We'll make them stay." Bo Weinberg, Schultz's main enforcer, was more explicit, promising to "break the skulls" of any controllers or collectors who quit the combination. When revenues dramatically decreased, Landau and Schultz speculated that, given Pompez's warning, this rebellious work action was perhaps the handiwork of Pompez trying to mount an insurrection. The Cuban-American, however, convinced the Dutchman that this was not the case; no further threats of physical harm were directed toward Pompez.[51]

Discovery of the funneling of Pompez's bank's funds to Hines was what everyone wanted to hear. Pompez first became aware in 1933 after being introduced to Milton Bernard, the combination's accountant, who informed him that for the purposes of filing tax returns George Weinberg was going to appear as his partner. The line of questioning again encroached into the area of hearsay that Judge Pecora had warned the prosecutor against. The judge interrupted Grimes to ask a few questions directly of Pompez. "Was that the only thing said on the subject of filing your tax return on all these occasions?" "No," Pompez replied, "they would talk about how long I was in the business and how much business I had, and bring my statements so he can fill up the books or fix up the books." Allowed to continue, Pompez recounted his discovery of an October 1933 entry for $10,000, money directed to the Monongahela Democratic Club, of which Hines was the president. Did he have proof? the judge asked. Although Pompez turned over a copy of the master sheet, he kept a duplicate of the sheet that listed all the expenses, he responded.

Escape from Schultz's outfit came in March 1934, he explained next. George Weinberg and Harry Schoenhaus informed the Cuban-American he was on his own to cover a shortage, since the syndicate's reserves were being directed to Schultz's defense. What was a "short-age"? the assistant district attorney asked him. A collector was respon-sible for all the money that his bank collected, Pompez explained. Some funds were loaned out, and if they weren't repaid, that came up as a shortage. If a collector was robbed, which had happened to his bank—at a loss of $15,000, Pompez noted—that, too, was considered a shortage. The circumstances under which their money disappeared didn't matter; the collector was still accountable to the banker to cover the shortage. In his case he owed about $25,000. That amount would be deducted out of the $115,000 profit his bank earned before calcu-lating his 40 percent share: Schultz owed him $36,000. When Pompez replied that he was going "to keep the business and work it for myself," since the combination was unable to cover the shortage and pay him, Landau's surprising response was that "it was all right with them."[52]

Finished with recounting his experience with Schultz as the pros-ecution attempted to link Hines to the various players in the con-spiracy, Pompez left the stand. Although they had voiced numerous objections to Pompez's testimony, Hines's legal team decided not to cross-examine him. They saw Dewey's calling of Pompez and other prominent figures involved in Harlem's numbers scene to testify as an attempt to smear Hines by association with a motley group of hench-men, assassins, extortionists, and numbers bankers.

By far the most reluctant of those who had turned state's evidence, George Weinberg took his turn on the witness stand after Pompez. Weinberg testified to Schultz's determination to "bring Pompez into line, to get a payroll from him or get a part of his business." The two conversed several times about Pompez "ducking them." Pompez's mul-tiple failures to follow through on promises to turn over his business frustrated Schultz. Weinberg witnessed Schultz's rising anger and de-livery of a final threat: "I am not going to take any more run-arounds from you. You either make up your mind that you are coming in or not. I am not going to let you stay in the business." Weinberg testified that Schultz's outfit never paid Pompez his percentage of the profits all the while that Schultz was withdrawing anywhere from $10,000 to $20,000 a month from Pompez's bank for "personal amusement" and "private expenses." The withdrawals whittled down the $100,000 reserves from Pompez's numbers operations to between $10,000 and $20,000. Moreover, Weinberg verified the story of the Cuban numbers man's escape from Schultz and of Dutch instructing Weinberg "to let both bankers quit the combination" and to "take all the business away from them he could." Dutch promised that once he took care of his legal troubles "he would get both Pompez and Ison back into the fold."[53] That never happened.

The prosecutors used Weinberg's testimony to make the direct connection between Schultz, numbers money, and Hines. Weinberg spoke of his personal interactions with Hines, offering further details of money exchanged for protection and connections. For example, Jimmy Hines had introduced him to District Attorney William Dodge. These were the connections that the protection paid for: it bought consideration, the transfer of overeager police officers intent on disrupting the numbers operations, and at times the outright dismissal of cases in court.[54] Continuously sparring with Judge Pecora as he sought to maneuver around limitations imposed on his efforts to introduce what Stryker contended was hearsay evidence, the district attorney pushed too far. In questioning one of his witnesses on September 12, Dewey openly spoke of Jimmy Hines's previous connection to the milk racket. Stryker objected. Judge Pecora declared a mistrial. The declaration set the Tammany leader free. Dewey pressed for scheduling a new trial immediately.

Trials Missed and Hits

The mistrial left questions unresolved, including the status of those who testified as state's evidence. The 1938 trial nonetheless had proven illuminating, confirming the suspicions about corrupt political figures cooperating with white criminals. "This amazing trial is bringing to light some things that every Harlemite knows," wrote an *Amsterdam News* journalist, "namely, that the evils from which the community suffers are largely imported from other sections of the city and financed and operated by white underworld racketeers with the help of Negro underlings." The trial seemed like politics as usual for others: it was not really about those living in Harlem but about those seeking power and greater office downtown. "The man on the street would tell you that Dewey was not as interested in cleaning up the numbers game as he was in getting a conviction against Hines," a front-page *Chicago Defender* article proclaimed, before stating that Dewey's success at trial would allow him to claim to have "broken the tie between numbers in Harlem and gangland. The Harlem barons are now going for themselves. They don't have to worry about the remnants of the Schultz mob."[55]

Harlem pondered what would become of those who had turned state's evidence. "Will Pompez and Ison go free?" asked a journalist in the *Amsterdam News* in its September 17 issue. "Will they be 'bumped off' by gangsters for testifying as they did?" Relieved of their twenty-four-hour security details, the numbers barons were unsure of their status: "They do not know if they are being held in technical custody, or walk the street free men." Unresolved legal questions aside, Pompez felt pleased to once again wander Harlem streets without the ever-present detectives. His Harlem friends greeted him "wildly" shortly after the declaration of the Hines mistrial. This allowed him to "breath[e] the Dewey-troubled air of Harlem without interference once again."[56] Pompez believed his constant trips downtown to visit the district attorney were over. The *Chicago Defender* was skeptical, stating, "That is his belief and beliefs don't mean much when a Tom Dewey is the man involved in your affairs." The Chicago paper contended that Dewey had relieved Pompez of his police bodyguards as a cost-cutting measure and as a political move. Despite the fact that the Hines trial was declared a mistrial, and having worked as district attorney in New York County slightly more than a year, Dewey embarked on a run for governor on the Republican ticket. Observers inside and outside of Harlem wondered aloud whether the release of Pompez and Ison was Dewey's effort "to snare Harlem votes."[57] Unsuccessful in his gubernatorial bid in that November's election, Dewey returned to prepare for the second Hines trial, slated to start on January 23, 1939.

Argued before General Session Court judge Charles C. Nott, Jr., Dewey secured the guilty verdict he had long sought against Jimmy Hines. Many of the same witnesses from the initial trial, including

Pompez and Ison, were called. One additional witness was Mrs. Dutch Schultz, who testified that Dutch had told her to forget she ever met the Tammany Hall political fixer. George Weinberg, however, did not reappear in court. Fearful that Schultz's mob associates had ordered a hit on him, and already despondent about having testified against Hines the first time around, he committed suicide on January 29. Judge Nott withheld this information from the jury until the scheduled day of Weinberg's testimony; his testimony from the first trial was instead read to the jury.[58] The jury took less than a day of deliberations to return their guilty verdict. Judge Nott rendered a sentence of four to eight years.[59]

The possibilities that existed for those in Pompez's generation were very different from those of his father's. Harlem was not the U.S. South; there were no laws in place here in Harlem that restricted access to public facilities, housing, or other institutions along racial lines as he had witnessed in the South that he had fled in 1910. But as he learned through direct experience, some in the North also wielded the law as a means by which to empower themselves and dominate segments of the population. That collaboration could transgress lines of class and respectability, as evidenced in the collaboration between Dutch Schultz and Jimmy Hines, master criminal and political fixer. Yet, less often did they involve the crossing of racial lines, demonstrating the enduring significance assigned to race, specifically the privileging of whiteness. The infamous partnerships formed between Schultz and the Harlem numbers kings were not about free choice but were instead a demonstration of a criminal mastermind able to operate from a position of racial privilege. "Harlemites are critical of the higher services he has rendered to the Negro in his attempt to obtain political office," reflected the *Amsterdam News* on Hines in the aftermath of the first Hines trial. "No one was able to recall a single Negro sponsored politically by Hines during the long years of his leadership and domination of the Harlem area."[60] Much to their dismay, as the Hines case affirmed most egregiously, those in the criminal underworld like Schultz could actually buy the political and legal influence that "Negroes" could only hope to attain.

Decades after the Hines trials, the retired Negro leaguer Leon Day commented to the historian Donn Rogosin that in testifying in the trials, Pompez had become "the only guy who ever snitched on the mob and lived to tell about it."[61] For certain, the killing of Dutch Schultz made the decision to testify easier for Pompez. Without Schultz as his protector, as the historian Mary Stolberg contends, whatever threat Jimmy Hines posed to those within the numbers world was significantly minimized.[62] But the threats on Pompez's life and others' were real enough that the district attorney provided police protection for him for three years and George Weinberg committed suicide.

Not only did Pompez testify against the mob and live, but Harlem accepted him back into its good graces, as did Negro-league baseball. Those in Harlem and in black baseball circles viewed him in a more complex manner than simply labeling him a criminal and a snitch. Rather, they interpreted his action through the prism of race and with an understanding of the economic realities of their time. This certainly influenced the stance taken by the local black press. The *New York Age* columnist William E. Clark, for one, labeled his crimes "no worse than those of bookmakers who accept bets on horses" and was happy to see him return to the Harlem streets. He was one of their own, someone who dealt with many of the same challenges as a "colored" person that they did.[63]

Travel was a defining characteristic of early Negro-league baseball, since most teams did not control their own ballparks. Successfully arranging exhibitions in between league games often made the difference between a profitable trip and a losing one. Pictured (from left to right): Pablo Mesa, Alejandro Oms, Bernardo Baró, Isidro Fabré, Tatica Campos, Pelayo Chacón, Juanelo Mirabal, José Junco, and Pompez (behind the wheel) (Charles Monfort personal collection)

Barnstorming after the season finished in the States was a regular occurrence for Negro leaguers. This squad organized by Pompez combined members of his Cuban Stars with African American players from other Negro-league teams. Pictured (from left to right): Isidro Fabré, Juan Pedroso, Rube Currie, Bernardo Baró, Valentín Dreke, Pablo Mesa, Alejandro Oms, Willard Brown, Oscar Levis, Frank Duncan, Marcelino Guerra, Jess Hubbard (Charles Monfort personal collection)

Located on 204th Street and bordered by Nagle Avenue and Academy Street, Dyckman Oval was renovated by Pompez in 1935. The *New York Age* claimed, "There is
no comfort that the fans can crave undone by Pompez Exhibition Co., Inc." (New York
Public Library)

Signed as a seventeen-year-old in 1923, the versatile Martín Dihigo (second from right) led the 1935 New York Cubans to a classic seven-game series against the Pittsburgh Crawfords for the Negro National League pennant. Voted into the National Baseball Hall of Fame in 1977, he is also enshrined in the Halls of Fame in Cuba, Mexico, Venezuela, and the Dominican Republic. Pictured here with fellow outfielders (from left to right) Justo "Cando" López, Alejandro Oms, and Lazaro Salazar (Transcendental Graphics)

The New York Cubans pitching staff at spring training, 1935. Martín Dihigo, who managed the squad, would also take turns on the mound. Pictured (from left to right): Heliodoro "Yoyo" Diaz, Manuel "Cocaina" Garcia, Luis "Lefty" Tiant, Rodolfo Fernández, John Stanley, Frank Blake, and Johnny "Schoolboy" Taylor (Transcendental Graphics)

CONTRACT

APPROVED BY THE

National Association of Negro Base Ball Leagues

Uniform Players Contract

IMPORTANT NOTICE—The attention of both Club and Player is specifically directed to the following excerpt from Article II, Section 1, of the Major-Minor League Rules:

"No Club shall make a contract different from the uniform contract and no club shall make a contract containing a non-reserve clause, except permission first be secured ....from the National Board or the Advisory Council. The making of any agreement between a Club and Player not embodied in the contract shall subject both parties to discipline by the Commissioner or the National Board."

IMPORTANT NOTICE—The attention of both Manager and Player is directed to the constitutional change which requires that all claims must be presented prior to the next annual meeting of the National League and within 60 days of the maturity of the claim.

Parties   The New York Cubans Baseball Club ....

herein called the Club and John A. Taylor ....

Recital   of Hartford........ lor 26 ROOsevelt St. Hartford......herein called the Player.

The Club is a member of the National Association of Negro Baseball Clubs. The purpose of these agreements and rules is to insure to the public wholesome and high-class professional baseball by defining the relations between club and player, between club and club, between league and league and by vesting in a designated Commissioner or National Board broad powers of control and discipline and decision in cases of disputes.

Agreement   In view of the facts above recited the parties agree as follows:

Employment   1. The Club hereby employs the Player to render skilled service as a baseball player in connection with all games of the Club during the year....... including the Club's training season, the Club's exhibition games, the Club's playing season, and any official series in which the Club may participate and in any receipts of which the Player may be entitled to share; and the Player covenants that he will perform with diligence and fidelity the service stated and such duties as may be required of him in such employment.

Salary   2. For the service aforesaid the Club will pay the Player an aggregate salary of $185.00 per month (May 1st to Oct. 1st) ...., as follows:

In semi-monthly installments after the commencement of the playing season covered by this contract, unless the Player is "abroad" with the Club for the purpose of playing games, in which event the amount then due shall be paid on the first week day after the return "home" of the Club, the terms "home" and "abroad" meaning, respectively, at and away from the city in which the Club has its baseball field.

If a monthly salary is stipulated above, it shall begin with the commencement of the Club's playing season (or such subsequent date as the player's service may commence) and end with the termination of the Club's scheduled playing season, and shall be payable in semi-monthly installments as above provided.

Loyalty   3. (a) The Player during said season will faithfully serve the Club or any other Club to which, in conformity with the agreements above recited, this contract may be assigned, and pledges himself to the American public to conform to high standards of fair play and good sportsmanship.

Service   4. (a) The Player will not play during said year otherwise than for the Club or for such other Clubs as may become assignees of this contract in conformity with said agreements; that he will not engage in professional boxing or wrestling; and that, except with the written consent of the Club or its assignee he will not engage in any game or exhibition of football, basketball, hockey, or other athletic sport.

(b) The Player agrees that while under contract or reservation he will not play in any post-season baseball except in conformity with the consent of club ....Agreement and Major-Minor League rules.

A 1936 New York Cubans contract signed by John "Schoolboy" Taylor, paying $185 a month. Although it lacked a reserve clause, this contract did include a renewal clause for the following season for $200 monthly. (Courtesy of Taylor Archives, Maureen Taylor Hicks, Curator)

After fleeing his January 1937 indictment in New York, Pompez hid out in Mexico City. He was apprehended on March 28, but his legal team delayed extradition until late October. Pompez (left) is pictured here with the Mexican federal police official Rafael Arredondo. (Associated Press)

After his extradition from Mexico, the haggard Pompez appears before the New York Supreme Court justice Ferdinand Pecora upon his return to New York City on October 30, 1937. Bail was set at only a thousand dollars in return for assurances that Pompez would testify against Dutch Schultz's mob associates. (Associated Press)

After Pompez completed his testimony, he informed the press that he was "through with the numbers racket for good" and that he would dedicate his energy to baseball: "The money may not be as fast, but it is much less troublesome in the end." (Associated Press)

The special prosecutor Thomas Dewey (front), only a month away from winning election as district attorney, watches a Negro-league game at the Polo Grounds along with his future assistant district attorneys Eunice Carter (front) and Paul Lockwood (rear, left), as well as Carter's husband, Dr. L. C. Carter. (Morgan and Marvin Smith Photographic Collection, Schomburg Center for Research in Black Culture, New York Public Library)

Enjoying front-row seats at a Negro-league game at the Polo Grounds, Pompez (far right) sits with (from left to right) the Negro National League commissioner, Ferdinand Q. Morton; Bill "Bojangles" Robinson, part owner of the Black Yankees; Roy Morse; and Joe Schoenfeld. (Morgan and Marvin Smith Photographic Collection, Schomburg Center for Research in Black Culture, New York Public Library)

From left to right: the 1943 Cubans starting outfielders, Francisco "Pancho" Coímbre, a Puerto Rican; Juan "Tetelo" Vargas, a Dominican; and Ameal Brooks, an African American, stretching before a game at Yankee Stadium. The trio reflected the international reach of Pompez's scouting. (Morgan and Marvin Smith Photographic Collection, Schomburg Center for Research in Black Culture, New York Public Library)

Even in the Negro National League, games were sometimes scheduled in smaller ball-parks because of the lack of access to major-league stadiums. This issue was resolved for Pompez's New York Cubans in 1944, when he secured an agreement with the New York Giants for the Polo Grounds to serve as his team's home park. (Transcendental Graphics)

The shortstop Horacio "Rabbit" Martínez (far left) would attract some interest from major-league clubs, but his physical appearance prevented his signing while the color line stood. Martínez would later make his mark on the major leagues as Pompez's scout in the Dominican Republic, steering him to the very best talent. (Negro Leagues Baseball Museum)

An advertisement for a Negro National League showdown versus the Newark Eagles at the Polo Grounds. After 1944, Pompez served as his own booking agent for events at the Polo Grounds, including bringing a second East-West Classic exhibition to New York in 1947. (National Baseball Library)

A young Orestes Miñoso (foreground; right) warms up with the Cubans prior to a Negro-league game at Yankee Stadium. A third baseman with the team from 1946 to 1948, Miñoso would later pioneer the racial integration of the Cleveland Indians and the Chicago White Sox.

(Transcendental Graphics; Negro Leagues Baseball Museum)

The 1947 squad featured the seemingly ageless pitching ace Lefty Tiant, who went 10–0 in regular-season action. The Cubans triumphed over the Cleveland Buckeyes in five games to take the best-of-seven series for the Negro League World Series crown. Pictured from left to right: (top row) Pedro Ulacia, Homero Ariosa, Pat Scantlebury, Lorenzo Cabrera, Rafael Noble, José María Fernández, Pedro Díaz, Barney Morris, Claro Duany; (middle row) Louis Louden, Orestes Miñoso, Pedro Páges, Martin Crue, Dave Barnhill, Silvio García; (bottom row) Lino Dinoso, Horacio Martínez, José Santíago, Chiflan Clark, James "Pee Wee" Jenkins, Lefty Tiant

The Negro-league great Ray Dandridge (center) briefly managed the Cubans in 1950. Pompez sold Dandridge's contract to the New York Giants mid-season, part of a working agreement that gave the Giants the first option on acquiring Pompez's talent. The Cubans folded shortly thereafter. (Transcendental Graphics)

Pompez (second from right) takes in a 1954 minor-league game with Juan Valdes (far left), Joe Cambria (far right), and a friend in Richmond, Virginia. Fellow owners in the Negro leagues, Valdes and Cambria collaborated on the entry of several Cuban players into major-league baseball after the Washington Senators hired Cambria as a scout in 1934. (Courtesy of the Lesley Rankin-Hill Valdes Collection)

Pompez was instrumental in the Giants' acquisition of outfielders Willie Mays (right) and Monte Irvin from the Negro leagues. The pair, along with Hank Thompson, another former Negro leaguer signed by Pompez, helped lead the Giants to a 1954 World Series victory.

(Transcendental Graphics)

Pompez (right) and friends at his desk in the office that served as the Cubans' head-quarters, located at 84 Lenox Avenue between 114th and 115th Streets in Harlem.
(Courtesy of the Lesley Rankin-Hill Valdes Collection)

The power hitter Orlando Cepeda barely made it out of the Giants' training camp in 1955. But Pompez advocated for signing the teenage Puerto Rican, whose legendary father, Pedro "Perucho" Cepeda, he had once sought to play for the Cubans. In 1958, Cepeda became the first unanimous winner of the National League Rookie of the Year Award, and he would go on to hit 379 home runs in a career that spanned seventeen seasons. He was inducted into the Hall of Fame in 1999. (Transcendental Graphics)

Felipe Alou (left) and Juan Marichal developed out of the Dominican talent pool opened by Pompez and Horacio Martínez. In 1992, Alou would become the first Dominican to manage in the majors with the Montreal Expos and later the San Francisco Giants. Marichal would win 243 games as a pitcher in the majors and, in 1983, be the first Dominican inducted into the Hall of Fame. (National Baseball Library, Cooperstown, NY)

On February 3, 1970, major-league commissioner Bowie Kuhn announces the formation of a special committee to elect Negro-league figures to the National Baseball Hall of Fame. Here Pompez (far left) sits at the dais alongside Kuhn and Hall of Fame president Paul Kerr; standing are Eddie Gottlieb, Sam Lacy, and Monte Irvin. (National Baseball Library, New York *Daily News*)

Ruth Seldon married Pompez in 1934 and stuck by him through highs and lows. The couple lived at 409 Edgecombe in Harlem and then in Woodside, Queens. Ruth was also the aunt of Edward Brooke, who would serve in the U.S. Senate representing Massachusetts from 1967 to 1979. (Courtesy of the Lesley Rankin-Hill Valdes Collection)

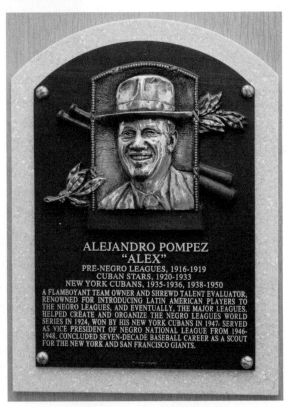

Pompez entered the Hall of Fame in 2006 after a special Negro-league election. His plaque joined those of Orlando Cepeda, Martín Dihigo, Monte Irvin, Juan Marichal, Willie Mays, and Willie McCovey— players he had signed into the Negro leagues or had helped the Giants acquire. (National Baseball Library)

ALEJANDRO POMPEZ
"ALEX"
PRE-NEGRO LEAGUES, 1916-1919
CUBAN STARS, 1920-1933
NEW YORK CUBANS, 1935-1936, 1938-1950
A FLAMBOYANT TEAM OWNER AND SHREWD TALENT EVALUATOR, RENOWNED FOR INTRODUCING LATIN AMERICAN PLAYERS TO THE NEGRO LEAGUES, AND EVENTUALLY, THE MAJOR LEAGUES. HELPED CREATE AND ORGANIZE THE NEGRO LEAGUES WORLD SERIES IN 1924, WON BY HIS NEW YORK CUBANS IN 1947. SERVED AS VICE PRESIDENT OF NEGRO NATIONAL LEAGUE FROM 1946-1948. CONCLUDED SEVEN-DECADE BASEBALL CAREER AS A SCOUT FOR THE NEW YORK AND SAN FRANCISCO GIANTS.

PART II

A WORLD MADE NEW

R esolution of the Hines trial created an opportunity for Pompez to remake himself. He declared to the reporters surrounding him at the courthouse: "I am through with the numbers racket for good." No more arrests, no more fleeing the country and leaving Ruth behind. From that point forward, he would dedicate himself to professional baseball. "The money may not be as fast," he told them, "but it is much less troublesome in the end."

Almost no backlash against Pompez took place within Harlem or Negro-league baseball. Acceptance back into Harlem's sporting world countered the loss of vast amounts of money and the allure of being a numbers king. Law enforcement and judicial authorities could disassemble his numbers operation, but taking away his social capital, business acumen, and baseball expertise represented a much different enterprise.

Over the next several decades Pompez recast himself once more, this time from a numbers king to one of baseball's greatest evaluators of black and Latino talent. That effort started with the revival of his Negro-league franchise. The black baseball business came with its own set of managerial challenges. However, none of Pompez's fellow owners would threaten to have him bumped off for failing to comply with their demands or for enjoying too much success with his individual franchise. The barriers to successfully restarting his Negro-league franchise were quite significant nonetheless. His New York Cubans had not operated the previous two seasons (1937 and 1938), and he no longer had Dyckman Oval under his control.[1] The return of Pompez and his

Cubans franchise pleased the *Chicago Defender* sportswriter Al Monroe, who observed that "even in the days when his other businesses were most discussed, his heart and soul were baseball." Pompez's team's return would fill a gap within the black circuit: "Time was when the Cubans ranked high in the doings of eastern baseball . . . When Pompez gave them up two years ago, however, they practically gave up baseball and have been almost a negative figure since that time."[2]

Pompez reentered the Negro leagues as the circuit was about to enjoy its greatest period of prosperity and fan support. This period of economic vitality proved all too brief, ended by a bigger development within baseball history: the launching of baseball's racial integration. The range of possibilities inside professional baseball changed dramatically between 1935 and 1947. The deaths of Nat Strong and Dutch Schultz had created critical openings in the sporting world that Pompez wisely took advantage of. He secured the lease to Dyckman Oval, renovated the site, and for the first time operated independent of a booking agency. (Others were coming to his Pompez Exhibition Company to book games at Dyckman.) This newfound freedom held the promise of a fresh start, of a revitalized black baseball circuit in the East and a Harlem numbers scene free of outside influence. But 1947 revealed that as a shadow institution, the foundation of the Negro-league enterprise had been partly built upon the loose, ever-shifting sediment of racist practice and racial ideas. Integration necessitated a new approach for a Negro-league entrepreneur.

Pompez seemingly ended the 1947 season on top of the black baseball world. The New York Cubans enjoyed their greatest season ever, winning the Negro League World Series. Yet he found himself atop an institution quickly reaching the end of its run. The public looked to the Negro leagues not as the circuit cultivating the future of integration but as a relic of a time many desired to relegate to the past.

As a Negro-league official and team owner, Pompez was forced by the events of 1947 to ponder whether black baseball had a future: If so, what would that look like? What role could he have in that revamped institution? As a baseball man and as someone who thrived for decades on his almost chameleon-like ability to blend into new surroundings and survive, he had to figure out whether another transformation was possible: whether he might be able to become an insider within organized baseball. Integration would offer him a final chance to transform himself. Drawing on what he learned in his decades of participating in the Negro leagues, he made himself an invaluable organizational man for a major-league ballclub. In so doing, he would position himself to leave a mark on the game's history by helping to change the face of modern baseball.

6

REBUILDING THE "LATINS FROM MANHATTAN"

That Alex Pompez will finally straighten himself out with the
law and return to his first love, baseball.
　　　—William E. Clark, New York Age, *December 31, 1938*

Restarting his Negro-league franchise required cash, a new home field, and a replenished team roster. Resuming his numbers bank to underwrite his baseball operations once again was no longer an option. Instead, Alex Pompez sought to have the money that had been confiscated when he was arrested in Mexico City returned to him. "Give Back My $180,000—Pompez to U.S.," read the headline of an *Amsterdam News* article that reported on the application he made in the Federal Court of the Southern District of New York. The U.S. government had impounded $180,000 of Pompez's money when he was arrested in Mexico City: $80,000 found among his possessions in Mexico City, and $100,000 confiscated in New York during Dewey's raids. A sticking point to this bold application to have the federal government return his money was not just the final disposition of his case. Still unanswered was whether the government would prosecute the dethroned kingpin for tax evasion, thereby teaching him the same lesson Dutch Schultz and Henry Miro had learned: the government requires one to pay income taxes regardless of the legality of that income. "If Pompez's story is true," *The Chicago Defender* remarked, "the United States government now holds more than $100,000 of his coin . . . This sum should prove ample to care for the delinquency of taxes charged against

Pompez." That money would also be more than sufficient to launch his Cubans.[1]

Approved as a full member by NNL owners at their April meeting, Pompez promised an attempt to lease Yankee Stadium for his team's home games.[2] That would not materialize. However, the $180,000 that he petitioned for did, as the *Amsterdam News*' Dan Burley "exclusively learned."[3] The Cuban-American still had much preparation to complete. There were transportation issues; he had sold his team's bus to Washington's NNL franchise. Then there was completing his team's roster. In April he named José Maria Fernández the Cubans' manager, his first NNL managerial stint; equally significant, this meant that Martín Dihigo was not returning. Signing pitchers Archie Jones and Connie Rector, Pompez continued the practice of mixing African Americans and Latinos on his team. The dispersal of his former U.S.-born black players among the other NNL teams when his Cubans team did not participate in the 1937 season constrained that effort; those NNL clubs retained rights to those players' services. As a result, the 1939 Cubans were disproportionately Latino; he would have to sign new African American players. Another significant challenge to his roster rebuilding was the continuing growth of the Mexican League as a summertime professional circuit, which provided Latino players another professional option.[4]

The rehabilitation of Pompez's public reputation received significant boosts throughout 1939. First, Judge Pecora handed down his sentence: no jail time, just a suspended sentence and probation. This, *The Chicago Defender* trumpeted on the front page of its June 10 edition, stood as "further proof that District Attorney Thomas E. Dewey was not interested in 'small fry' other than as links that would lead to the conviction of higher ups." The *New York Age* likewise celebrated that Pompez was given his freedom for his "damning testimony" in the Hines trial. Pecora even made a special concession, allowing him to travel on business with the New York Cubans and to file his probation reports by mail.[5]

Pompez also launched a new sporting venture, managing professional boxers and promoting boxing matches. His previous involvement in boxing had been limited to hosting matches at Dyckman Oval, where enthusiasts witnessed some of the day's more exciting and well-known black and Latino boxers: Kid Chocolate, Kid Gavilan, Sixto Escobar, and Spanish Harlem's local favorite, Pedro Montañez. Pompez's involvement was now more direct, as he personally managed the careers of boxers in addition to arranging fight cards. He agreed to promote boxing matches at Harlem's State Palace, slated to open that fall. Acquiring his license as a boxing manager, he signed his first fighter in September, the Chicago-based African American featherweight boxer Joe Law. The first bout scheduled for Law pitted him against the Puerto Rican boxer Pedro Hernández on October 16 at the St. Nicholas Arena on Sixty-sixth Street and Broadway. The Hernández-Law tussle did not come off; Law would later box two bouts at Rockland Palace. In addition to managing boxers, Pompez increased his involvement in the local "colored" boxing scene by forming a partnership with William Pressley to promote weekly cards at Rockland Palace. According to the *New York Age*, Pompez had been considering promoting boxing in Harlem for some time, and securing an "excellent" business partner in Pressley sealed the deal, as the two aimed "to secure the services of the best fighters available."[6] Formerly the Manhattan Casino and located on the southeast corner of 155th Street and Eighth Avenue, Rockland Palace served as a central venue for Harlemites to enjoy all kinds of entertainment. For decades, Rockland hosted the very best of the time's jazz musicians, such as Charlie Parker, political gatherings where Harlemites heard Father Divine or Paul Robeson speak, and basketball games. And as he had done at Dyckman, Pompez promoted boxing cards that featured U.S.-born blacks and Caribbean natives from English and Spanish-speaking islands. His entry as a boxing promoter at Rockland Palace placed it back as the "center of boxing in Harlem," according to *The Chicago Defender*. The New York Boxing Commission would sanction the fights, the Chicago paper reported, "which means the best of the big shots can be obtained for the Saturday night shows." The new boxing scene at Rockland unfurled on November 18 with "an all-star card" featuring Jersey Joe Walcott and William Joyce.[7]

This new venture allowed Pompez to cultivate new revenue streams within Harlem's sporting world. After all, no longer operating a numbers bank meant he was not producing revenue year-round. Additionally, his involvement in building up Harlem's boxing scene dovetailed with his efforts to rebuild his New York Cubans and giving Harlem a truly competitive Negro-league team.

Señor Pompez and Papa Joe

An additional boost to Pompez's reputation came from the loyalty expressed by several of his New York Cubans players. Second baseman Antonio "El Pollo" Rodríguez impressed major-league scouts with his skillful play. In June 1939, the New York Giants offered the lighter-skinned Cuban a contract to sign with their Chattanooga farm team, their highest minor-league affiliate. But the "white Cuban," as the *Amsterdam News* described him, rejected the offer. Instead he opted to continue performing with the Cubans. "Pompez is my friend. He brought me here," the infielder explained through an interpreter to the *Amsterdam News*. "With Pompez I can do a lot of things . . . I know the offer from the Giants might mean more money and greater fame, but I like playing with my own people and for Pompez."[8]

Although Rodríguez would play in the Giants organization the following season, his initial decision indicated a level of comfort with Pompez as well as the accommodations the owner made for the cultural adjustments his foreign-born players faced. On and away from the playing field, Pompez approached the issue of cultural adjustment directly and in a manner that stood in stark contrast with that of the Washington Senators. With Joe Cambria as the Senators' scout in Cuba, Washington signed hundreds of Cuban prospects, starting in 1933; most proved "can't make it" instead of "can't miss." These prospects encountered an extremely alienating situation upon arrival. They might have played on well-manicured fields and in stadiums with more modern amenities than those they had left behind in Cuba, but the cultural terrain was riddled with divots and traps and was largely slanted against them.

Joe Cambria's familiarity with Cuban players when hired by the Senators came from his own involvement in the Negro leagues and from the relationship he had forged with Pompez. The two made quite a pair, sharing similar backgrounds. Both sons of immigrants, each had earned his wealth in other business pursuits that provided the capital to venture into professional baseball: Cambria owned a series of laundry and dry-cleaning stores throughout Baltimore. Cambria made things happen through sheer force of will and a charming personality. As a scout for the Washington Senators through 1962, he would become the most recognizable white American face in Cuban baseball circles without learning more than a smattering of Spanish. But his indoctrination in Cuban baseball began in the Negro leagues. In 1932, Cambria bought into the ownership of the Baltimore Black Sox. During the next two seasons his Baltimore team would play exhibitions against Pompez's Cuban Stars, exposing the Italian-American to the talent available in the Caribbean and starting a professional relationship with Pompez that would extend into the era of baseball integration.

Working beyond the purview of the guardians of organized baseball's color line, Pompez and Cambria forged a collaboration that would lead to Cambria's signing a couple of his earliest Cuban players. That collaboration started with Ismael "Mulo" Morales, a tall Cuban outfielder who came to Cambria's attention as a member of Pompez's Cuban Stars in 1932. Cambria and Pompez entered into a unique agreement in which Morales would acquire a different kind of "seasoning" from what prospects who continued to play with the Cuban Stars received: cultural exposure.[9] Unfortunately, as with dozens of Cubans signed by Washington, an all-too-familiar problem emerged that dimmed Morales's major-league prospects: his inability to communicate with his teammates and manager in English. *The Washington Post* noted that on several occasions the Cuban was unable to communicate with Washington's multilingual catcher, Moe Berg, during a brief August stay with the big-league club.[10] The following year Washington sent Morales down to the minors early in spring training; he would never appear in an actual major-league game.

Cambria, unlike Pompez, could find work within organized baseball well before integration. After several years of working informally with the Senators, Washington owner Clark Griffith officially hired Cambria as a scout in 1934. Griffith hired him as much for the cost savings his approach to scouting could yield as for his eye for talent. Griffith "rates Cambria slightly below a blindfolded tailor's dummy," Shirley Povich wrote in *The Washington Post*. "But he gambles heavily

on the law of averages that some day Cambria will turn up with a genuine 'find' among the hundred of youths he shepherds into organized
baseball."[11] However, Cambria was no dummy: he used his own network of bird-dog scouts throughout Cuba to spot talent; he could then
make his official assessments.

The first major-league organization to have an official scout working the Caribbean beat, the Senators accounted for over 40 percent of
the Latino players (thirteen of thirty) to debut in the majors between
1935 and 1945. The arrangement that Griffith made with Cambria
called for the scout to receive a commission for each Cuban prospect
who secured a roster spot on either the Senators or one of their minor-
league teams. In other words, the more players who made the grade,
the more commission Cambria received.[12] The Senators organization,
however, remained largely indifferent about the cultural challenge
they laid before their Cuban prospects, who typically spoke little or no
English. Additionally, despite their heavy scouting in Cuba, the Senators did not bother to relocate any of their four minor-league affiliates—
Charlotte, North Carolina; Chattanooga, Tennessee; Panama City,
Florida; and Selma, Alabama—from the segregated South. This meant
the team's Latin American prospects faced a double burden that their
white teammates did not: Latinos not only had to demonstrate their
skills on the field but they also had to survive in a racially hostile
environment; they were forced to live in a Jim Crow setting with local
segregation laws, segregated housing and facilities, and the reality
that few accepted them as fellow whites but many saw them as unwel-
comed foreigners.[13]

An understanding of the complexities of race, culture, and national
identification shaped the approach that Pompez developed to address
what Latino players encountered in the States. His travels between
Florida and Cuba in his youth, his migration to New York City, and his
trips throughout Latin America exposed him to the cultural and ethnic
divides that existed inside and outside of Harlem. Spread throughout
Harlem, the businesses he operated and the places he resided transcended simple delineation between "Black" and "Spanish" Harlem.
In fact, he never lived in Spanish Harlem; his longest affiliation with a
Harlem neighborhood of Latinos was with Little Ybor, where Afro-
Cubans from Ybor City settled. That was where he opened his first

business, the cigar store that doubled as the center for his work as a numbers controller. As his numbers business grew, the controllers who worked for his bank were scattered throughout Harlem. The headquarters for his baseball operations were always in central Harlem, with the New York Cubans' offices initially located at 200 West 135th Street (on Seventh Avenue). Familiarity with Harlem's neighborhoods and people thus enabled him to build a network of homes and friends to house his ballplayers and ease their cultural adjustment.

For Negro leaguers from the Caribbean, the U.S. South, or anywhere else, there was no place more vibrant and exciting than Harlem. His first stroll down 125th Street captivated Missouri native and Negro-league great Jimmy Crutchfield, who experienced "a feeling of freedom I had never felt before." The black mecca had everything, especially for men who were young, black, and professional. At the nightclubs and after-hours speakeasies scattered throughout Harlem's neighborhoods, they could listen to black musical rhythms fused together by sons and daughters of Africa who came from all strands of the diaspora. The smells of African-influenced cuisine were likewise ubiquitous; Latin scents wafted along with those of West Indian and southern food. For a reporter like Alvin White, who lived there from the mid-1920s through the late 1930s, Harlem was "much more than an entertainment oasis where whites could enjoy a quality of music found nowhere else . . . Harlem was 116th Street and Park Avenue at the international market of an international community with foreign born blacks—British, French, Dutch, Danish, Spanish, and even a few Swedes—proud of the separate heritages they brought with them from the island, and celebrating, of all things, Queen Wilhelmina's or Juliana's birthday, or singing the Marseillaise on Bastille Day."[14]

Rodolfo Fernández recalled this vibrancy upon arriving in Harlem as a twenty-one-year-old pitcher with Pompez's Cuban Stars in 1932. Rather than have Fernández find his own housing, Pompez arranged for him to stay in an apartment in Little Ybor. For a rookie playing in a new land, this made quite a difference. "And it is not as it is now, where a Latino arrives and wherever you go one can hear people talking in Spanish," Fernández stated. The *barrio latino* was nearby, and only walking distance to movie theaters, restaurants, and Spanish-language newspapers. "It had everything," Fernández remarked. Rafael "Ray" Noble and Armando Vásquez shared similar stories about housing arrangements the Cubans owner made for his young players. The arrangements had a particular purpose: the host family for some was selected to ensure that a young player did not suffer an extreme case of homesickness; in other instances, a Jamaican or West Indian family might be chosen to help a player develop his English-speaking abilities.[15] Homes like that of Juan Valdes were a vital part of this network. Valdes was a migrant from Ybor's Cuban-American community like Pompez, and his home at 15 West 107th Street served as a cultural center, a home away from home where players could gather to eat Cuban food or drink *café cubano*, listen to boleros or mambo, swap the latest gossip, and renew acquaintances with compatriots.

This community would be where Fernández and fellow Cuban Negro leaguer Armando Vásquez returned after their playing days ended; they knew that its members took care of one another. For Fernández, this knowledge came from his own role bringing Cuban great Cristóbal Torriente to Harlem in 1935. His skills eroded, Torriente was unable to land a roster spot in the Negro leagues. Worse yet, his health suffered from years of hard living and drinking. With no job or prospects, the once-feared slugger went to the hotel where the New York Cubans stayed in Chicago when they played the American Giants. Fernández came across Torriente in the hotel lobby seeking out manager Martín Dihigo: Torriente was looking for a lifeline. Dihigo called Pompez to see what they could do. The Cubans owner decided to hire Torriente as a coach to work with the players on the Cubans and the Havana Cuban Stars. Spending his next three years living in Harlem, Torriente died of tuberculosis at age forty-four in 1938; fellow ballplayers would buy his coffin and pay for the return of his body to Cuba, where Torriente was buried in a national cemetery.[16]

Challenged for Talent

Jorge Pasquel and Pompez established their acquaintance in a Mexico City jail in 1937 when the Mexican business magnate visited the imprisoned numbers king. Two years later the pair would compete over signing Latin American talent. The driving force behind the Mexican League, Pasquel sought to acquire the very best talent from anywhere without regard to color. Thus he immediately began to raid the Negro leagues and to sign Latino players from throughout the Americas. Unsurprisingly, Pompez would be the most drastically affected within either the Negro leagues or the majors.

In 1939, Pompez's Cubans lost the services of the ace pitcher Schoolboy Taylor to the Mexican League. Taylor signed a deal that paid him $100 per game and called for him to pitch twice a week—$800 a month if he made all his starts. Playing in Mexico meant that the Connecticut native no longer had to play in a segregated league or endure segregated travel and accommodations.[17] Black newspapers recognized the impact of this and other signings. As the 1939 season drew to a close, *The Chicago Defender* observed that Pompez was "faced with a difficult job in assembling players, as the leading Cuban players had gone to Venezuela and Mexico."[18]

Of course, Pompez was not the first Negro-league owner to suffer defections. While he remained in a Mexico City jail, across the Caribbean the upstart Dominican summer league began extracting its own chunk of talent from the Negro leagues. The Pittsburgh Crawfords lost Satchel Paige, Cool Papa Bell, and eight other players, while their crosstown rivals the Homestead Grays lost Josh Gibson to the Dominican circuit. When Pompez's legal woes shelved the New York Cubans, the team's top Latino players—Martín Dihigo, Lázaro Salazar, and Luis Tiant, Sr.—all found employment in the Dominican league. For all the Dominican jumpers, NNL president Gus Greenlee delivered stern words: "These men must realize that the league is far larger and more powerful than they are." Greenlee threatened to bar the jumpers from the Negro leagues for one year if they failed to report. The *Amsterdam News* linked the Dominican raid directly to the disbanded New York Cubans, blaming Dihigo and Salazar. Labeling the pair as instigators, Greenlee threatened legal action.[19] Team and league officials nonetheless vacillated on how to discipline players who jumped to the Dominican circuit when a few sought to return to the Negro leagues in 1938. In the days preceding the new campaign, NNL owners voted to delay the imposition of fines and suspensions against the jumpers and to give members of the 1936 New York Cubans who had not signed a 1937 contract a chance to air their case before announcing disciplinary measures.[20]

Unlike the Dominican summer league's meteoric appearance and disappearance, the Mexican League proved a much more enduring threat as Pasquel tapped into the Negro-league talent pool of African American and Latino players. The Negro leaguers were attracted to the Mexican League's higher salaries and better quality of professional life compared to what the United States offered. Latinos flocked to the new summer circuit as well, leaving U.S. teams on both sides of baseball's racial divide as well as coming from all over Latin America. Dihigo, Salazar, and Silvio García—star Cubans from the Negro leagues—joined the procession to Mexico. So would the Cubans Roberto Estalella, Roberto Ortiz, and Gilberto Torres, among others, as well as the Puerto Rican Luis Rodríguez Olmo from the majors. There they joined U.S.-born blacks who had also ventured south, headlined by the future Hall of Famers Paige, Gibson, and Cool Papa Bell. A scant four years into Pasquel's raid on the Negro leagues, the U.S. circuit had lost thirty-six frontline players; the Mexican League would sign over one hundred Negro leaguers.[21]

Negro-league owners tried to fight back. Rufus "Sonnyman" Jackson, the money behind the Homestead Grays, literally took matters into his own hands. In early July 1943 he caught A. J. Guina at Forbes Field asking questions about several Grays before a game against the Cleveland Buckeyes. Noticing his accent, Jackson inquired whether Guina was Mexican. When he answered in the affirmative, Jackson had him forcibly ejected after allegedly physically threatening Guina— who happened to be the Mexican consul in Pittsburgh. None too pleased, Guina filed an official complaint and had Jackson arrested. Although Guina later failed to report in court, leading to the dismissal of the charges against Jackson, the episode nonetheless illustrated the level of antagonism. Jackson was not apologetic in the least: "I don't care if they send Pancho Villa, they're not getting to get to my players." NNL owners had in fact already pursued formal legal channels to repel the "Mexican Menace." Yet that proved futile. State Department officials would deny visa requests for Negro leaguers seeking to travel to Mexico, but players could gain entry into Mexico with a visitor's pass and, once there, have their status altered to allow them to stay for the duration of the Mexican League season.[22]

Negro-league owners banded together and imposed a blacklist that penalized players for jumping to the Mexican League. The blacklist backfired, failing to compel players to stay and actually encouraging some jumpers to remain in Mexico. Indeed, the blacklist missed the reason why African Americans and Latinos had jumped south of the border in the first place: the salaries paid by Mexican League teams far surpassed what Negro-league owners were either willing or able to pay. In 1939, the Mexico City Diablos Rojos paid Newark Eagles third baseman Ray Dandridge a salary four times what Newark had paid him the previous year. Two years later Josh Gibson left the Homestead Grays to sign with Veracruz for $6,000—$2,000 more than what the Grays had offered the power-hitting catcher.[23] A suspension for departing for a league that paid more, traveled less, and offered an integrated setting on and away from the baseball diamond was no deterrent.

The growth of the Mexican circuit had the most enduring impact on the New York Cubans. Whereas other Negro-league teams encountered departures of established U.S.-born players, the Mexican League drew from Pompez's primary talent pool: Latin America. The Mexican League was doubly attractive to Latinos, since Mexico was a Spanish-speaking society and did not racially segregate whites from blacks. The attractiveness of Mexico produced regular player defections that made finalizing the New York Cubans roster late into the spring an annual ritual. The Cubans owner shared with *The Chicago Defender* the level of uncertainty that arose in 1940, expressing worry when five of eleven players scheduled to report from Cuba had yet to appear at the Cubans spring training camp. Had they, too, been recruited to play in Mexico? he wondered. Such defections forced an annual scramble to fill out his roster with talented players and thus complicated his ability to field a highly competitive team.[24]

Suitors for his talent came on two fronts. Not only did Pasquel's Mexican League beckon, but major-league organizations also sang a siren call. Since their inception as the Cuban Stars, Pompez's team had welcomed Latinos from the lightest to the darkest in skin tone; the Negro leagues never discriminated among Latinos. Occasionally, Caribbean players whom Pompez signed drew interest from major-league organizations. Team executives like Clark Griffith used a simple mantra to defend such signings before fellow big-league officials, the press, and the public: these men are not black; they're Cuban, Puerto Rican, or Venezuelan. This clearly played on racial ambiguity, but it nonetheless provided the main means through which Latin American players of different gradations of skin color were ushered into organized baseball at a time when African-Americans were entirely excluded and the majority of Latinos were deemed to have too "Negroid" an appearance.

The offers intensified from the late 1930s up through the moment the majors undertook integration. Toward the end of the 1942 season, the Washington Senators expressed interest in the Cubans infielder Carlos Blanco. The Senators' offer underwhelmed Pompez: it was far less than what he would accept for such a talent. However, "Pompez was more concerned in getting Blanco into big time baseball than the money and told Griffith he could have Blanco," Frank A. "Fay" Young recounted in *The Chicago Defender*. Their interest in Blanco dissipated after a Senators scout observed the Cubans playing an exhibition game in Waterbury, Connecticut. "The Washington club's representative was disappointed in two things in Blanco," Young noted. "One was his hair was not the wavy Spanish type but was more Negroid. Second was that Blanco was too dark. He had hoped to find Blanco of a decided [*sic*] Spanish type." The Blanco episode reiterated the fickle nature of racial perceptions. Blanco continued with the Cubans in the Negro leagues "while some of his former mates are now in minor league baseball in the East. One who has more Negro blood in his vein than Blanco gets by because his skin is near white."[25]

Protests organized during World War II heightened public awareness of organized baseball's color line and discrimination against U.S.-born blacks. On several occasions in the mid-1940s, journalists from the black press and Socialist newspapers successfully forced major-league teams to hold tryouts for Negro-league players. Two New York Cubans drew wide notice as serious prospects: Schoolboy Taylor and David Barnhill, both lighter-skinned U.S.-born blacks. A hard-throwing right-hander, Taylor dominated the high school and local amateur baseball scene in his hometown of Hartford, Connecticut, before starring on the 1935 Cubans squad. In making a pitch for baseball integration that October, a *New York Age* editorial advanced the then twenty-one-year-old pitcher as a serious candidate to integrate organized baseball, stating "Taylor conducts himself with credit to the race both on and off the diamond." Taylor struck out twenty-five batters in one high school game, and his pitching exploits at the Hartford high school drew major-league scouts, including one from the New York Yankees.[26] Interest disappeared once the scout learned that Hartford's pitching ace was black.

Dave Barnhill debuted with the New York Cubans in 1941 and impressed immediately. The slightly built pitcher quickly moved toward the top of the list of players sportswriters mentioned as worthy of a major-league tryout. Black sportswriters, joined by a small group of white sportswriters from mainstream dailies and Socialist papers, actively advocated for integration. Lester Rodney and Nat Low provided ardent support in their *Daily Worker* columns and also worked behind the scenes. The pressure they mounted seemingly succeeded when, in late July 1942, Low announced that the Pittsburgh Pirates' owner, William Benswanger, had agreed to a tryout on August 4 for three Negro leaguers: Barnhill, the Baltimore Elite Giants second baseman Sammy Hughes, and his teammate the catcher Roy Campanella. It proved to be another false start in the campaign: the date came and went with no tryout.[27] Following the tryout's failure to materialize, Low received criticism for selecting those specific prospects. Critics believed Barnhill was a valid selection but contended "the other two were not the outstanding Negro players in their positions." That criteria other than recognized playing ability and on-field accomplishment were involved in selecting black prospects for major-league tryouts was understood by those in black baseball. For example, while noting that Satchel Paige was baseball's greatest drawing card since the days of Babe Ruth, the *Defender* article labeled Paige "too old" and not a wise selection either.[28]

A formal statement issued by Major League Baseball commissioner Judge Landis had raised hopes that major-league tryouts were within the realm of possibility. Other major-league insiders verbalized a lack of opposition to such tryouts. Brooklyn Dodgers manager Leo Durocher stated in a mid-July 1942 article in the *Daily Worker* that he would hire black players if not prevented from doing so by Landis. Unnerved that a major-league manager placed the blame for an inability to sign blacks at his door, Landis called Durocher in for a sit-down. After meeting with the commissioner at his Chicago office, Durocher denied having made the statement against Landis quoted in the *Daily Worker*. Landis then delivered a statement that showcased his legal training and writing talent honed during his tenure on the judicial bench: "Negroes are not barred from organized baseball by the commissioner and never have been during the 21 years I have served," he insisted. "If Durocher, any other manager, or all of them, want to sign one, or 25, Negro players, it is all right with me. That is the business of the managers and the club owners. The business of the commissioner is to interpret the rules of baseball and enforce them."[29] His cleverly worded statement denied his culpability for the absence of black players in organized baseball. Landis was not the originator of organized baseball's color line, but he was by no means actively working toward its elimination.

Black baseball sportswriters and integration supporters had dared to dream that the timing was right: the nation was at war against the pernicious racist ideology of Nazism; Americans of all colors and ancestry were involved in the war effort, on the battle front in the Pacific and European theaters and in defense industry plants as workers; a patriotic fervor and the idea of shared humanity had seemingly taken the nation. Integration advocates sensed an opening to push ahead with their campaign, one that would have additional false starts but would not bear actual fruit for several more years.

In the 1930s, minor-league teams and a handful of major-league organizations tested the resolve of their league rivals by acquiring Latino players who were increasingly racially ambiguous: Were they white, black, or somewhere in between? In some instances Pompez cleared the way for his players to leave the Negro leagues. He did so with the knowledge that America's game was not just about what happened inside the white lines of the baseball diamond. His life experience made him exceedingly aware of the power play between those seeking to widen and those seeking to limit access to institutions and opportunities by either altering or maintaining current racial restrictions. The stakes in professional baseball were clear: inclusion in organized baseball meant access to a more economically secure livelihood for individual players, although in an alienating environment. What remained unclear was how this inclusion would work to change racial understandings about Latinos as a group, and to what extent the inclusion of Latinos would transform the workings of baseball's racial system.

The owners also dealt with a threat of a very different kind: the growing popularity and antics of the Ethiopian Clowns. NNL and NAL owners felt that the team owned by Syd Pollock besmirched the standing of black baseball. The quality of baseball Pollock's team played was not the issue; his Clowns won the 1941 *Denver Post* semipro national tournament. The problem for Negro-league owners was the showmanship that accompanied their ballplaying. Much like the Harlem Globetrotters in basketball, entertainment shtick was a major part of the team's appeal as they barnstormed throughout the country. Negro leaguers found the Ethiopian Clowns' routine a blot on their racial enterprise. "The painting of faces by the Clowns players, their antics on the diamond and their style of play was a detriment to Negro league baseball," stated a resolution owners approved that forbade the scheduling of any contests with Pollock's team.[30] "While all Negro league teams employed a bit of showmanship in the countryside," the historian Donn Rogosin observes in describing what disturbed Pompez and his fellow owners, black baseball teams had long abided by an unwritten rule wherein they "insisted on the primacy of their professional baseball."

The Ethiopian Clowns ventured into professional black baseball as the lone exception to this code, drawing interest as much for being black entertainers as for their athletic performance. The fact that the Clowns' Jewish owner (Pollock) along with Abe Saperstein (originator of the Harlem Globetrotters, who also served as the Clowns' booking agent) were willing to have their players don face paint, perform comedic routines on the field, and use other antics upset the black baseball establishment. The problem: the Clowns management's willingness to "conform closely to the racial stereotypes of the period" through these antics. Such practices were anathema for most Negro-league owners and players; they had labored for years seeking respect for the black institution and as professionals. Pompez claimed that no foreign-born player would engage in such "humiliating activity." The black press often struck a tone that was no less clear, with one publication declaring: "The team has been capitalizing on slap-stick comedy and the kind of nonsense which many white people like to believe is typical and characteristic of all Negroes."[31]

Criticism about the lack of opportunities for U.S.-born blacks was also levied at Pompez during his three decades operating teams in the black baseball circuit, specifically about how he filled his team's roster. In the 1920s, New York City sportswriters asked why he refused to hire native-born blacks, one even accusing him of racial prejudice. When he reentered the Negro leagues in 1935, his new plan of liberally mixing native-born blacks with Latinos was likewise criticized. It was doomed to fail, a *New York Age* columnist observed. Pompez nonetheless persisted. The *New York Age* noted the distinctive composition that continued until the Cubans dropped out of league play after the 1950 season: "The Latin entry of the Negro National League is perhaps the most unique one in the country. Half Latin American and the other half from the good ole Los Estados Unidos."[32] It is small wonder, given the New York Cubans' diversity, that the *New York Age* and the *Amsterdam News* proclaimed the Cubans "Harlem's Own" and "The Latins from Manhattan."[33]

Black baseball owners faced a common set of management issues with the entry of the United States into World War II. The institution of mandatory registration for the Selective Service created a talent vacuum in both the major-league and the Negro-league circuits. As white major leaguers exchanged their baseball uniforms for those of different military branches, major-league organizations turned to Latin America like never before. Between 1939 and 1945, Latinos enjoyed their highest rate of debut in the majors to date. The Mexican League also continued to recruit them, and, after the United States entered the war in 1941, their numbers also increased in the Negro leagues. Foreign-born Latinos offered, at least initially, the advantage that they were not U.S. citizens and not likely to be called into military service. This loophole, which drew protests from major-league teams that did not use foreign-born Latinos, was closed in April 1944 when the Selective Service Commission declared that all Latin Americans who entered the United States on a six-month work visa were "resident aliens" and would have to either register for the draft within ten days or leave when their six-month visas expired. The ruling had its effect: the Washington Senators lost three Cuban players who returned immediately to Cuba rather than face the possibility of being pressed into U.S. military service.[34] A number of Latinos with major-league experience opted for the Mexican League and joined a southward migration of talent, meeting up with Negro leaguers Ray Dandridge, Lloyd Davenport, and Theolic Smith, among others, who had been lured south by the cash of Mexican baseball impresario Jorge Pasquel. Because the majority of his players were not from the continental United States, Pompez's baseball operations were more deeply affected by wartime restrictions than the other Negro-league franchises were. A fear of submarine attacks during the winter of 1941 caused serious travel concerns between the Caribbean islands and the United States, hampering Pompez's ability "to provide passage from Cuba for several of his players."[35] Such safety concerns complicated finalizing the 1942 Cubans roster—this, on the heels of a 1941 season during which the Cubans topped the NNL in the second half before being whitewashed by the Homestead Grays in a playoff doubleheader before fifteen thousand at Yankee Stadium.

In addition to the wartime talent drain, Negro-league team officials encountered travel restrictions and rationing of products used in the production of game equipment. Spring training was cut short and conducted much closer to home to comply with the Office of Defense Transportation. The two Negro leagues also conducted fewer interleague matches and barnstorming exhibitions. Governmental calls for rationing of gas and rubber (tires) forced teams to rely on train service for much of their transportation instead of their own buses.[36] Despite the rationing, the Negro leagues enjoyed a boon in attendance as African Americans in urban centers enjoyed higher-paying, more stable employment, which increased their discretionary income. Compelled to stay close to home to seek out entertainment due to the broad travel ban, they came to Negro-league games in numbers never before seen.

Finding New Ground

The new terms of operations prompted Pompez to contemplate a franchise move to Washington, D.C., for the 1942 season. *The Chicago Defender* reported on developments in the District of Columbia's black baseball scene after an owners' meeting in Baltimore. The Homestead Grays' Cum Posey expressed disappointment with the level of support that fans in the capital exhibited the previous year. Frustrated with a lack of proper support, Posey released a few dates at Griffith Stadium for others to fill. However, when Pompez explored the possibility of making Griffith Stadium the home grounds for his Cubans, the Grays executive team of Posey and Sonnyman Jackson "decided that baseball should do well in the capital city this summer" and kept Washington as one of their franchises two homes. Outmaneuvered, Pompez returned to looking in the New York area for a proper home ground for his New York Cubans.

The effort to find his Cubans a new home continued until 1944, when Pompez forged an agreement with the New York Giants to lease the Polo Grounds. Located at the northern edge of Harlem on 155th Street and Eighth Avenue, the ballpark was the most accessible home grounds for Harlem fans ever used by Pompez's Cubans. After Dyckman Oval was gone, Harlemites had trekked all over New York City and even across the Hudson River to Paterson's Hinchliffe Stadium and Newark's Davids' Stadium to watch the Cubans perform. The Polo Grounds were literally within walking distance. Fans could stroll northward from the center of Harlem—from 125th or 135th Street along any of its north–south arterials: St. Nicholas Avenue, Amsterdam Avenue, or Edgecombe Avenue—up to the ballpark built on Coogan's Bluff.

Those who filed into the Polo Grounds to witness the New York Cubans perform offer a striking counterpoint to perceptions that Harlem was a Negro mecca consisting solely of English-speaking blacks. The *Cleveland Call and Post* estimated that at least 30 percent of fans at the Cubans home games at the Polo Grounds were Latino. The diversity of the spectators who filled the stands lingered in the recollections of New York Cubans players Rodolfo Fernández, Charlie Rivera, and Armando Vásquez. It was also the memory of Negro leaguer Jimmy Robinson, who grew up in Harlem and whose aunt lived a couple of blocks from the Cubans' business office on 114th Street. Similarly, Everard Marius, a Harlem-born man of West Indian parentage, recalled going to the Polo Grounds as a youth with his friends who were U.S.-born and foreign-born blacks. Marius contrasted this with his father's generation: baseball had replaced cricket as sport of choice, providing a cultural practice that bonded black youths from diverse origins into neighborhood teams and contributing to their notions of being members of the same racial community in ways that their own parents did not quite (or want to) understand or embrace.[37] The Harlem that Marius and his contemporaries grew up in was strikingly similar to what Pompez and his generation had experienced a decade or so earlier. There, they interacted with men and women of different national origins moving back and forth between what later became clearer lines of distinction. It is the power of history and historical memory that either erase these lines of distinction—as captured in oral interviews with individuals who lived in Harlem during this era—or reinscribe them through selective silences that hide the contributions the New York Cubans and Pompez made to Harlem's social life.

The Negro leagues, like other black-dominated businesses, retained special meaning in a community adversely affected by segregation and discriminatory practices. In the midst of the Depression, the Negro leagues possessed one advantage over Major League Baseball at the box office: admission prices to Negro-league games cost far less. Prices for the Cubans 1935 home opener ranged from $0.45 for the bleachers to $0.55 for general admission to $0.85 for a box seat. By comparison, general admission ("upper-stands") to a New York Giants game at the Polo Grounds cost $1.10.[38] Games at Yankee Stadium, the Polo Grounds, and Ebbets Field were special events for Harlemites, providing them an opportunity to witness their own performing in these well-manicured major-league venues. It was a social event to be seen where fans wore their Sunday best and ticket prices were commensurate. A September doubleheader between the Negro National League All-Stars and Satchel Paige's barnstorming Santo Domingo Champs at the Polo Grounds in 1937 cost fans $1.10 for general admission, $1.65 for a box seat, and $0.55 for the bleachers.[39]

Showcase events in these ballparks shaped the memories, histories, identities, and sense of community of Negro-league players and spectators, whose presence interrupted the conventions that came with segregated sports: on these occasions there was no racially segregated seating. "Fans who have seen the teams of the Negro National League play at Dyckman Oval say they prefer to see these boys in action to seeing many big leaguers," a *New York Age* editorial proclaimed, "because they play with more spirit and present a more colorful game."

The *Age* then went so far as to claim that it was "a well known fact" that attendance at Negro-league and interracial exhibitions in the city the previous two or three years were larger than those for big-league games.[40] Notwithstanding the doubtful veracity of that claim, there is some validity to the assertion that the spirit of crowds at Negro-league games differed substantially from that at major-league contests. Through the annals of American sports history, black Americans openly celebrated when Jack Johnson beat Jim Jeffries and listened raptly to Joe Louis's titanic fights with white adversaries. So, too, did they cheer when Negro-league all-stars defeated white stars on and off U.S. playing fields. These events not only formed a "structure of feelings," they produced a tapestry of understanding that wove a sense of collectivity, pride, and affirmation into the accomplishment of black athleticism.[41]

The occasions that the NNL rented Yankee Stadium or the Polo Grounds revived debates about booking agents, since the Yankees and Giants had long insisted on using agents instead of working directly with the local NNL owners. This practice bothered Pompez and Black Yankees owner Jim Semler. First, it reduced their revenue stream: they received their cut only after paying the agreed rental and booking agent's fee.[42] Second, fellow NNL executive Eddie Gottlieb, the white owner of the Philadelphia Stars, served as booking agent for Negro-league games at Yankee Stadium. This meant the New York–based Negro-league team owners were forced to pay Gottlieb a percentage to book games in their hometown. Pompez and Semler were most directly affected; this minimized the benefits of operating in the nation's largest black market, with more than 458,000 black residents.

Booking agents did provide important services that reduced the amount of staff a Negro-league franchise had to employ: Ed Gottlieb Sporting Enterprises handled all aspects of hosting a game; a team owner basically just had to have his squad show up at the stadium. Gottlieb's outfit handled publicity, printed tickets and window posters, distributed advertising materials to local stores, and advertised the event in newspapers.[43] But for his part, Pompez knew he was more than capable of handling such details. No other Negro-league owner had Pompez's range of experience: he had operated his own ballpark (Dyckman) as a multisport venue; he had booked sporting events since the

1910s, starting with his stint working with Nat Strong and more recently as a boxing promoter at Rockland Palace; and he had arranged barnstorming trips throughout the Caribbean for his own Negro-league teams. Clearly, as a former numbers king, he did not lack the practical knowledge of running a business—and now he was solely operating a legitimate enterprise.

A fractious voting bloc formed in the early 1940s, split between NNL owners operating in the New York metro area (Pompez, Semler, and the Manleys) and those who did not (Cum Posey, Tom Wilson, and Gottlieb). Paying the Philadelphia-based Gottlieb 10 percent of their gate for booking games in their hometown irritated Pompez and Semler. The two New Yorkers vocalized their displeasure at a contentious owners meeting in February 1940, stating that "New York was their territory and league games ought to be booked by the [resident] club owners or the league." They directed their ire at NNL president Tom Wilson, owner of the Baltimore Elite Giants, for allowing the unfair practice to persist. Wilson responded by reminding them that five of the six owners had previously consented to Gottlieb's booking the events at Yankee Stadium and that Wilson had personally agreed not to take 10 percent for such league promotions as had the previous president Gus Greenlee. Rather, he had chosen to turn that money over to Gottlieb because the Stars owner "could save the league money." Gottlieb, he continued, had successfully lowered the rental fee at the Stadium from $3,500 to $1,000. Semler demurred, insisting that he should be entrusted with Yankee Stadium promotions. That idea was quickly dismissed; *The Chicago Defender* noted that a 1939 promotion Semler organized at Randall's Island had "netted four league clubs exactly $12 and the expenses were greater than any of the games promoted by Gottlieb at the Yankee stadium." Nevertheless, Effa Manley insisted, "the league ought to be run for colored by colored." Her declaration was an ironic jab at Gottlieb, the NNL's only recognized white owner; Manley herself had two white biological parents, although she was raised by a black stepfather and her white mother in a black neighborhood in Philadelphia.[44]

Dissatisfied with Wilson's leadership, the New York faction tried to unseat him at the February 1940 meeting. Effa Manley nominated *Amsterdam News* publisher Clilan B. Powell, championing the position of an independent league president. She had the support of Semler and Pompez, but the other owners objected "on the grounds that [Powell] was hand-picked and came from the New York area." Posey protested that Powell's newspaper had only recently begun to publish the league's activities. The NNL owners left their Chicago meeting deadlocked: Wilson and Powell had garnered three votes each. Reconvened two weeks later in Gottlieb's Philadelphia office, the NNL owners reelected Tom Wilson, with some diplomatic wrangling from Pompez to break the stalemate. The *New York Age* sportswriter Buster Miller intoned sharp words for all participants in the dispute except Pompez, who "stamped himself as the shrewd business man [by refusing] to be deterred from the business at hand in order to participate in a factional squabble." The *Age* pilloried the Manleys and Semler for their insistence "upon a president who is a business man without being a baseball man" and likewise blasted the Wilson faction for seeking to maintain "a baseball man without being a business man." Thus it was left to Pompez to broker peace. Cognizant that they were otherwise deadlocked, he spoke of the "best interest of the league" and recommended retention of all the same officers from the previous year; the battle to unseat Wilson would be saved for another season.[45]

The arrangement would continue to generate resentment. The following January the owners voted to consolidate the secretary and treasurer positions, forcing Manley out of the inner circle. At their Baltimore meeting, NNL owners approved a tentative working agreement regarding promotions at major-league parks—an agreement whose details were to be finalized by a committee of Wilson, Cum Posey, and Ed Bolden.[46] Bickering continued; resentment lingered. A Baltimore *Afro-American* article published almost three years later cited a New York sportswriter who derided the NNL owners for enacting an "Uncle Tom" move in retaining Wilson as president, "thereby keeping Ed Gottlieb in the driver's seat, dictating to the owners about promotions and league business." This derailed more significant issues from receiving attention, such as the league's publicly declaring its support for tearing down organized baseball's color line.[47]

The diverse makeup of Pompez's New York Cubans, part of his broader effort to provide Harlem baseball fans with a team to call their own, brought to the fore many of the same questions Harlemites confronted in their everyday interactions. These questions centered on making a community that saw its ethnic diversity as a resource to build with—instead of a community that saw its diversity as a constant source of division and strife. In this manner, the New York Cubans truly captured the continuing transformation of Harlem from a European-American enclave at the beginning of the twentieth century to a black cultural mecca by middle of the twentieth century. No figure within Negro-league baseball could negotiate this complex terrain better than Pompez. His experience growing up in segregated Tampa had first exposed him to the power of racialized perceptions that divided white from black in a Jim Crow town. Even among Tampa's Cuban émigré community, color lines were drawn that separated the lives of Cuban compatriots, as described by fellow black Cuban Evelio Grillo, who grew up in Tampa a generation after Pompez. The baseball entrepreneur knew all too well the impact of such lines on his own life, and how they were doubly complex when someone was both Latino and black. No dividing line could be drawn through him: he lived in both worlds. His Harlem was multilingual, not English only. His Harlem world was full of differences yet filled with people dealing with similar struggles to maintain their human dignity in a society where they were constantly reminded that race mattered. It was this community to which he endeavored at long last to bring a Negro National League pennant and a Negro League World Series title.

7

GLORY DAYS

*The big league teams are taking most of them now, and I have
a very small field to pick from.*
　　　　　　—*Alex Pompez*, The Pittsburgh Courier, *June 1945*

The Brooklyn Dodgers' signing of Jackie Robinson on October 24, 1945, shook the professional baseball world. A major-league team had finally taken a very real step, not just making a halfhearted offer of a tryout as the Pittsburgh Pirates had done in 1942, or hosting a sham tryout for talented black players as the Boston Red Sox did in April 1945, or offering coy denials about no rule, written or otherwise, that denied black players the opportunity to perform in the majors. Integration was in its infancy, and those who had long campaigned for the demolition of organized baseball's color line rejoiced. Black baseball owners scrambled. They were in an unenviable position: as business-people, they operated an entity whose finished product—talented black players—was now a desired commodity and in need of protection; as "race" men and women, they could not protest too vociferously that a formerly segregated institution had begun to open its doors to blacks. Thus, Pompez and his fellow Negro-league owners faced the monumental challenge of retooling what had been created as a "shadow" institution to serve the nonwhite community of baseball fans into a league serviceable for the new integrated era. Critics and supporters alike told them to "get their house in order," which proved much more difficult than expected.

NNL owners set out to disprove that theirs was more "a racket" than a professional organization, as Brooklyn Dodgers president Branch Rickey had charged when he signed Robinson. At their January 1947 gathering at Harlem's Hotel Theresa, NNL owners finally unseated Tom Wilson as league president and elected the circuit's first independent top executive, Reverend John H. Johnson, chaplain of Harlem's St. Martin's Episcopal Church. The death of Cum Posey swung the vote that ended Wilson's decade-long hold on the league's top post as Posey's replacement, Sonnyman Jackson, aligned himself with Pompez, Manley, and Semler—all numbers men in the past—in casting a 4–2 vote for Johnson; Wilson and Gottlieb, unsurprisingly, voted to retain the status quo.[1]

Johnson's election reflected the hope that new leadership could persuade those who wielded power within organized baseball of the mutual benefits of having the Negro leagues as a partner in desegregating the national pastime. The new NNL president joined the re-elected vice president, Pompez, and instituted a series of reforms that raised the league's professional standards and strove to build up the circuit's good name. The reforms addressed concerns organized baseball officials previously expressed about the structure and operation of Negro-league baseball: the form of the official contract, the execution of the league schedule, the behavior and background of black baseball owners themselves. Johnson knew this rehabilition effort involved public relations, since major-league officials were hesitant to publicly partner up with Negro-league owners in the racial desegregation of organized baseball. Moving mountains seemed easier than budging Major League Baseball commissioner Albert "Happy" Chandler and other big-league executives from their entrenched position that black baseball must conform to their vision of how it ought to operate before entering into any official collaboration.

In late February, Johnson released a statement titled "On the Status of the Negro in Baseball" to counter comments made by Chandler to the Associated Press and point out the continued lack of recognition from organized baseball. The Negro-league executive cited the September 1945 report written by New York Yankees executive Larry McPhail that recommended that the major leagues "take action to strengthen the Negro Leagues and to admit them into Organized

Baseball 'after their house had been put in order.'" The Negro leagues had done just that, and he believed the time had arrived for organized baseball to accept the applications of the two Negro leagues. Despite the reforms, their formal applications for admission to the National Association of Professional Baseball were rejected in December 1947. This denial meant that more than two years after McPhail's recommendations, the Negro leagues still possessed "no status, no voice, no rights, no relationship at all to the Major or Minor Leagues." The NNL president reiterated black baseball's poignant plight: "Forced to carry on as best they can, limited and handicapped, competing against the vast resources of Organized Baseball, struggling to survive." Additionally, while the Negro leagues were denied admission, Johnson lamented that "new white leagues not better organized than ours and with players inferior to ours in skill have been accepted." The "only feasible solution" for the NNL president was the admittance of the Negro leagues into organized baseball, for it "would provide the Major Leagues with rich resources of colored talent to draw upon, and would give many colored players, of Robinson's caliber with a broader opportunity for development."[2]

No challenge to the Negro leagues' hold on black talent proved greater than the major leagues once they launched racial integration. In retrospect, one might have anticipated Branch Rickey's 1945 signing of Robinson in the marked increase of Latinos signed by major-league clubs in the early 1940s. That ended a near monopoly the Negro leagues had enjoyed on darker-skinned Latinos, especially since the Latin American players major-league teams signed were more racially ambiguous than in decades past. Sportswriters such as Lester Rodney of the *Daily Worker*, Shirley Povich of *The Washington Post*, Sam Lacy of the Baltimore *Afro-American*, and Dan Burley of the *New York Age*, among others, debated the impact that the shift to Latino players had on baseball's color line even before Robinson had been signed by Brooklyn.

The start of baseball's "great experiment" increased demand for Latino talent, as it made all Latinos eligible to sign and not just the lighter-skinned ones, who had enjoyed limited access since the early 1900s. These were the glory days for Latinos in the Negro leagues: the era of Orestes Miñoso pacing the New York Cubans offensive attack before he became "Minnie" in the majors; Horacio Martínez displaying his slick fielding, which some argued merited his inclusion in the first wave of integration pioneers before he became instrumental in the opening of the Dominican talent pipeline; the powerful hitting of Silvio Garcia, which prompted Rickey to consider the Cuban as the potential color-line breaker. These and other lesser-known Latino players vaulted Pompez's "Latins from Manhattan" to the Negro league's upper echelon. Black baseball fans recognized their excellence by voting Latino players as regular participants in the Negro leagues' East-West Classic. From the 1935 classic through the 1947 contests, Martín Dihigo, Alejandro Oms, Miñoso, and Martínez were regular representatives of the East All-Stars; over two dozen Latino players appeared on the East rosters during this span.[3]

Even with new opportunity beckoning, some Latinos hesitated before venturing north to play, aware of the hardships earlier sojourners had encountered. News of Robinson and Johnny Wright and then Roy Campanella and Don Newcombe signing with the Dodgers did motivate some Latinos to sign with the New York Cubans or other Negro-league teams (instead of going to Mexico). Concerns about racial perceptions in the States had long represented a critical factor in the decisions of talented ballplayers who grew up in Cuba, the Dominican Republic, Puerto Rico, Mexico, or Venezuela. Black Latinos had to weigh more than the cultural dislocation they would encounter: they also had to decide whether venturing to the States was worth the psychological toll that came with playing segregated baseball as a black Latino.

Changing the Rules of Engagement

The signing of Jackie Robinson changed the terms under which major-league teams engaged the Caribbean pool of baseball talent. Competition for this talent had already intensified, even before the Dodgers had inked Robinson. That had prompted Pompez to complain to the *Pittsburgh Courier* sportswriter Wendell Smith that major-league teams were taking "most of them now" six months before the Robinson signing. Indeed, the Robinson signing posed a significant challenge to his ability to secure players for his Cubans team. When NNL owners convened in January 1943, the circuit's player shortage ranked high on their agenda. Scores of Negro leaguers, such as Monte Irvin and Leon Day, had answered the call to serve and joined the military. War production industries had taken dozens of players away from professional baseball diamonds. Departures created multiple roster openings on Negro-league clubs, vacancies that executives increasingly filled with Latinos.[4] The composition of the Indianapolis Clowns, for one, started to resemble the New York Cubans. The 1944 Clowns roster included Leo Lugo, Antonio Ruiz, and Armando Vásquez playing alongside the African American players Lloyd "Pepper" Bassett, "Buster" Haywood, and Johnny Williams. The trend of signing Latinos increased after the Dodgers signed Robinson. The 1946 Negro-league season featured four teams (the Baltimore Elite Giants, the New York Black Yankees, the Indianapolis Clowns, and the New York Cubans) with a handful of Latino players on their rosters instead of just one or two.

In the first week of June 1944, Pompez announced that he had negotiated a deal with New York Giants owner Horace Stoneham to lease the Polo Grounds as the New York Cubans' home field. The relationship between Stoneham and Pompez would flourish over the ensuing years, creating unique opportunities for both the Cubans and the Giants franchises. For now, the lease agreement liberated Pompez from having to work through Eddie Gottlieb as a booking agent to arrange showcase events in New York City. Equally significant, this also meant the ballplayers who wore the Cubans uniform would play at least twenty league home games in the major-league park, potentially gaining increased exposure to big-league scouts.[5] The loss of top players Claro Duany, Lázaro Salazar, Alejandro Crespo, and Silvio García precipitated the team's slide into the NNL second division in 1944. The franchise's troubles continued the following season. Winning only one of their first twelve NNL games in the first half, the Cubans also endured inclement weather and injuries. "I have never seen such weather since I started bringing teams here from Cuba more than twenty years ago," Pompez lamented to Wendell Smith in late June after rain canceled three straight Sunday dates at the Polo Grounds. Moreover, injuries prevented many of his team's players from suiting up in the games the Cubans did play. "Right now, seven of my best players are hurt, and some of those who are playing are bandaged up," Pompez informed Smith. "My best pitcher, Dave Barnhill, has a sore arm, and six others look like they are veterans of World War II." Despite the weather issues and the injury-depleted lineup, the events he organized at the Polo Grounds reportedly drew more than three hundred thousand spectators.[6]

The looser attitude toward signing Latinos exhibited by major-league organizations during the war added further difficulty to Pompez's effort to field a competitive team. "There was a time when I could get all I wanted, but theese [sic] Cincinnati Reds, Washington Senatoors [sic] and minor league teams are taking them like anything," he complained to Smith.[7] The signings had a new wrinkle: these organizations were acquiring players they had refused to sign before World War II largely due to their physical appearance. Pompez could not compete with major-league organizations financially, so he emphasized his reputation as a "good" man who took care of his players. His reputation led to a "favorite yarn" that Harold Preece recounted in the *Baltimore Afro-American.* "A teacher in one of the country schools asked her class to tell her the name of Cuba's Ambassador to the United States," Preece wrote. After a pause one of the pupils raises her hand and responded, "I know who he is . . . He's Senor Alex Pompez."[8] The anecdote captured popular sentiment about the work he did for those long neglected by organized baseball, earning him title of "Cuba's unofficial goodwill ambassador to the United States."

Latino players followed a peculiar pattern of participation in the major leagues. Over four dozen foreign-born and U.S.-born Latinos appeared between 1902 and 1945. As a reflection of the capricious policing of baseball's racial divide, thirteen Latinos would perform in both the black baseball circuit and the major leagues during this Jim Crow era: Oscar Estrada, Ramon "Mike" Herrera, and Tomas "Tommy" de la Cruz all played for Pompez's Cuban Stars in addition to time in the majors. As a study of U.S. racial norms, Latino participation and movement between the segregated leagues of "organized baseball" and the Negro leagues exposes the knowing manipulation of racial understandings that justified the inclusion of some Latinos while excluding the majority of them. Indeed, the key to this group's participation in the segregated majors was the public portrayal of them as not being U.S.-born blacks.

Horacio Martínez, the slick-fielding Cubans shortstop from 1935 until 1947, felt the impact of this truth. The Dominican impressed many within Negro-league and Latin American baseball circles, becoming a highly sought-after player. In 1943, sportswriters offered his name as a potential barrier breaker in the majors. The *Daily Worker* writer Nat Low cited the Brooklyn Dodgers as a possible destination, given its "weakness" at shortstop. Mistakenly referring to Martínez as "first, last, and always a Cuban," the *Norfolk Journal and Guide* writer Lem Graves noted that there were "plenty of Cubans playing big league baseball, no fairer than Martinez." The problem, as was the case with dozens of other Latino players, was Martínez's hair. That was what Pompez informed the sportswriter, admitting to previous opportunities to sell Martínez to the Washington Senators or other clubs "if 'Rabbit' had possessed the slick hair." A vocal contingent would have likely objected to the shortstop's selection as baseball's integration pioneer, since they "will want to see an American Negro of unmistakable origin playing in the majors before they will see in baseball the slightest semblance of true democracy."[9]

Familiarity with this history prompted Branch Rickey to briefly contemplate, but ultimately forgo, signing Silvio García—Martínez's replacement on the New York Cubans—to dismantle baseball's racial barrier. A Negro-league all-star, García possessed the talent to play in the majors but lacked the right skin color and citizenship, being clearly black and also a Cuban. Rickey's signing of García would not have eliminated all of the ambiguity that the Washington Senators, the Cincinnati Reds, and other major-league organizations had played on in justifying their signing of "mulatto" Cubans or Latinos. Players like Pedro Dibút, Roberto Estalella, and Tommy de la Cruz were Cuban and not black, organizational officials explained. García did not represent the optimal prospect through which Rickey and the Dodgers could shatter the ambiguity that had long sustained the color line's system of racial exclusion.[10] In the end Rickey opted to sign Jackie Robinson, a U.S.-born, college-educated black man. Although coming too late for black Latinos such as Martín Dihigo and Lefty Tiant who had starred on Pompez's Negro-league clubs, the dismantling of the color-line system created a new era for all Latinos. The success of Robinson and then Larry Doby as unambiguously black men in the majors enabled Latino players of African descent who followed, such as Orestes Miñoso and Luis Tiant, Jr., to acknowledge their race and ethnicity when they entered organized baseball. No longer did Latinos of "visible" African ancestry have to evade those policing the racial divide as de la Cruz, Estalella, and possibly others had done.

Acutely aware of how much racial integration was going to alter the professional baseball landscape, Pompez found himself in the middle of an intense competition for Latino talent among himself, the Mexican League, and organized baseball. The Mexican League's raid on major-league rosters inflamed the situation, daring to challenge the supremacy that the majors had long held for white American players. This effort to woo players away from U.S.-based leagues was not new. Pompez's Cubans had suffered departures for the Mexican circuit of all levels of talent, from the established star to the young player on the rise, since 1938. In its preview of the 1946 Negro-league campaign, *The Chicago Defender* listed sixteen former New York Cubans who spent the 1945 season in Mexico; the list included pitchers Dihigo, Schoolboy Taylor, and Ramón Bragaña along with former starting Cubans Lázaro Salazar, Claro Duany, and Carlos Blanco. Rather than unnerve Pompez, especially considering the energy he expended in replenishing his team roster, the situation drove his competitive spirit as he sought to get some of his players back and to locate new ones.

Pompez found irony in major-league owners' complaints to the mainstream press about the temerity of Mexican League teams "raiding" their rosters. In a sit-down interview at his New York Cubans office with a *Cleveland Call and Post* sportswriter, he recounted how "everybody was snickering and giggling over our predicament" when black baseball owners protested Branch Rickey's "snatching" Jackie Robinson and John Wright from the Negro leagues. Rickey's signing the two Negro leaguers without compensating either the Kansas City Monarchs or the Homestead Grays was not business as usual, he insisted. After all, he and Joe Cambria had in times past made arrangements to transfer players' rights from his Negro-league team to one of Cambria's minor-league teams. "Now I can laugh for all my fellow Negro club owners," he told the scribe, observing that major-league owners were "scrambling and beating their breasts and hollering 'Stop, thief!'" after the Mexican League signed the Dodgers outfielder Luis Olmo and the New York Giants players Danny Gardella and Nap Reyes. "I have done a little snatching myself," he boasted to the Cleveland sportswriter of his signing of Silvio García, Santos Amaro, and Alex Crespo, three of the Mexican League's top players from the previous year. "They all jumped my club to go to Mexico," he explained. "Now they have jumped the Mexican League to return to the Cubans." The most prized catch was García, whom the Dodgers manager, Leo Durocher, described to a New York sportswriter as "the best I ever saw" after witnessing him play in 1941 spring training exhibitions between Brooklyn and a Cuban all-star team (composed mainly of Pompez's players). "He can do anything Marty Marion can do and he can do it better."[11] With such high praise from Durocher, it is no small wonder that Branch Rickey was willing to at least scout García as the player to pioneer integration for the majors.

Competition also occurred over emerging players, as seen in the case of Miñoso, whose first professional season in the Cuban League in the 1945–46 campaign was impressive. His play caught the attention of one of his Marianao coaches, José María Fernández, veteran manager of the New York Cubans. In that vein Fernández communicated with Pompez about the infield prospect and received authorization to sign Miñoso. Jorge Pasquel also wanted to sign Miñoso, traveling with his brother Bernardo to Cuba to recruit the young Cuban. The three met at Havana's Rio Hotel, where the Pasquel brothers made their play. "What I saw stunned me; I had never seen so much money in my life. Thousands and thousands of American dollars in assorted bills," the future Cuban star recalled. They offered him $10,000 to play in Mexico; $30,000 if he signed on for two seasons. He turned down the Mexican oil tycoon, informing him that it was his dream to play in the United States. Instead he signed with Pompez's Cubans, which would allow him to fulfill "the dream of every black baseball player anywhere." Instead of the five-figure salary Pasquel offered, he received $300 a month in the Negro leagues, drawing $150 salary and $5 per diem for meal money.[12] Success in acquiring young talent—Miñoso along with pitcher José Santíago and catcher Rafael Noble—in addition to reacquiring players from the Mexican League helped elevate the New York Cubans to respectability in 1946.

Pompez was known within baseball circles as a diplomatic figure able to broker peace, and his election as Negro National League vice president in 1946 gave him an increasingly important role in league affairs. This standing was tested when a player strike threatened the

1946 East-West Classic at Washington's Griffith Stadium. Negro-league officials could scarcely afford the public relations disaster of its all-star showcase canceled due to a players' strike. Players from the West (Negro American League) squad engaged in a sit-down strike after their pre-game practice, refusing to take the field unless owners agreed to pay each player $100. The players well knew that the East-West Classic was the biggest attraction of the entire Negro-league season, producing the single most significant gate. Players wanted a greater share of the Washington exhibition, a second East-West game to be held that season. The players' strike dragged on for fifteen minutes as the Griffith Stadium crowd of sixteen thousand, who had paid $3 for box seats and $2 to sit in the grandstand, waited. Speaking for NAL players who refused to take the field, the Cleveland Buckeyes' Willie Grace told the Homestead Grays' See Posey, the Baltimore Elite Giants' Vernon Green, and Pompez in the impromptu negotiations: "You folks asked us to take $50 because you didn't know how it was going to draw here the first time. You got a park full of people and we think we are entitled to $100." Although the NNL squad was uninvolved, Pompez hoped to save the circuit embarrassment. "This sort of thing every time we have an all-star game has got to stop," he replied to Grace. "You're doing nothing but sending your own baseball to ruin." This was not the first players' labor action at an East-West Classic. Two years earlier the East squad had demanded $200 to play the Classic in Chicago and returned to the field only after owners conceded to their monetary demand and promised that there would be no reprisals for their collective action. Now, although initial reports credited NAL president J. B. Martin, *The Pittsburgh Courier*'s Wendell Smith wrote that it was Pompez who provided his personal assurance that the striking players' demand would be met (in the event that the other owners refused to comply) in return for preventing the disastrous cancellation of the all-star contest.[13]

The following year, NNL owners granted Pompez the opportunity to host an East-West contest at the Polo Grounds. The move to host two all-star contests annually allowed fans in the East a chance to partake of the gathering of black baseball's best. The scheduled July 29 contest gave Harlem fans only their second chance to witness Negro-league all-stars performing in their hometown. (The first had been organized by Gus Greenlee in 1938.) Owners had previously discussed a permanent shift of the annual classic from Chicago to New York. However, concerns over whether New York City's baseball fans' "zest for Negro baseball" rose to the level of that of black baseball fans in Chicago quashed that conversation. Hosting a second "dream game" in the East was the compromise position that pleased owners but would spur players to demand better compensation for their participation.[14]

Hosting the Classic was the Cubans owner's chance to bring the strongest aggregation of Negro-league talent to perform before New York's black baseball faithful. Preparations, including placing ads in the *Amsterdam News* and the *New York Age* to spur interest, gave him confidence in a large turnout. "Baseball's Dream Game" read the quarter-page advertisement in the July 26 *Amsterdam News* announcing ticket sales for the East-West Classic, which were available at four locations, including the New York Cubans' headquarters at 84 Lenox Avenue. "Tickets are going like hot cakes for this 'natural,'" he informed the *Amsterdam News*. "Who was it [who] said New York is not a baseball town? The fans here will turn out, if you've got something to give 'em," he declared confidently. Noting that a record crowd of 51,000 had attended a night game between the New York Giants and Brooklyn Dodgers, Pompez quipped, "We're not expecting quite that many, but can anybody say we haven't got an attraction?" In his capacity as NNL vice president, he invited major-league scouts and executives to attend the showcase. A memo to major-league owners asked them to "please come see our all-star game and what we have to offer." This approach, according to sportswriter Sam Lacy, represented a drastic change in approach among black baseball owners, who only two years earlier were "raving mad with sportswriters who were advocating integration." Wendell Smith extolled the Cuban "señor," referring to him as one of the "pillars of Negro baseball" who insisted that the "future of Negro baseball depends on smoother operation and a sane and honest policy throughout."[15]

The 1947 East-West Classic featured seven New York Cubans who appeared before hometown fans. Those selected to represent the East (NNL) included second baseman Silvio García, third baseman Orestes Miñoso, catcher Lou Louden, right fielder Claro Duany, and pitchers Luis Tiant and Pat Scantlebury, along with José María Fernández as a coach. The contest at the Polo Grounds, the *Amsterdam News* announced, would feature "five players the scouts rate as sure bets for the major leagues." The five touted by the paper included four (Danny Bankhead, Monte Irvin, Sammy Jethroe, and Miñoso) who would later play in the majors; the fifth, Gentry Jessup, would appear in the minors. Another five players who participated in the contest would also appear in the majors: Joe Black and Luis "Canena" Márquez for the East; Artie Wilson, Quincy Trouppe, and Vibert Clarke for the West.[16]

The showcase event was an unqualified success, a testament to the hard work of the committee headed by Pompez and to the hunger among Harlem's fans for high-caliber baseball. While the East squad disappointed, losing 8–2, New York City fans did not: they streamed out of the subway stop at 155th Street, spilled out of jammed buses at the gates of the Polo Grounds, and exited from a convoy of taxis and private cars that lined up 158th Street, St. Nicholas Avenue, and surrounding side streets. In all, 38,402 fans paid to enter through the turnstiles to watch the Classic; inclusive of invited guests, the overall crowd totaled nearly 42,000. New York papers hailed it the "largest crowd ever to have witnessed a Negro contest in the East," easily more than double the previous year's crowd at Griffith Stadium.[17]

Challenge of Integration

The decision in 1945 to go north to play for the New York Cubans versus going to Mexico was a fortuitous one for Orestes Miñoso. Playing home games at the Polo Grounds, the New York Cubans were the Negro-league team closest to the unfolding events with the Brooklyn Dodgers and Jackie Robinson. Branch Rickey set the terms for how he would pursue racial integration in organized baseball, bucking its gentlemen's agreement to bar blacks by signing Robinson. The level of opposition within the major leagues' executive leadership was palpable: Rickey later stated that the fifteen other team executives voted against his signing a black player.[18] Yet despite that lack of institutional support, the Dodgers executive also decided unilaterally not to deal with the Negro-league executives as stakeholders in the project of integration. Instead he took the October 24 press conference announcing Robinson's signing as an occasion to besmirch the Negro leagues. Accused of "raid-ing" the black circuit by Negro-league executives, he answered by im-pugning the Negro organizations in baseball as "not leagues . . . As at presently administered they are in the nature of a racket." The charge levied by Rickey attempted to place public opinion squarely against the black institution created in the shadow of the racially exclusive major leagues. *Racket* was a loaded label, one that New York City residents recalled from Tom Dewey's recent anti-vice campaign. Washington Sen-ators owner Clark Griffith disagreed with Rickey's tactical approach to integration, although he too averred that no agreement existed between organized baseball and the Negro leagues that set fees for the transfer of players. Griffith nonetheless declared, "We still can't act like outlaws in taking their stars" and that organized baseball should compensate Negro-league teams like any other league in purchasing its players.[19]

Integration did not catch Negro-league executives unawares: many of them knew that it would one day become reality. Rather, what truly surprised them was that organized baseball team and league officials steadfastly refused to work with them as shared stakeholders in the integration of America's game. For them, integration was a cause that aimed to improve the lives of the formerly excluded. Civil rights and social equality were goals that Negro-league owners had publicly advo-cated away from the playing field and also brought to their league events when they held fund-raisers for the Urban League, the "Stop Lynching" campaign, the NAACP, and other organizations committed to improving the lives of those in "colored" communities. That is one reason why Negro-league officials sought to use Judge Landis's 1942 statement about "no rule, written or unwritten" barring black players as an opening: at minimum, it was a public declaration that they could increase pressure on major-league teams to give excluded black and Latino players an opportunity. In the days after Landis's statement, NAL president Dr. J. B. Martin shared with sportswriter Fay Young what turned out to be an overly optimistic vision of how integration would work. Martin "doubted that there would be any wholesale raids," believing that major-league clubs signing Negro leaguers would "deal with the [Negro-league] club owners in the same method that these organized ball clubs deal with the minor league club owners."[20] Rickey shattered that illusion.

Once Rickey signed Robinson without compensating the Monarchs, Negro-league owners had to scramble. Two weeks after Robinson's signing, they convened at Harlem's Hotel Theresa to assess how best to protect their investment and racial enterprise. Together they drafted a letter to major-league commissioner Happy Chandler, defending their institution and insisting that they operated professional leagues with constitutions and player contracts similar to those used in organized baseball. They called the manner in which Rickey pursued Robinson's signing "a flagrant violation of an ancient baseball law." Reconvened at Chicago's Hotel Grand a month later, the owners voted to adopt a player contract identical to that of the major leagues, a move aimed to gain further legitimacy in the public eye and in organized baseball.[21]

The collective lack of preparation for the onset of integration was evident in the different approaches taken by NNL owners. Cum Posey was a begrudging advocate of integration at best; suffering from failing health, he would die of cancer in March 1946. Already saddled with a reputation as an ineffectual leader, NNL president Tom Wilson held true to form: his public statements on the impact of integration on the Negro leagues held little sway with the public or with organized baseball officials. The Manleys and Pompez took a more proactive approach in seeking protection from Major League Baseball raids. Their plan hinged on transforming the Negro leagues into a high-ranking affiliated minor league focused on the development of black players for entry into the integrated major leagues. Achieving this aim required recognition from organized baseball. So they, along with NNL secretary Curtis Leak, visited the downtown office of Louis F. Carroll, a Manhattan lawyer whose clients included the National League, the Yankees, and the Dodgers. The attorney pointed to territorial rights as a major issue to resolve before any affiliation was formed between the Negro leagues and organized baseball. George Trautman, president of the National Association of Professional Baseball Leagues (NAPBL), also saw territorial rights as the "biggest obstacle" to the admission of the Negro leagues into organized baseball. He, too, denied admittance to the Negro leagues based on the position that its franchises played in the same "protected" regions of other minor-league clubs already within the NAPBL.[22]

While NNL owners attempted to negotiate through formal channels, sportswriters and other advocates of integration used public pressure in an effort that yielded headlines but not the desired results:
meaningful tryouts. Often orchestrated by a journalist supportive of
integration, on several occasions Negro-league players appeared at a
major-league team's spring training camp to demand an official tryout.
Jackie Robinson himself participated in one such event in March 1942,
appearing along with Negro leaguer Nate Moreland at the Chicago
White Sox camp in Pasadena, California, and seeking out Chicago's
manager Jimmie Dykes to ask for a tryout. Dykes's response presaged
what Durocher would state that July: "Personally, I would let Negro
players into the major leagues, and I'm sure most of the other managers agree with me. But the matter is out of the hands of us managers.
It's strictly up to the club owners and Judge Landis. Go after them!"[23]

Boston city councilman Isadore Muchnick and sportswriter Wendell Smith did exactly that, embarking on a campaign to compel the
Boston Red Sox to offer a tryout to black players. A blue law still on
the books forbade paid entertainment on Sundays and required unanimous approval of the city council to grant permission. Muchnick threatened to withhold his vote unless the Red Sox tried out black players.
Muchnick's political maneuver worked: on April 16, 1945, Jackie Robinson, Sam Jethroe, and Marvin Williams—Negro leaguers recommended by Smith—underwent a tryout at Fenway Park. Boston's
management was much more interested in fulfilling its end of the political arrangement with Muchnick than in truly evaluating the three
talented black players. The day would be most remembered for an unidentified Red Sox official's allegedly yelling "Get those niggers off the
field!" during the tryout. The experience would rank among the more
humiliating Robinson underwent in professional baseball. The trio never
heard back from the Red Sox.[24]

Robinson was by no measure the best or most talented player to
perform in the Negro leagues in 1945. That, of course, was not the
criterion Branch Rickey used in determining whether Robinson was
the best candidate to integrate organized baseball. Robinson twice
endured the emotionally bruising impact of showing up for a major-
league tryout for naught. Given his brief time in the Negro leagues, not
everyone was convinced the former all-American football star had the
baseball talent to succeed in the majors: baseball was arguably the

fourth best sport for the multisport star at UCLA. Pompez counted himself among those unconvinced Robinson was a budding big-league star. In fact, he told *The Sporting News* in March 1946 that the Homestead Grays pitcher John Wright was more ready for "fast company" than Robinson. That comparison stands among his most flawed assessments as a talent evaluator. Unable to handle the adjustment as an integration pioneer, Wright washed out in the minors and returned to the Negro leagues within the year. However, Pompez's direct exposure to Robinson had been limited to one game—the 1945 East-West Classic in which Robinson went 0 for 5 at the plate.

Competition for his players continued to come on two fronts. Better money offered by the Mexican League lured away the stars Martín Dihigo and Silvio García from his Cubans. The profound difference in money caused a spike in salaries earned throughout Latino baseball. Sportswriter Maximo Sanchez noted in January 1947 that players who had performed in Cuba drawing $200 to $300 monthly salaries a few years earlier were now paid from $700 up to $1,200 monthly in Mexico. New York's star infielder Silvio García took advantage of this opportunity, drawing $1,200 a month as player-manager of Matanzas. But the start of racial integration of organized baseball slowed the movement south of the border.

The Dodgers enjoyed an up-close view of Pompez's players during spring training in 1947 when Branch Rickey had both the Dodgers and Montreal Royals (their top farm team) conduct spring training in Cuba. The hope was to avoid segregated conditions in Florida and thereby allow Jackie Robinson and the organization's other black prospects to practice with their white teammates and to freely compete in interracial exhibitions. In late March, Brooklyn played a series against a Cuban all-star squad that included every single member of Pompez's starting nine: he had granted "a week's grace" for them to report to the team's spring headquarters in New Orleans.[25] Several New York players impressed their Dodgers opponents—none more so than Miñoso, who had previously enjoyed a successful Negro-league rookie year in 1946.

The New York Cubans starting third baseman caught the eye of Dodgers scout Clyde Sukeforth, Branch Rickey's right-hand man, who had previously scouted Robinson. Word emerged from Dodgers spring training camp that Montreal was ready to offer a contract to the young Cuban. Sukeforth, according to the *Baltimore Afro-American*'s Sam

Lacy, had his eye on Miñoso from the moment of the scout's arrival on February 20. After hearing his scout's glowing reports, Rickey granted Sukeforth permission to sign the talented Cuban third baseman. Surprisingly, Miñoso spurned the Dodgers organization offer. "I'd rather play with Cubans," the budding star told Sukeforth "with little more than a shrug of his shoulders." The Dodgers put forth their version of a full-court press to sway Pompez's all-star to join Brooklyn's organization, sending the Montreal Royals' head man, Mel Jones, and two more of the Dodgers top scouts to woo the young Cuban. After their efforts likewise failed, Rickey dispatched his own son. The answer to each was the same: "No want to leave Pompez. He treat me good, I no leave him." The Dodgers entreaties, which continued well into the 1947 season, infuriated Pompez, since Rickey avoided directly negotiating with him. "Nobody from the Brooklyn organization questioned me about buying Minosa [sic]," the Cubans owner complained to the *Amsterdam News*. The Dodgers were not Miñoso's only suitor that winter, as Jorge Pasquel again tried to bring him to the Mexican League. That required a direct intervention. When Pompez heard that the Mexican League agents were in Cuba "monkeying around with my players," he remarked, "I grabbed a plane and went down to Cuba pronto."[26]

The New York Cubans and other Negro-league franchises continued to operate in 1947 fully aware that Jackie Robinson's debut with the Dodgers had profoundly altered the professional baseball landscape. Integration had long been an aspiration within the black community. Yet the terms and conditions through which mainstream institutions undertook desegregation concerned many of those involved in the campaign for social equality. Baseball was no different in this regard. Negro-league executives worried about the manner the leaders of organized baseball were addressing the underlying issues that had been involved in the creation of segregation in the first place. Their worry proved justified.

A Pennant Run

The 1947 season started with much promise for Pompez's New York Cubans. Almost an entire roster of players had departed for the Mexican League over the past several seasons: the sensational Martín Dihigo now headlined with Torreon, and star pitchers Ramón Bragaña and Schoolboy Taylor hurled for Vera Cruz and Monterrey, respectively. Hit with continuing player losses, the Cubans owner responded in typical fashion, attracting prodigal players back in addition to acquiring new talent from the Caribbean and Latin America.

The 1947 season that ensued was historic on a number of levels for Harlem fans. Of course, the season marked the beginning of baseball's "Great Experiment," but it would also represent the zenith of the New York Cubans in the Negro leagues. The addition of the strong-hitting Claro Duany and Lorenzo Cabrera to an already potent lineup that featured all-stars Miñoso, Silvio García, and Rafael Noble propelled the Cubans to their best season ever. The team featured ballplayers who in the coming years would enter organized baseball: Duany, Cabrera, Miñoso, Noble, José Santiago, Pat Scantlebury, Lino Diñoso, and Martin Crue. A handful of them—Miñoso, Noble, Santiago, Scantlebury, and Diñoso—made it all the way into the majors. Pitching would make the biggest difference for the Cubans, featuring the ageless wonder Lefty Tiant, fellow left-hander Scantlebury, and hard-throwing right-hander Dave Barnhill. The undefeated (10–0) forty-year-old pitching wonder Tiant would enjoy his greatest season in black baseball. (His then seven-year-old son, Luis, would became a right-handed major-league pitcher and would win 229 games.) The Cubans owner couldn't contain his enthusiasm in a mid-season interview. "Our baseball has a golden opportunity to get places this year," Pompez exuded confidently to the *Baltimore Afro-American*'s Sam Lacy. The sportswriter was a bit less sure about the Cubans staff. "On their good days, guys like Barney Morris, Luis Tiant and Pat Scantlebury will give any team a real run for the dough. But on their bad days, they're just like so many creampuffs in the middle of traffic." The Cubans' track record did not inspire much confidence for Lacy: he picked the Cubans for the middle of the pack in the NNL.[27]

Title aspirations suffered an early setback when NNL president Johnson declared the newly reacquired Duany temporarily ineligible pending investigation. Opposing teams had raised a howl, arguing that the Cuban outfielder had returned without incurring any punishment for jumping to the Mexican League. At issue was whether the five-year ban that Negro-league officials had imposed on jumpers applied to Duany. In Johnson's case, imposing discipline on Mexican-League jumpers signaled the league president's ability to administer discipline and thereby demonstrate the league's power over individual team owners; this went to the core of whether the black circuit was a legitimate enterprise that merited official recognition from organized baseball. Nonetheless, Pompez protested the suspension, claiming that New York had released him for failing to hustle during his previous tenure and insisting Duany was not a jumper.[28] NNL president Johnson decided to reinstate Duany.

Although Pompez confidently told Joe Bostic of the *Amsterdam News* that his 1947 team "was the best that the Cubans have ever had," the New York Cubans muddled through their May schedule.[29] When the hitters were smashing the ball about the park, the pitching faltered; when pitchers were shutting opponents down, the Cubans bats fell silent; if the bats and pitching seemed on, the steady defense disappeared. But Pompez remained confident, if not overly hopeful, that his Cubans would find their collective stride. The Cubans rallied to finish the NNL first half in second place, trailing only the Newark Eagles. The squad surged in the second half, prompting Bostic to comment in mid-July: "Taking a good look at the New York Cubans in the Polo Grounds Sunday you could reach only one conclusion . . . they are the best all around team in the National League and there's no reason why they shouldn't win the pennant."[30] By mid-August the NNL pennant was clearly within their grasp. A sweep of the Baltimore Elite Giants extended the Cubans' lead to three games and buoyed Pompez's hopes. "I think I've got the best team in the country," he remarked to Sam Lacy. The second-half performance changed Lacy's tune as well. "From top to bottom, they've got power, speed, hustle and brains. They should win in a walk."[31]

"Alejandro Pompez is baseball's No. 1 enigma," Lacy observed in a *Baltimore Afro-American* profile of the New York owner. "No one seems to know what to do with or about the mild-mannered owner of the New York Cubans, whose team is currently headed for the Negro National League pennant." The Cuban-American owner cut quite the figure: "Graying somewhat at the temples and over the ears, Pompez, nevertheless, still maintains the physique of a man fully capable of defending himself in any test of physical strength." His description of the longtime team owner ranged from the physical to mental: "His capabilities do not end there. He knows a lot more than the ordinary human about to take care of himself in other things . . . Therein lies the mystery of him." Panic did not set in for the Cubans owner when Branch Rickey signed Jackie Robinson and Johnny Wright or when the Dodgers executive later acquired Roy Campanella and Don New-combe. When other black baseball owners began to tear their hair out and sought each other out for "sympathetic shoulders upon which to cry," he went along "his easy-going, unaffected way . . . Nothing disturbed him, it seemed," Lacy wrote. "If the majors wanted to snatch his men, if they had any thought of sapping the strength of his organization by lifting his key players, Alex Pompez gave no sign that he would be the least bit concerned."[32]

Preemptive action figured largely in Pompez's rather successful strategy of retaining Latino players, or recruiting back those who had departed for Mexico. Before bringing players north, he would tout the advantages of their signing with him: he would look after them, share his knowledge of racial attitudes, and protect them from the full brunt of segregation. Lacy saw in his approach something that other Negro-league owners could not offer as they attempted to fend off raids from either the U.S. major leagues or the Mexican League. "The fact of the matter is that when the Pasquels were sniping at the major leagues and making fabulous offers to star players in the colored loops, Pompez was quietly conducting his own little raids in the land of charm and romance." His quiet, diligent way of scouting talent and building relationships with players in the face of increasing com-petition for Latino talent gave him the ability to constantly bounce back from what seemed like devastating setbacks. The evidence: he convinced Silvio García and Alex Crespo to return to the Cubans in 1946 after the pair enjoyed highly successful campaigns in Mexico; when Crespo opted to head back to Mexico in 1947, Pompez secured Claro Duany, the 1946 Mexican League batting champion. This in-deed bolstered his confidence that he could handle the challenge before him.

Declining attendance dimmed the financial outlook, as did cancel-lations due to the bad weather that seemed to follow the New York

Cubans for much of the 1947 season. Because of a limited choice of open dates in the schedules of big league parks, it was virtually impossible to reschedule league contests, a situation that had long resulted in an imbalanced ledger of games played in the final league standings. This was precisely what NNL president Johnson sought to avoid. Aware that the Cubans had had nineteen rained-out games—and therefore had played eighteen fewer games than the Newark Eagles—he ordered Pompez's club to schedule twelve makeup games between September 1 and the final day of official league play on September 14 to reach a minimum of sixty games by season's end. The Cubans endeavored to fulfill the NNL president's order; there would be no scheduling of additional exhibitions to build up Pompez's coffers. The Cubans swept a three-team doubleheader at the Polo Grounds on September 11, defeating the Eagles in the first game and the Philadelphia Stars in the second to reach sixty league games. Although they had played thirteen fewer games than Newark, the Cubans' winning percentage—over .700—placed them well ahead of Newark's .554 winning percentage and allowed them to claim Pompez's first pennant in his thirty years in the Negro leagues.[33]

New York entered the postseason series on a hot streak, winning sixteen of their last eighteen league games. The Cleveland Buckeyes also strode confidently into the Series, envisioning their securing a second Negro League World Series title in three years. One Cleveland player boasted to the *Amsterdam News*: "We'll knock those Cubans over in nothing flat, and if the series goes over five games, I'll be the most surprised man in baseball.

"We're not playing the Latins from Manhattan cheap," he continued, "but we're confident of a quick victory. Remember how we knocked over the powerful Homestead Grays in four straight in the '45 series? The Grays team was a stronger one than this Cubans team."

The *Amsterdam News* writer Joe Bostic saw a more balanced series matchup. He gave Cleveland the advantage with its combination up the middle, rating Cleveland's catcher Quincy Trouppe, second baseman Leon Kellman, and center fielder Sam Jethroe superior to New York's catcher Louis Louden, second baseman Horacio Martínez, and center fielder Pedro Páges. However, the scribe rated the left side of the Cubans infield, shortstop Silvio García and third baseman Orestes

Miñoso, above Cleveland's duo of Al Smith and Joe Atkins. Offensively, the two teams were potent. But the key difference maker was Sam Jethroe, who led the NAL in five offensive categories, including runs scored and stolen bases. Nevertheless, the reconstituted Cubans offense validated Pompez's hard work as they led the NNL in batting and had six regulars post a batting average over .300: Lorenzo Cabrera, Chiflan Clark, Duany, García, Louden, and Miñoso. Predicting a much more competitive World Series than others, Bostic still went with Cleveland over the hometown Cubans.[34]

Rain had plagued the Cubans' entire 1947 campaign, and the opening of their quest for the Negro-league title was no different. Inclement weather delayed the Friday night contest three times at a soggy Polo Grounds before a diminished crowd of 5,500. Rain ultimately prevented completion of the contest, a 5–5 tie called after six innings. Although not tagged for the loss, Cleveland had roughed up the Cubans onetime ace Dave Barnhill, who left the game in the second inning trailing 5–0. The Cubans' big bats came through with a Cabrera run-scoring double sparking a three-run outburst that tied the game in the fifth inning, an inning before the torrential rains prompted the umpire to call the game.[35] New York's pitching faltered again in the first completed game of the series two days later at a Sunday afternoon game before nine thousand fans at Yankee Stadium. Cubans manager José María Fernández did not give the undefeated Lefty Tiant much leeway, pulling the pitcher in the first inning after Cleveland put three runs across the plate. The sloppily played game in which Cleveland committed four errors and New York three turned into a seesaw affair. New York battled back from 3–0 and 7–3 deficits to tie the game at 7. The Buckeyes rallied off a tiring Lino Diñoso, who had held them scoreless for four innings before their outburst gave them a 10–7 victory and the initial advantage as the series headed to Philadelphia for one contest and then to Chicago for the next two games.[36]

The two initial contests shook the Cubans manager's confidence in his frontline pitchers. Instead of going to Scantlebury or Barnhill, he turned the ball over to Barney Morris. The move worked: Morris hurled a five-hit shutout and New York scored six times in the ninth inning to tie the Series at one game apiece.[37] Before a dismal crowd of 1,739 at Philadelphia's Shibe Park, Barnhill followed with his own strong pitching performance, shutting down Cleveland's vaunted offense except for a four-run rally in the eighth after the Cubans had amassed an 8–0 lead. New York catcher Noble led the offensive onslaught, hitting a towering grand slam that struck the top of the left-field roof as the Cubans secured a 9–4 victory and a two-to-one series advantage.[38] Their pitching woes apparently behind them, the Cubans arrived for game four at Chicago's Comiskey Park. Good hitting, standout fielding highlighted by Horacio Martínez's two fielding gems, and a strong pitching effort by Diñoso paced the Cubans to a 9–2 victory in front of a paltry crowd of 2,048 fans whom the *Chicago Defender* described as "half-frozen."[39]

Tiant took to the mound in game five in Chicago, but the magic touch he had enjoyed throughout the season escaped him. New York found itself trailing 4–0 in the third inning with their ace on the bench again. Just as in the rain-shortened game at the Polo Grounds, Scantlebury came on in long relief and deftly handled the Cleveland batters. The Cubans mounted a comeback by taking advantage of the Buckeyes' shoddy defense, pushing three runs across in the sixth inning and another in the seventh inning. Entering the eighth frame down 5–4, game three's batting star Noble stepped to the plate with two on and once again proved himself in the clutch, slamming a two-run double to put New York ahead 6–5. It was a pennant-winning hit, as Scantlebury made sure it stuck. Pompez and his New York Cubans finally had a Negro-league championship, winning four straight on the road after dropping the first official contest.[40]

Seasons of Change

Operated out of Harlem's Lenox Avenue with the Polo Grounds as its home field, this quintessential New York team won its lone Negro League World Series championship, having played games in four different cities. Far from a departure from standard practice, this was a Negro League World Series tradition. Low attendance figures for the five games, where the crowd failed to reach five digits even once, reflected more than poor weather conditions. Rather, it illustrated that the attention of black baseball fans had turned away from the Negro leagues and to Jackie Robinson the barrier breaker. Getting the latest news on Robinson's diamond exploits was one of Harlem's newest obsessions. That was evident on September 11 when the National League–leading Dodgers traveled to St. Louis to play the Cardinals, while the New York Cubans, in the midst of their own pennant run, hosted the Newark Eagles at the Polo Grounds. A murmur among the 4,500 fans grew into a roar in the middle of the Cubans-Eagles game. The cheers were not for the Cubans scoring or for making an outstanding defensive play but rather for the news coming across the radio airwaves and the wire ticker: Robinson had blasted a game-tying home run against the Cardinals. That moment encapsulated where the minds and hearts of black baseball fans resided; the Negro leagues, at least in the East, could no longer captivate their interests.

Indeed, fans who previously strolled through Sugar Hill and Harlem streets to catch the New York Cubans battling the Philadelphia Stars or Homestead Grays at the Polo Grounds were now taking the IRT to Brooklyn to see Jackie Robinson. Black baseball fans as well as the black sporting press voted for integrated baseball with their feet, dollars, and attention. The entrance of Robinson and Larry Doby into the major leagues clearly overshadowed the 1947 Negro League World Series, which pitted the New York Cubans against the Cleveland Buckeyes. That these two Negro-league teams made the 1947 championship series highlighted an irony: both came from towns that were the launching points of integration with the Dodgers' and Indians' signing of Robinson and Doby, respectively. The Cubans and Buckeyes matchup was largely ignored by the sporting press, especially in New York City, with the Dodgers and their pioneering star Robinson facing off against the New York Yankees in the Major League World Series. That series captivated baseball fans everywhere and further energized those committed to the desegregation of baseball. Conversely, the assumption that black baseball fans would venture to see the Cubans face the Buckeyes motivated league officials to schedule series games in Philadelphia and Chicago in addition to the home parks of the two contending teams. They didn't come: fewer than five thousand fans witnessed Pompez's Cubans reach the pinnacle of black baseball.

Pompez nonetheless sought to take advantage of New York's first championship by arranging a barnstorming engagement in his father's native Cuba. Ever the promoter, he formed a preliminary agreement for a five-game series against the Havana Cubans, owned by his long-time associate Joe Cambria. A minor-league team composed primarily of lighter-skinned Cubans, the Havana team had won the Class C Florida International League championship. The proposed series would be much like the exhibition that his Cuban Stars had played against Abel Linares's Cuban Stars in Puerto Rico three decades earlier: a battle for bragging rights; a chance to prove which club could claim to be the best "Cuban" team. Pompez got his publicity machine working to disseminate word about the series. The Associated Negro Press distributed the announcement to all its subscribers, reporting the two teams were to face off in Havana from October 4 through October 7 in a series expected to draw over 150,000. The New York City–based *La Prensa* also reported the slated showdown in its September 18th issue, highlighting how the New York Cubans were set to travel in unusual luxury, departing from New York by train on Wednesday, October 1, for Miami, then flying to Havana—a far cry from the steamship that had taken Pompez's first team of Cuban Stars from Puerto Rico to the U.S. mainland in 1916.

Despite claiming the Negro League World Series championship, the New York Cubans lost money in 1947—lots of it.[41] The series was a financial bust; neither participant made money. Pompez claimed to have lost $20,000 for the season. This off-season would involve contemplating which of his talented players could be sold to major-league organizations to balance the ledger. The winter would likewise require time dedicated to finding fresh talent to replace whoever was sold. The Cubans' owner again contemplated selling the team.[42]

It soon became clear to Pompez that this industry was doomed to fade away if unable to prove itself useful to organized baseball. Throughout the 1947 season Negro-league owners had sold their players to major-league baseball organizations. He was no different. In June he sold four players to the Norfolk Royals for $5,000, money that was critical to his team staying out of the red. Yet these transactions between the Negro leagues and major-league organizations underscored the imbalance in power between the executives who had maintained a color line in their organizations and those who had formed a circuit to deal with that race-based exclusion. Effa Manley could barely contain her sense of injustice at the manner in which organized-baseball officials almost unilaterally dictated the process of integration. She knew white big-league officials would offer much more money to purchase Negro-league players if the Negro leagues received formal recognition. And then there was Branch Rickey, still trying to lure Negro leaguers away without negotiating with Negro-league owners, all the while cloaking himself with the shroud of higher morality. She found Rickey's actions offensive: he was snubbing the Negro-league owners while attempting to take advantage of popular support for integration by snatching players away or offering absurdly low purchase prices. After learning that Rickey had bypassed her and Abe to deal directly with Newark Eagles pitcher Don Newcombe, Manley asked sportswriter Sam Lacy, "What will become of colored baseball leagues if players are picked out by major league owners without consulting the team management?"[43]

With Jackie Robinson's debut on April 15, 1947, major-league officials took advantage of the wide support racial integration enjoyed within the African American community. The success of Robinson and Doby in 1947 and 1948, each leading his team to the World Series in successive seasons, sparked a rush on acquiring black talent. In the decade that followed, Latin American players who would have started the U.S. portion of their baseball careers playing for Pompez's New York Cubans now entered straightaway into organized baseball. This was yet another sign that the era of black baseball as a major force in the professional baseball world was nearing its end. Knowledge of this enabled major-league officials to place Negro-league owners in an unenviable position, especially when it came to negotiating the price for acquiring these players. Before, black players were untouchables. Now a handful of big-league organizations actively scouted these players and pressured Negro-league teams to sell cheap and to get on board with integration, or to get out of the way. Moreover, journalists and black civic leaders were ready to label Negro-league owners obstructionists for placing their personal financial interests ahead of the collective civil rights cause. The approach the major leagues took to integration—signing away the best black and Latino prospects and undercompensating Negro-league clubs that had developed those players—effectively zapped the energies of Negro-league officials and bankrupted the teams that had scouted, signed, and developed the formerly excluded talent.

Pompez felt the pressure to change with the times, especially after the "Negro press" singled him out for not doing so quickly enough. Black sportswriters actively reported rumors of which Negro-league players were being pursued by which major-league organizations. Their columns detailing ongoing negotiations with officials in organized baseball intensified the pressure Negro-league owners felt to privilege the collective good (integration) over their self-interest (securing the best price). Player departures were nothing new to Pompez. Since the 1920s, a handful of his Latino Negro leaguers had gained admittance into the major leagues or their minor leagues based on their racial ambiguity: their ethnicity and color allowed the perception that they were not clearly black. Those were typically negotiated transactions, involving brokering access for players that otherwise would have been excluded from organized baseball due to its color line.

Closing the Circuit

Integration made the talent Pompez had acquired and developed into a desirable commodity, and he insisted that big-league organizations properly compensate him. This stance drew derision from black sportswriters in general and the *Chicago Defender* sports columnist Fay Young in particular. In an August 2, 1947, column Young reported that Orestes Miñoso would sign with the Dodgers after the East-West Classic. Underwhelmed by Brooklyn's offer, Pompez turned them down, opting to retain his star infielder through the 1947 campaign. Young blasted Pompez, claiming that the owner was impeding progress and asking too much for a player whom the sportswriter deemed no more than a Class C minor leaguer.[44]

A year later it was the same story: Fay Young castigating Pompez and other Negro-league executives for making excessive demands. "Negro Club Owners Fail to Deal Fairly with Major Leaguers," proclaimed a 1948 headline for a *Chicago Defender* article in which Young chastised the New York Cubans executive for having declined another Dodgers offer to purchase his star infielder Miñoso. A year removed from his New York Cubans' winning the Negro League World Series, Pompez remained insistent on waiting for the right offer for Miñoso. This time it was Cleveland Indians owner Bill Veeck trying to convince Pompez to lower his reported asking price of $25,000 for Miñoso. The major-league owner won out, purchasing the infielder and pitcher José Santiago for Cleveland for $15,000 after the 1948 Negro-league season. The *New York Age* offered a context for the sale: Pompez was $20,000 in the red in operating the 1948 New York Cubans. The sale of Miñoso and Santiago would cover most of the season's financial losses. Miñoso added his own wrinkle to the story, stating that he had asked Pompez for a cut of the transaction. "I ask him for $1,000 or no report. I tell him I want to buy a new car," Miñoso informed *The Sporting News*. "He think it over. I got it."[45]

With his New York Cubans in dire financial straits, Pompez contemplated selling the team before the 1948 campaign. "[The] 1947 World Champions are on the auction block," reported Marion Jackson in his *Atlanta Daily World* column in early February. More than $250,000 had been spent over the previous ten years to build a winner; now "the red-ink splattered" Pompez was asking $50,000 for the Cubans franchise. A "lack of support" and "Jackie Robinson" had resulted in a "financial flop" at the gate and produced his desire to sell.[46] Finding no serious takers, the New York Cubans played out the 1948 season.

The NNL disbanded after the 1948 season, effectively ending organized black baseball in the East. The Homestead Grays and the Black Yankees opted to cease operations as league teams. The Manleys wanted to sell the Newark Eagles franchise; whether they sold or disbanded, they would personally be out of black baseball. The Philadelphia Stars and Baltimore Elite Giants hoped to latch onto the Negro American League, as did Pompez. The NAL had six existing teams: the Kansas City Monarchs, the Chicago American Giants, the Memphis Red Sox, the Birmingham Black Barons, the Cleveland Buckeyes, and the Indianapolis Clowns. A nine-team league would not work if three former NNL teams joined: one team would always be idle. The Negro-league executives discussed possible solutions that off-season: the NAL needed to have either eight or ten teams. At their meeting in Chicago in November, Pompez informed the other owners of his willingness to play independent ball rather than see Philadelphia and Baltimore forced out of league play. After all, he had lost tens of thousands of dollars and was directly competing with the Brooklyn Dodgers and, after July 1949, the New York Giants for the entertainment dollars of Harlem's black baseball fans. Neither of Philadelphia's major-league teams had integrated; thus, the Philadelphia Stars faced only the occasional visit of Jackie Robinson's Dodgers and Larry Doby's Indians. Baltimore was not yet a major-league town, with the Orioles a member of the International League, a high minor league. So it made more sense to continue both those Negro-league franchises than the Cubans.

Pompez's proposal to drop from organized black baseball spurred conversation in the black press. The Cubans executive commented on the difficulties he and the other owners encountered in scheduling games in the eastern circuit. "There were times," he told the *Chicago Defender*'s Fay Young, "that Baltimore and the Homestead Grays had to protect their home city parks, Baltimore and Washington, that for three Sundays in a row the best the Cubans could do was to play the Philadelphia Stars." Booking the Newark Eagles for a Sunday date at the Polo Grounds proved just as difficult; the Eagles had to book Sunday home games lest they lose priority in booking the potentially lucrative Sunday dates at Newark's Ruppert Stadium. Unable to schedule three of the other five NNL teams meant either booking the Philadelphia Stars or the Black Yankees. "Fans got tired of seeing the same clubs perform." That left the Cubans' head man with bringing to the Polo Grounds teams unknown to Harlem and New York City fans; these games failed to draw and he suffered heavy financial losses.[47] This placed black baseball on the verge of losing Pompez, who, Fay Young reminded readers, had "been in baseball ever since we can remember anything concerning Negro baseball in the East." Just as important, the other owners knew of Pompez's reputation as a fair and trustworthy executive, someone who "had always paid his players, [and] lived up to his agreements with other owners." The six NAL owners voted to admit the three former NNL teams; the matter of locating a tenth franchise would be taken up later. The merger meant that Pompez and Reverend John H. Johnson lost their executive positions; NAL owners elected J. B. Martin as league president.[48]

Forced to build new revenue streams, Pompez entered an agreement with the New York Giants that off-season. Starting in 1949, his Cubans would operate informally as a farm team for the Giants—the first time a Negro-league team served in such a capacity for a major-league organization. The arrangement gave the Giants the first option to purchase New York Cubans players whom the big-league organization deemed ready for organized baseball. In exchange, the Cubans would play their home games exclusively at the Polo Grounds at a discounted rental rate and Horace Stoneham's director of scouting and player development, Carl Hubbell, would seek out Pompez's guidance on which Negro-league players the Giants should sign.[49]

The first transactions between the Giants and the Cubans took place in the middle of the 1949 season and raised questions about the ultimate purpose of Pompez's Negro-league franchise as a professional enterprise. In June, Pompez sold the Cubans' starting catcher, Rafael Noble, player-manager, Ray Dandridge, and starting pitcher Dave Barnhill to the Giants for $21,000. The sale of Dandridge might have taken away the Cubans' manager for the 1949 season, but it did position the veteran third baseman one step away from fulfilling his last significant goal in professional baseball, donning a major-league uniform. The transaction also presented Barnhill with the chance to prove his mettle within organized baseball, which had been denied him when the 1942 tryout with the Pittsburgh Pirates never materialized. However, mainly due to his younger age, Noble would be the only one of this trio to appear with the Giants; Dandridge would be enshrined in the National Baseball Hall of Fame for his Negro-league exploits.

The transactions between Pompez's Negro-league club and the Giants provoked some controversy. Sportswriter Joe Bostic questioned whether the sale was "a good thing or bad from the point of view of the Latin organization." The sale of Barnhill and Dandridge, two players past their prime, weakened the ball club both on the field and at the gate. What was Pompez's goal with the New York Cubans operation? Bostic asked: Was it "to have a good team or to get money from selling players?"[50] The sale of its strongest players would not benefit the Cubans in its quest to draw fans, he pointed out. Declining attendance could not be solely attributable to "the advent of Negro players into organized baseball," the sportswriter insisted; rather, Negro-league teams in New York and elsewhere were not drawing fans due to "the lack of aggressive exploitation and promotion."[51] The journalist's critique failed to fully appreciate how much integration changed the context in which the Negro leagues had to operate in order to survive, especially in the East. Black baseball fans were not willing to support what they viewed as a minor-league operation when they could support black major leaguers.

Each transaction with the Giants brought Pompez's financial ledger a little closer to operating in the black, but it was never enough to make the team profitable. The Cubans slashed ticket prices for their Polo Grounds games for the 1950 season: box seats were reduced from $2 to $1.50 and general admission lowered from $1.25 to $1; bleacher seats remained at $0.60. Hoping to stimulate attendance, Pompez bragged that his Cubans had sent the most players into organized baseball of all Negro-league teams. In a March 1950 *Chicago Defender* article he stressed the circuit's continuing role in the development of "Negro" talent. And for that to continue, baseball fans "must increase their support of teams in the Negro National Leagues," for, the veteran owner exclaimed, "without this support, the clubs can not exist, thus wiping out the opportunity for the Negro players."[52]

In the early months of the 1950 season, Pompez's tone revealed his weariness at trying to stay afloat in a sea of debt with no sight of potential rescue. That was the impression made on Joe Bostic after a discussion with Pompez. "Alex has never said so in too many words," Bostic wrote in his May 6 column, "but when you talk to him, you can't help but notice that faraway look in his eyes as he seems to be contemplating the past days of glory that were highlighted by the sparkling play of Oms, Chacon, Oscar and the like. Then there have been those of later vintage such as Martinez, Dihigo, Rodriguez, Garcia, Vargas and many others." To Bostic, Pompez was coming to a sobering realization, which the sportswriter eloquently described: "He realizes as well as any other that the time is rapidly running out both for Negro baseball as such and for him, as an active importer of galloping gems. The major league ivory hunters have discovered the islands are caches of raw talent and are bush-beating with unlimited bankrolls as probing sticks. That kind of competition must eventually wash away the independents such as our friend Alex."[53]

Bostic was both right and wrong about what the future held for "our friend Alex." His days as an owner were indeed numbered. After the 1950 season the New York Cubans withdrew from the NAL. His team, like most that had pressed on in the East since 1947, had drowned in that sea of debt. The future of blacks in professional baseball had become the domain of Jackie Robinson's Brooklyn Dodgers and of the New York Giants, who were likewise committed wholeheartedly to the enterprise of integration.

The glory days of Negro-league baseball in the East had come to an end. Pompez would continue in a new capacity and over the next two decades distinguish himself as one of baseball's premier talent evaluators. His domain would be the Caribbean and the rest of Latin America as well as the surviving black talent pipeline in the States. He would build on his Negro-league experience and network in locating Latino and African American talent for the Giants organization. In so doing, he adapted with the times; it was a life lesson forged in his childhood by his father's death, which left him and his siblings along with his mother to survive on the largesse of family and the Cuban community in Tampa and Key West. As Pompez had done time and again, he retooled, doing what he did best, reinventing himself and pressing forward.[54]

8

SCOUTING THE AMERICAS FOR GIANTS

The big door of the Dominican was opened by Pompez . . . It's not only the talent that he brought in, it was a relationship. Anywhere and everywhere they played baseball—Panama, Colombia, Venezuela, Puerto Rico, Cuba—Pompez was a legend. —Felipe Alou

In early January 1951 the black press announced that the Negro American League would enter its new season minus two teams. Those two teams captured how much had changed in black baseball in just over three years. In September 1947 the New York Cubans and Cleveland Buckeyes had battled for the Negro League World Series title; now both franchises were out of league play. The Cubans' demise closed the era of Negro-league baseball in New York City. Pompez's franchise, claimed sportswriter Dan Burley, was "the first to feel the full effects of the new situation of Negroes in the big leagues," catching "the brunt of everything" when Robinson broke baseball's color line.[1]

Professional opportunities declined precipitously for blacks in the first decade of baseball integration. Major-league organizations were slow to sign blacks, while fewer Negro-league teams existed after the Negro National League's collapse in 1948. Older, less-heralded players tried to latch on with an NAL team or returned to the workforce. Hoping to land a spot on either a minor-league or major-league roster, talented veterans shaved years off their ages to stimulate interest among big-league organizations. Promising young prospects started to bypass the Negro leagues and signed directly with major-league organizations. Such was the case of the fireballing pitcher Bob Gibson, who played professional basketball with the Harlem Globetrotters before signing with the St. Louis Cardinals. Players were not the only ones within the black baseball world affected by the start of integration. Employment opportunities also diminished for team managers, business managers, trainers, black umpires, and others who had been employed in off-the-field capacities in the Negro leagues. Regardless of their position, the NNL's demise resulted in a permanent return to their communities. The fortunate eventually found work as teachers, post office workers, janitors, or high school baseball coaches.

A select number of Negro leaguers successfully made the transition to off-the-field positions in organized baseball. Buck O'Neil received the most notice of these Negro leaguers: he was hired as a scout for the Chicago Cubs in 1955 and over the next two decades signed future Hall of Famer Lou Brock and other talented black ballplayers, such as Joe Carter and Lee Smith. He would also become the first African American to coach in the major leagues. Longtime Negro-league catcher Quincy Trouppe developed his keen eye for evaluating talent while managing in the Negro leagues and the Puerto Rican winter league; he would bring future big leaguers Roberto Vargas and Vic Power north after managing them in Puerto Rico in 1949. After Trouppe had enjoyed an extremely brief stint in the majors with the Cleveland Indians in 1952 at the age of forty, the St. Louis Cardinals hired him as a scout. Collectively, the scouting efforts put forward by the likes of O'Neil, Trouppe, John Donaldson, and Chet Brewer, among others who followed, influenced the pace of major-league integration, affecting which players were put into position to pioneer integration on different major-league teams. However, the Negro-league figure who would make the greatest impact in the early decades of integration was Alex Pompez.

The end of his New York Cubans' formal run did not end Pompez's involvement in black baseball or his commitment to the players who were part of its legacy. Much to the contrary, he maximized the opportunities created by integration and facilitated the entry of black and Latino players into organized baseball, which kept former and current Negro leaguers in the public eye. First, his experience as a hands-on Negro-league team owner was the basis of his work as a scout for the New York Giants. Second, starting in 1948 he organized barnstorming tours for the Black All-Stars, headlined at various moments by Jackie Robinson, Roy Campanella, and Willie Mays. In so doing, he parlayed his years as a baseball entrepreneur into a new career in the major leagues. Over the next two decades, he signed dozens of U.S.-born and foreign-born players who integrated various minor leagues and made a significant impact in the majors.

Integration Matters

The 1950s were a decade of transition on and away from the professional baseball diamond. In 1954 the Supreme Court issued its landmark decision in *Brown v. Board of Education of Topeka, Kansas,* which called for desegregation of public schools. The *Brown* decision would expose the cauldron of feelings about race and opportunity as some whites erupted in protest over school busing in communities throughout the nation, while others celebrated the *Brown* decision as an affirmative step toward fulfilling the American promise. Neighborhoods became sites of conflict as pioneering "colored" families moved into previously segregated areas. Sidewalks hosted hostile welcoming parties. White protesters hurled epithets at "invaders" and launched bricks and Molotov cocktails through the windows of the aspiring black families' homes. Such scenes played out time and again in cities and their suburbs throughout the industrialized North and Midwest. This served as a backdrop to the ongoing drama taking place on the baseball diamond.

The confluence of events was stirring. On May 1, 1951, baseball fans gathered at Comiskey Park in Chicago's Southside to witness the integration of the White Sox. The mixed multitude cheered Orestes Miñoso, acquired a couple of days earlier from Cleveland, as he made his debut as the team's first black player against the 1950 World Series champion New York Yankees. Fans would continue to come throughout the summer to see a resurgent White Sox team paced by Miñoso. Meanwhile, in Cicero, a suburb on Chicago's western edge, several nights in mid-July saw an estimated two to five thousand whites rioting over Harvey Clark's moving his "colored" family into a local apartment building. The continued racial disturbance forced Governor Adlai Stevenson to call in the National Guard to quell the race riot. The two events revealed that cheering for integration in the national pastime at the big-league ballparks did not translate into acceptance of integration in local neighborhoods. That was a lesson the Clark family in Cicero and Jackie Robinson likewise learned in Stamford, Connecticut, when buying a home. Just as the *Brown* decision later did not immediately end school segregation, Robinson's debut in the majors did not instantaneously eliminate racially discriminatory practices throughout organized baseball. In both cases, the process of desegregation merely began to unfold, and most major-league teams did not pursue integration with any deliberate speed.

Active pursuit of previously excluded African American and Latino talent made the Brooklyn Dodgers, the Cleveland Indians, and the New York Giants exceptions to the norm in the majors. Collectively, their acquisition of this talent compelled teams to confront the legacy of discriminatory practices that by then had become standard parts of baseball operations. Integration pioneers of organized baseball from the lowest minor leagues up through the majors encountered segregated spring training sites (which most teams begrudgingly changed over time), segregated hotel accommodations on the road, and indifference if not outright hostility to their plight from teammates and front-office personnel. The varied organizational approaches to integration, along with the uneven pursuit of black and Latino talent, reiterated that race and integration indeed constituted, as Gunnar Myrdal claimed, an American dilemma, one that lay largely in the hearts and minds of whites who openly or subtly resisted integration of schools, neighborhoods, workplaces, and even the national pastime.[2]

Black and Latino players entered uncharted terrain as the process of integration unfolded at an uneven pace throughout organized baseball. The minor leagues were not always welcoming of the new "colored" players, as Felipe Alou would learn firsthand in 1956. Coming out of spring training, the New York Giants assigned their Dominican prospect and two African American players to their Lake Charles minor-league team in the Louisiana-based Evangeline League. The state's

Jim Crow laws forbade integrated facilities and interracial competition. Local police enforcing these laws prevented Alou and his U.S.-born black teammates from dressing in their team's locker room and from playing in Lake Charles games. In fact, the trio was forced to observe their white teammates compete from the park's "colored" section in the outfield bleachers. When local officials refused to budge, the Giants were forced to ship Alou back to Florida and reassign him to another farm team. Unsettled by the experience, he contemplated quitting on the long ride to Cocoa Beach, Florida, just getting on a plane to the Dominican Republic and resuming his university studies. Two things stopped him: he lacked the money to purchase the ticket, and he thought of the disappointment that his flight would cause to the two men who had fought for him to get a chance, Horacio Martínez and Pompez.

Aware that the dismantling of baseball's color line made available all Latino talent, the Giants had moved fully into the Latin American market. John "Jack" Schwarz, the successor to Carl Hubbell as the Giants' director of scouting, described how the organization initiated its involvement in Latin America in a 1984 letter to *The Wall Street Journal*: "We realized there was a huge talent pool that hadn't been tapped," Schwarz wrote. "We were fortunate enough to be able to hire Alex Pompez . . . He traveled to the Dominican Republic with Frank (Chick) Genovese to pass judgment on the players, and persuaded a former shortstop of the New York Cubans, to show them the best players in the Dominican Republic." A moral imperative to end segregation did not motivate the organization's decision to pursue black talent and to wade into the Latin American talent pool, according to Chub Feeney, the Giants' vice president and team owner Horace Stoneham's nephew. "Of course we knew that segregation was wrong," Feeney informed sportswriter Roger Kahn. "My uncle knew it and I knew it, but pure idealists we were not. Competing in New York, against the Yankees and the Dodgers, the resource we needed most was talent . . . In 1949, the Negro Leagues were the most logical place to look for talent."[3] Nonetheless, the impact of the Giants' decision was profound, on and off the field, in the league standings and the financial ledger. "The Giants never made a better investment," opined longtime *San Francisco Chronicle* sportswriter Art Rosenbaum in a 1962 *Baseball Digest* article. "Not only has Pompez scouted for outstanding stock but he has acquired some of today's stars for practically no down payment."[4]

Integration involved extensive work, much of it beyond public view and not actively discussed outside baseball circles. Into this fray entered Pompez in 1950. No other Negro-league figure was as well positioned to deal with the changing baseball world. Unlike his fellow Negro-league owners, he had extensive experience evaluating and acquiring talent from throughout the Americas and an established network of contacts in Cuba, the Dominican Republic, Puerto Rico, Venezuela, and Mexico. His interpersonal skills were unmatched among those scouting for major-league organizations: he was bilingual, familiar with national cultures throughout the Spanish-speaking Caribbean and Mexico, and fully capable of traversing the local and national black baseball circuit in the States.

In hiring Pompez, the Giants were the first major-league organization to extend integration beyond the playing field. Their incorporation of his front-office and scouting expertise resulted from the relationship he had established with Giants owner Horace Stoneham and the culmination of Pompez's indispensable role in the team's acquisition of Monte Irvin and Willie Mays, among other Negro leaguers. Indeed, through the Negro-league owner's work in setting up a showcase for the Giants scouting director, Carl Hubbell, to personally witness the young Mays perform at the Polo Grounds and in facilitating the organization's signing of the future superstar, Pompez proved that he himself would be a valuable addition to the organization.

Once the Cubans dropped out of the NAL in 1950, and given the Giants' early success in acquiring black talent, the Giants decided to hire Pompez to his scouting post. In so doing, the team harnessed the expertise Pompez had developed over three decades in black baseball and put the Giants organization in position to maximize its scouting effort in the Latino market.

Lessons learned as a Negro-league owner proved vital to Pompez's work as the principal figure responsible for the flow of black and Latino talent into the Giants organization. The talent he secured through his scouting and the behind-the-scenes work done to prepare these players for the challenge of pioneering integration remains one of baseball's lesser-known success stories. Starting in 1948 and signing talent for the organization through the early 1970s, he had a direct hand in the Giants' acquisition of future Hall of Famers Willie Mays, Monte Irvin, Willie McCovey, Juan Marichal, and Orlando Cepeda. These players, along with Felipe Alou and his brothers Jesús and Mateo ("Matty"), Willie Kirkland, and José Pagán, among others, kept the Giants a first-division National League team from the 1950s into the late 1960s, competing with the Dodgers and the St. Louis Cardinals for the National League pennant.

Pompez served as an inside man within black baseball for the Giants during these initial years of integration. He knew the black circuit's talented players: their playing strengths, their character, and mental fortitude. Monte Irvin was the first Negro leaguer the Giants signed through their inside connection. Acquired during the 1948 Cuban winter season, the hard-hitting outfielder who spent his summers playing for the Newark Eagles had originally signed with the Brooklyn Dodgers. However, Eagles owner Effa Manley claimed Irvin's rights remained with the Newark franchise, which she was in the process of selling to a Houston ownership group. Branch Rickey relinquished his claim, unwilling to compensate Manley for Irvin's services. Manley then turned around and sold the veteran standout to Stoneham's Giants for $5,000—clearly not what the talented black player would have fetched had he been white.

Hank Thompson also entered the Giants fold that winter. For him it was a second chance. Two years earlier, he and Willard Brown had become the majors' first pair of black teammates, However, their month-long stint with the St. Louis Browns was disastrous: the pair had been signed as part of a halfhearted attempt at integration by the Browns. Fortunately for Thompson, Pompez was more convinced of his big-league ability based on his performance in the Negro leagues and in the Cuban circuit than by his lack of success with the Browns. Willard Brown was not as fortunate in that regard: he never returned to majors.[5]

Stoneham boasted of the acquisitions; Harlem fans who had called for the Giants to sign a black player could at last rejoice. "We scouted numerous Negro teams as well as teams in the Mexican, Cuban, and Puerto Rican leagues for several seasons in the hopes of coming up with really good players," the Giants executive declared to the *New*

York Age writer Dan Burley. "This winter, though, was the first time our scouts were satisfied." A major difference from previous years was that the Giants now had Pompez in their employ to advocate for "Negro" players in the organization.

Black All-Stars Barnstorm America

In addition to scouting talent in Cuba and elsewhere in the Caribbean, the entrepreneurial Pompez began organizing off-season barnstorming tours for the Black All-Stars. The first tour featured Brooklyn Dodgers teammates Jackie Robinson and Roy Campanella on a team composed primarily of Negro National League stars. Robinson decided to participate in the 1948 off-season tour to stay in playing shape—this versus hitting the banquet circuit, as he had after the 1947 season. The 1948 tour started in Atlanta on October 11 and included stops in Memphis, Houston, Birmingham, Dallas, and New Orleans over the following three weeks. The Black All-Stars were slated to face the American Association all-stars in Atlanta, and the *Atlanta Daily World* excitedly publicized the impending visit by Robinson, Campanella, and the Black All-Stars, which featured the NNL players (and future major leaguers) Miñoso, Irvin, George Crowe, and Pat Scantlebury, supplemented with New York Cubans Chiflan Clark, Lyman Bostock, Sr., David Barnhill, and Raul Lopez.[6]

The Black All-Stars' barnstorming tours would enjoy a brief period of popularity, one that promoters not normally involved in black baseball attempted to capitalize on. In October 1950 the *Amsterdam News* reported that Pompez, along with Campanella, Don Newcombe, and Larry Doby, were subjects of a lawsuit filed by Lester Dworman and Ted Worner. The plaintiffs' affidavit contended that the ballplaying trio declined to renew their contracts, believing they deserved better compensation. The suit sought to restrain the three players from touring with Pompez's group and, moreover, alleged that Pompez was attempting "to undermine the plaintiffs' established barnstorming tour and conduct one of his own."[7] Dworman claimed he and Worner had formed the idea of having "outstanding major league Negro baseball players" conduct a barnstorming tour of southern states in August

1949. The pair lined up Jackie Robinson for the tour and then had Pompez complete the barnstorming team's roster. The crux of the lawsuit was a "renewal clause" in the players' contracts that covered a 1950 tour. While Robinson renewed, Campanella balked, as did Newcombe and Doby.

The holdouts preferred to play on a tour organized by Pompez, someone they had known since their Negro-league days and who possessed a reputation for taking care of *all* his players. This was not the case with Dworman and Worner in the eyes of the protesting players. Robinson and Campanella had arrived "at loggerheads" after comparing paychecks following the 1949 tour, according to coverage in the black press: Robinson had been much better compensated than Campanella, even though much of the promotional material had prominently featured both. But with the renewal clause invoked, the trio was compelled to join Robinson for the 1950 tour.[8] The pay dispute caused a split after the 1950 tour: Robinson and Campanella would headline different barnstorming tours. The split did not surprise sportswriters. "Coolness" had prevailed between the Dodgers teammates for much of the 1950 tour. After the Black All-Stars played in Atlanta, sportswriter Marion Jackson observed that while the two stars "still get together for publicity purposes," the pair went their separate ways after the games. In an interview with Jackson, Campanella expressed resentment at being "forced by contractual arrangements" to participate in this barnstorming tour. "You know what that tour made last year?" he asked Jackson. "It made $100,000. I should have got $10,000," the Dodgers catcher proclaimed. Robinson also shared his sentiments with Jackson. "If I could," Robinson informed him, "I would quit on this tour too. But the man has an option on my services and I've got to go through with it." Campanella was upset not only about being pressured to fulfill his contractual obligation but also about learning that Dworman and Worner had coaxed Robinson into participating in the 1950 tour by inserting a "percentage" clause into his contract that guaranteed him a percentage of the gate in addition to his salary. Robinson, unsurprisingly, agreed to the sweetened financial agreement. But his failure to share this information with Dodgers teammates until afterward—and the fact that organizers had compelled them into participating—upset Campanella.[9]

Freed of his contractual obligations after the 1950 tour, Campanella placed his lot in Pompez's hands, allowing the former Negro-league owner to handle the arrangements for future tours of the Black All-Stars. Most of the top black major leaguers joined "Campy's" squad for the 1951 tour: Newcombe, Doby, Irvin, Willie Mays, Luke Easter, Harry "Suitcase" Simpson, and Hank Thompson. Their choice was not so much an indictment of Robinson but rather of Dworman and Worner, who had taken advantage of them.[10] Troubles surfaced again in 1951 over the services of Easter, Doby, and Sam Jethroe. Lawyers got involved as Pompez and Worner secured orders to prevent the three players from touring for the other side. The *Atlanta Daily World*'s Marion Jackson worried about the feud; specifically he was concerned that Pompez was "giving up service to anti-semitic [*sic*] talk about Ted Worner, Jewish promoter of Jackie Robinson's all-star unit." Jackson hoped both parties would "call off the racial angle to their propaganda," stating "it has never been to the credit for one minority to play Hitler's game against another."[11]

The conflict between the two promoters had as much to do with notions of race and loyalty as it did financial concerns. Worner was an outsider to black baseball, but the public relations man was an insider on Madison Avenue. His loyalty was to his most marketable asset: Jackie Robinson. Prior to the 1949 tour, New York City radio station WMCA had lined Worner up to produce Robinson's radio show. As he recounted the story, Robinson approached him about promoting that year's tour, complaining that the 1948 tour had been "completely disorganized." Worner jumped at the opportunity. The financial arrangement he set is what contributed to Campanella's and most of the other black major leaguers' preferring to tour strictly with Pompez: promoters kept 40 percent of the net gate, Robinson received a percentage, and the others (including Campanella) were paid flat guarantees. However, Pompez handled pay differently with his Black All-Stars. Birmingham Black Barons outfielder Jessie Mitchell, who toured with the team in 1956, attested to how the entrepreneur took care of his players: "When you played for Pompez . . . you always got cash after the game. He'd just take the gate money, peel off what he owed you, and say, 'Thank you very much.'"[12]

Pompez had seen this before—the different treatment of blacks when it came to collaborative ventures with white businessmen. He was adamant that Campanella's All-Stars be paid and given the same guarantees that the Dodgers, the Indians, the Giants, and even the minor-league Minneapolis team had received for playing exhibition games at Atlanta's Ponce de Leon Park. This stance drew the ire of Marion Jackson, especially after Pompez pulled "Campy's all-stars" from an exhibition game against Gil Hodges's barnstorming team of major leaguers. "Money does strange things to the conscience of men," Jackson jotted in his October 18 column criticizing Pompez's stance. "The deal which prevented Roy Campanella's outfit from playing Gil Hodges' all-stars is repulsive to our stomach," he continued. "Promoters had a chance to cement sports-racial goodwill in the South as initiated by Branch Rickey, Earl Mann, the Dodgers and [the Atlanta] Crackers. Yet for greedy dollar they compromised all that decency and fair play for stands in this area, the state and South."[13] Despite Jackson's criticism, advocacy for the best financial interests of the Campanella All-Stars is what allowed Pompez to maintain the favor of Campanella and black major leaguers: his loyalty stood with those he had worked with since 1916—black ballplayers.

In the fall of 1952, word circulated that Robinson and Worner would not be conducting a tour. Robinson was turning his attention elsewhere: opening a department store in Harlem, fulfilling media commitments, and engaging in charitable activities. Meanwhile, Campanella and Pompez gathered at Campy's Harlem liquor store to finalize details for their upcoming tour. With Pompez as the organizer, Campanella's tours were distinct from Robinson's: his were a racial enterprise "handled by Negroes and playing dates are booked by Negroes," whereas Robinson's had white businessmen in control. Marion Jackson put aside his previous protestations about the vigorous advocacy for Campanella's barnstorming troop to celebrate Pompez's commitment to the enterprise of black baseball. This commitment was evident in his scheduling games against Negro American League clubs in the hope of building interest in the hometown clubs. "All of this is the work of Alex Pompez," Jackson declared. "He does not want organized Negro baseball to die. He wants the Negro American League to continue."[14]

Hits and Misses

Traveling with the Black All-Stars on their postseason barnstorming tours greatly aided Pompez's work for the New York Giants. Stops in Memphis, Birmingham, and other southern towns for interracial competition against white major and minor leaguers provided him with up-close views of black talent. Witnessing prospects perform in this setting, and with their signing with the Giants a possibility, Pompez gained critical insight into their personalities in addition to their ball-playing abilities. This was vital to assessing each player's fit for organized baseball, and strengthened his claims of a player's preparedness to partake in the pioneering wave of black players crashing onto organized baseball's shore.

Public opinion of the Giants changed with their signing of black players. One black newspaper proclaimed that the Giants "don't have any inhibitions against the signing of Negro players," noting that former Negro leaguers Artie Wilson and Rafael Noble were among those competing for roster spots to join Monte Irvin and Hank Thompson on the 1951 Giants. The *Amsterdam News* saw the possibility of the Giants competing with, if not supplanting, the Dodgers for the rooting interests of black fans.[15] The 1951 squad indeed competed for the hearts of black fans in Harlem and throughout New York City. The team's newest star, Willie Mays, did much to elevate the team's standing. The young center fielder was the most significant Negro leaguer acquired through its black baseball connection, Pompez.

By this point the Giants talent czar, Carl Hubbell, had established the practice of calling on Pompez to conduct a "cross-check" whenever a Giants scout evaluated a Negro-league talent. A glowing report on Willie Mays from scout Eddie Montague—Mays was the best player he'd ever seen—prompted Hubbell's secretary, Jack Schwarz, to call Pompez for his evaluation about the Birmingham Black Barons center fielder and whether he was worth the $10,000 purchase price. "Can't miss," Pompez reported back.[16]

Glowing reports and investing "big" money in signing a Negro-league prospect required that Hubbell personally witness Willie Mays perform. This had to be done clandestinely to avoid alerting other big-league teams that the Giants were closing in on signing Mays. And if Hubbell was to get his man, then he would have to rely on Pompez working his connections within the sporting press and on Tom Hayes, owner of the Birmingham Black Barons, to keep matters quiet. When Birmingham visited the Polo Grounds in June 1949, Pompez ensured that the advance publicity for the Black Barons' visit that appeared in New York City papers made no mention of Mays.

The stage was set; this was the showcase for Hubbell to observe the phenom. Entrusted with player development through the Giants' farm system, Hubbell had to be convinced of the quality of the young Negro leaguer before signing off. Signing Monte Irvin, Hank Thompson, and other seasoned Negro leaguers involved less uncertainty because they had a professional track record; Mays was eighteen years old. The Black Barons' center fielder's work in the field and at the plate in the Polo Grounds that afternoon delighted Hubbell. No further demonstration needed: Must sign this gem.

The Giants' inside man within black baseball was vital in the execution of this transaction. "White scouts in Negro baseball were travelers in a foreign land," historian John Klima later observed. But this land had been Pompez's domain since the 1910s: he knew the score, the terrain, and the negotiations involved. A Willie Mays was as rare a find as a Martín Dihigo; one must do everything to ensure the acquisition of such a "can't-miss" prospect. Subterfuge continued until Mays's signature was on the Giants contract. Nowhere within the game recaps of Birmingham's June 1949 contests versus the New York Cubans did Mays's name appear; box scores were not even printed in the *New York Age* or the *Amsterdam News*.[17]

The gamesmanship involved in signing Willie Mays to a bonus of $10,000 at a time when white players of lesser promise were receiving signing bonuses of upwards of $100,000 (or $60,000 in the case of Mays's future Giants teammate Mike McCormick) reveals the different economic scales used by major-league teams. The very best of black prospects, and even those seasoned Negro leaguers, received far less than the average white prospect in the form of a signing bonus. Clearly talent and future promise as a ballplayer were not the criteria for determining the bonus—race was the overriding factor. And the Giants would take advantage of this financial reality within organized baseball; black and Latino prospects came on the cheap. However, the way the Giants, through the work of Pompez, addressed the potential pitfalls for these black and Latino newcomers to organized baseball would place the organization ahead of its big-league contemporaries.[18]

A rookie center fielder in 1951, Mays helped elevate the Giants to the top of the National League. The regular season ended in a tie with crosstown rivals the Brooklyn Dodgers. Their memorable three-game playoff ended with Bobby Thomson's game-winning "Shot Heard Round the World" that landed the Giants in the World Series against the New York Yankees. The Giants lost the series in six, but the future looked bright with budding superstar Mays in center field and the veteran Irvin in left, and an infield featuring Alvin Dark at short and Eddie Stanky at second along with first baseman Whitey Lockman and Hank Thompson at third.

Once Mays emerged as a superstar for the Giants, several attempted to claim credit as *the* person responsible for his acquisition. Chief among those was Giants scout Eddie Montague, who shared his version of discovering Mays with *Look* magazine in 1954 and, in so doing, minimized Pompez's active involvement throughout the Giants' pursuit of Mays. The Giants scout told the magazine, and insisted to his dying days, that he had found Mays on his own while scouting Mays's Birmingham teammate Alonzo Perry. In one version of the scout's tale, Boston Braves scout Bill Maughn pointed him in Mays's direction instead of spending time evaluating Perry. "I had no inkling of Willie Mays," Montague would later recount, "but during batting practice and fielding practice, my eyes almost popped out of my head when I saw a young colored boy swing the bat with great speed and power . . . I also saw his great arm during fielding practice, and during the games his speed and fielding ability showed up."[19]

Montague's claim to sole discovery, however, is artfully dismantled by the historian John Klima in his detailed description of Mays's last days as a Negro leaguer. Montague watched Mays perform in Birmingham in mid-June, over a month after Carl Hubbell had personally witnessed Mays perform in the showcase Pompez had arranged at the Polo Grounds. The reason the Giants did not attempt to sign the teenager then was the restriction enforced by the major-league commissioner that Mays had to graduate high school before any team could ink him to a contract, even though Mays was already playing as a professional in the Negro league. Montague was sent to Birmingham along with Pompez to negotiate the transaction between the Giants and the Black Barons, not as the team's sole emissary. And it was in the capacity of the liaison between the Giants and Tom Hayes, a fellow Negro-league owner, that the Cuban-American participated in the acquisition of Mays for $10,000.[20]

"The Giants wanted Pompez in Birmingham to buy Mays from the Black Barons so there would be no confusion at all," George Genovese, another of the Giants' scouts, shared with Klima. Giants owner Horace Stoneham, Genovese explains, "felt bad because the Cubans ball club was [Pompez's] living and his business." And, as Stoneham and everyone else were quickly realizing, given the success already enjoyed by black ballplayers in the majors such as Jackie Robinson, Larry Doby, and Monte Irvin, the Negro leagues were not going to last much longer, particularly in the East. In Genovese's mind, the hiring of Pompez was directly connected to the Mays signing and built on the earlier relationship the Cubans owner had established with the Giants head man. "Stoneham felt that he owed Pompez something, so he brought him in after they got Mays." Klima goes further. "Pompez had done what no Negro League owner had done or would do again. He had won the trust of a major league owner."[21]

Relying again on Pompez and their bevy of scouts, the Giants nearly landed Henry Aaron in 1952. The Alabama native had been playing for the NAL's Indianapolis Clowns, starting as a seventeen-year-old that season. "You got to check this Aaron out"—that was the word about the Clowns' new shortstop from Armando Vásquez, a first baseman on the Clowns who had previously played on the New York Cubans. Heeding his former player's suggestion, Pompez alerted Hubbell, who sent another Giants scout to evaluate Aaron. That scout left unimpressed with Aaron's one-for-four performance at the plate; his evaluation stated Aaron would never hit major-league pitching. More confident in his former player's word than in that of the initial scout, Pompez insisted that Aaron be reassessed by another scout. That scout, Gene Thompson, the Giants' chief scout in the Midwest, saw what the first could not; he recommended to Hubbell that they sign Aaron.

Plans to sign Aaron encountered a roadblock: Hubbell, Jack Schwarz, and Gene Thompson did not know how to contact Clowns owner Syd Pollock to initiate the process of negotiation. As with Mays's signing, discretion was necessary so as not to alert other big-league teams that the Giants were on Aaron's trail. Schwarz recalled the effort to contact Pollock: "I found out who the owner of the Clowns was from Alex Pompez . . . Normally, Alex would offer to call the Negro League team owner to introduce me, as he did when we bought Willie Mays from the black undertaker [Hayes] in Memphis, Tennessee, who owned the Birmingham Black Barons."[22] Evidently, Pompez and Pollock were not on the best of terms: he did not offer to make this call of introduction. Perhaps he still harbored resentment toward Pollock for homing in on "his" turf in the Negro leagues and their subsequent competition for Cuban players. First the white businessman had organized the Havana Red Sox and stocked the club with some of Pompez's players, headlined by Pelayo Chacón. In response, the Cubans owners successfully convinced Negro-league owners to pass a ban on scheduling games with Pollock's team. Pollock likewise accused Pompez of stealing players, such as Lefty Tiant. Then there were the antics associated with Pollock's Indianapolis Clowns, like King Tut and Spec Bebop; the war paint that players at times donned; and the comedic routine, all part of the Clowns' shtick. Pompez, Cum Posey, and other NNL owners decried all this, feeling that it lowered the professional standards associated with their league. Finally, there was Pollock's alliance with Ted Worner, who had vied with Pompez over control of the Black All-Stars barnstorming tours.

The whole Aaron purchase was a muddled affair, with two teams ready to purchase Aaron; Pompez hesitant to act as a go-between; the Giants' Schwarz believing he had secured a deal with Pollock for $10,000; Schwarz requesting confirmation of their sale agreement via telegram from Pollock, which never arrived; the Clowns' owner informing Boston Braves general manager John Mullen that Aaron had been sold to the Giants for $15,000; Mullen reminding Pollock of the Braves' thirty-day option on the purchase of Aaron, to which the Clowns' owner had previously consented for $10,000; Schwarz sending a second telegram for "same deal as outlined in previous" while increasing Aaron's monthly salary to $350; and Aaron initially refusing to sign the Braves contract after having spoken with Giants scouts and believing that part of the purchase price would go to him. In the end, the young shortstop would become the property of the Braves, the organization for which he would perform his greatest feats.[23]

Public feuding between the Pompez-Campanella camp and Jackie Robinson and his backers flared up again during the 1953 off-season. Robinson's departure from the Black All-Stars to focus on other interests did not take him out of the sporting spotlight. The press and the American public constantly turned to Robinson for his opinion on the day's social issues and seemingly mundane sporting matters. Many interjected what they believed would be Robinson's stance into their own positions when controversies erupted over race relations, desegregation, and the proper approach to addressing local permutations of the race question. Such was the case when the Jackie Robinson's All-Stars traveled to Birmingham in November 1953 on a tour organized by Ted Worner and Pollock. Robinson's All-Stars included four white major leaguers: Ralph Branca, Gil Hodges, Mickey Vernon, and Bobby Young. The team planned to buck local Jim Crow practices and thereby score a victory for race relations and integration by scheduling integrated contests in two NAL towns, Birmingham and Memphis. However, local city ordinances in both cities prohibited not interracial competition—a "colored" team playing against a white team—but rather racially "mixed" teams composed of whites and nonwhites competing against segregated teams of either whites or "colored" players.

Pompez decried the stance Robinson took in taking a "mixed team" through the South in an interview with the *Chicago Defender*'s J. Don Davis. "Jackie Robinson made a great mistake in taking a mixed team into Memphis," he insisted. "The publicity is embarrassing in more than one way. It is not good reading for the liberal areas." The former Negro-league owner aimed his ire at the backers of the Robinson All-Stars, criticizing Pollock's role in the NAL. "The Negro American league is a joke. Owners of the Clowns and Monarchs run the so called loop . . . Birmingham and Memphis gets the crumbs of the bookings." Another source of his displeasure with the Robinson All-Stars came from "Jackie's tie-up with promoters of another racial group." Not surprisingly, Worner's recollection about the fan response to the 1953 tour differed from Pompez's. "The white guys on the team was a big, big draw" for black fans, who "just loved seeing the white guys playing with the black team," Worner recounted. Birmingham sheriff Bull Connor was not a fan of the team's makeup. Two of his men visited Worner in his Birmingham hotel room in the days before the scheduled game; they wanted to impress upon him that breaking the law would be dealt with harshly. Despite Worner's enthusiasm, the four white major leaguers on the Robinson All-Stars opted against traveling to Birmingham, citing fears of race riots possibly breaking out should they personally appear on the mixed team. Robinson's squad played the Birmingham game as an all-black team. That decision to acquiesce to local authorities prompted Pompez to comment that the backer should have been willing to go "all of the way with the program." As it played out, the segregationists won a public victory and the repercussions of Worner's provocative moneymaking scheme remained something that blacks in Birmingham had to live with and not Worner.[24]

Off-season barnstorming tours by black major leaguers lost much of their appeal by the mid-1950s. The 1954 tour headlined by Campanella drew only 60,231 fans for its twenty-six games, averaging approximately 2,300, about half of the previous year's average. Pompez blamed poor attendance on a combination of bad weather that canceled the tour's Atlanta dates and a "lack of publicity on the part of the local promoters." The dramatic decline continued the next year despite new headliners Mays and Aaron, drawing 34,789 fans. Continued reluctance to challenge prohibitions regarding racially integrated teams in certain southern cities prompted accusations that Pompez was "bowing to the White Citizens' Council line in excluding Caucasians who wanted to make the tour." The 1956 tour would again star Mays and Aaron on a team of black major leaguers opposite the Negro American League All-Stars, which included the future country singer Charlie Pride and the Harlem-raised Jimmy Robinson. Fewer than 15,000 fans passed through the turnstiles. "Deep South fans are retaliating on the box office against tan major leaguers who have been barnstorming the area," the *Atlanta Daily World* proclaimed in October. "This punitive attitude is due to the disdain which the big leaguers have exhibited towards Dixie fans during previous tours in Dixie." Pompez offered his own explanation, blaming the dismal turnout on the absence of any Dodgers players and stating that area fans were "almost 100 per cent followers of the Dodgers."[25]

After almost a decade of organizing postseason barnstorming tours through the South, Pompez decided the end had come for such tours. In February 1958 he placed the "Roy Campanella and Willie Mays

All-Stars" tour bus for sale in an advertisement in *The Sporting News*: "Flexible Bus, 25 Passenger, New Motor, New Tires, Reclining Seats, Greyhound Type, Excellent Interior, Fully Equipped." The bus had originally been purchased for $12,000, but Pompez was willing to accept $2,500.[26] His new strategy was to go international. In 1957 the team toured the Dominican Republic, Panama, and Nicaragua. Handling the Panama arrangements was the nation's general sports director, Gil Gonzalo Garrido, who had played for the New York Cubans from 1944 through 1946. The 1957 tour ended with a swing up California's Pacific Coast. Much had changed in the baseball world: the Dodgers and Giants franchises had both announced they were relocating to Los Angeles and San Francisco, respectively.[27]

The Hope of Spring

Integration was an uncharted realm of experience for most within organized baseball. Talented African American and Latino players learned the lifelong lesson that more than talent was required for them to secure a genuine chance at a lasting professional career. They had to persevere despite the cultural adjustments involved in pioneering integration, whether one was a foreign-born Latino or a U.S.-born black prospect. By 1955 Carl Hubbell and Jack Schwarz had placed Pompez in charge of the organization's Latino prospects during the minor-league spring training camp in Melbourne, Florida. This forward-thinking intervention recognized that cultural adjustment could affect a Latino prospect's ultimate success—how sometimes handling living in a new land was as significant as learning to hit the curveball or, in the case of pitchers, mastering how to vary the speed on their pitches. The former Negro-league team owner would serve these players as a cultural translator—a U.S. Latino who understood their cultural backgrounds and who could interpret social norms and U.S. cultural practices for the prospects.

The Melbourne spring training facility where prospects tried out and minor-league assignments were decided was fraught with tension. Scouting and developmental personnel gathered each day to assess the prospects and determine whom to sign, the amount of signing bonuses, and where to assign them within the Giants' minor-league system. At these meetings, Pompez often waged a lonely battle against the impatience, benign neglect, or perhaps even tacit racism of colleagues not yet fully committed to racial integration. He stood as the unwavering advocate of African American and Latino prospects at these daily conferences: steadfast in his commitment to ensure that these prospects received a fair and thorough evaluation. Reflecting on his days as one of those prospects, Orlando Cepeda declared emphatically: "Pompez had to fight for us to stay, for us just to be given a chance." "Alejandro Pompez had 100 per cent to do with my career," Cepeda explained to one sportswriter. "In 1955, the Giants wanted to release me from spring training and he begged the Giants not to let me go because I had a future in the big leagues. And he fought with them until the end."[28]

Everyone in the Giants camp knew of the daily meetings, especially the prospects. They knew that, after the meetings, more were sent home than were offered contracts and a minor-league assignment. The sight of the graying Pompez walking toward their dormitory rooms after a meeting frayed their nerves and sent their minds racing: How should they read the stern look on his face, the shaking of his head, the tone of his whispered voice, or the pace of his gait as he ambled toward them? Was he bearing bad news? Were they the ones being released? Or was he upset once again at his colleagues for shortchanging a prospect on a signing bonus? Whatever the case, more than a few players took to hiding when they saw him making his way toward their rooms.

A strapping teenager from Mobile, Willie McCovey feared the post-meeting appearance of the balding Pompez during his 1955 tryout. "I was scared to death," he later recalled. "There were a lot of good ballplayers in that tryout camp—Orlando Cepeda, Jay Alou, and José Pagán. I figured I'd soon be on a bus back to Mobile." Throughout spring training McCovey witnessed Pompez informing other prospects that they were being released after the evaluation meetings. Then, as spring tryouts neared their close, there Pompez stood at his door with "that look." McCovey was certain his return ticket had been punched. "Why don't you hit?" he asked the young first baseman. "I don't know. I'm trying. I'm doing the best I can," the Alabama native replied. Then Pompez delivered the surprising news: McCovey had misread his look.

"You got a contract," Pompez informed him. "You've been disappointing here. but we're going to take a chance. We know you have potential."[29]

Helping the Giants' young African American and Latino players realize that potential involved special measures, which began with advising and even mentoring players at spring training. Pompez introduced the young prospects to the rules of social and racial engagement. This was their first time in the States and the initial exposure to Jim Crow segregation for most, if not all, of the foreign-born Latinos trying to land a contract with the Giants. Pompez's attempts to alleviate the culture shock that these Latinos inevitably experienced included supervision of their living quarters, making roommate assignments, and imparting cultural lessons to prepare them for encounters with the media and the American public. After several years he institutionalized the method of teaching these lessons, holding formal classes on language and cultural adjustment at the Giants' minor-league facility during spring training.

Accommodations were made on every hand. The Giants broke stride with some discriminatory practices while at times seemingly conforming to others. The dormitory that housed their prospects featured a peculiar form of integrated accommodations. Players slept in the same dormitory but there were no mixed room assignments. White prospects enjoyed rooms on the dormitory's first floor; black and Latino recruits were assigned a cluster of rooms on the second floor. Pompez initially set up roommate assignments with Dominicans rooming with other Dominicans, Cubans with Cubans, and Puerto Ricans with fellow Puerto Ricans. And there were plenty of Latinos to accommodate. The Giants had thirty-four "tan" players in their farm system in 1957, according to the *Chicago Defender*'s count. That number included more than Spanish-speaking Caribbean Latinos: Panamanian Vibert Clarke, Virgin Islander Valmy Thomas, African Americans McCovey and Leon Wagner, and Bahamian shortstop Andre Rodgers, who later that year became the first of his countrymen to appear in the majors.[30]

 Not all of the Giants' attempts to facilitate the success of their new black or Latino players worked. In 1950, while Willie Mays was spending his first season in organized baseball with the club's Trenton minor-league team, the Giants assigned a Latino player who had formerly played on the New York Cubans to be Mays's roommate when the team traveled on the road. That effort fell flat; the Latino player was dispatched from the Trenton club within a month. "The arrangement was contrived," according to Mays's biographer James Hirsch, who states that Mays, a self-described country boy, "disdained the newcomer as a showboat from the big city." Hirsch's harsh criticism of the organization's effort fails to acknowledge two elements involved in this particular proactive attempt's not succeeding: Mays had little professional experience performing in a multicultural setting and even less exposure to Latinos. His two abbreviated seasons with the Birmingham Black Barons meant he had participated in only a couple of series against the New York Cubans and its bilingual, multicultural band of players. Indeed, the big city and the Spanish-speaking players who performed on its premier Negro-league team were quite foreign to the Alabama-raised teenager. Additionally, the "contrived" label diminishes not only the behind-the-scenes work of Alex Pompez, Carl Hubbell, and Horace Stoneham in acquiring black and Latino talent from the Negro leagues and the Caribbean but also their efforts to address issues that players indubitably would confront as part of integrated baseball's pioneering generation.

As evident in Mays's rejection of his Latino roommate in Trenton, these efforts were not uniformly well received by the African American and Latino players in the Giants organization. And reception mattered. The organization's player development officials protected their prized prospects, and those who might impede their progress were released. Cultural differences between the U.S.-born blacks and the foreign-born Latino prospects also mattered, influencing their relationships as they worked their way up through the minors. Resentment at times arose, especially as the aspiring minor leaguers observed any "special" treatment members of either group received. Joking in Spanish among the Latino prospects was viewed with suspicion by the English-speaking players, white or black. Likewise, Latino players resented it when their North American teammates poked fun at their efforts to speak in English and however else they demonstrated that they were strangers in a new land. In such ways, everyday perceptions of Latinos, African Americans, and white Americans manifested themselves in how these players related to one another, inside the clubhouse as well as beyond the playing field.

The pioneering of racial integration in minor-league towns and the newness of this realm of experience—of whites, blacks, and Latinos all playing together as teammates in organized baseball—was the backdrop to their story. There were a few exceptions. Monte Irvin had already played in Cuba and would also play in Puerto Rico; he had experience playing on integrated teams. Orlando Cepeda recalled Negro leaguers who visited his father's Ponce home while they played in the Puerto Rican winter league. But for the most part, and especially for white Americans and many southern-born blacks, integration was entirely new.

Dominican Felipe Alou counted himself among those who benefited from Pompez's spring training rap sessions. Signed in November 1955, he attended the Giants' minor-league camp the following spring. A nightly ritual emerged in which a group of Latinos loaded into Pompez's Packard; he then drove them to a local ice cream parlor. He did this to safeguard the young men from the Jim Crow environs. "Racism was very strong at that time in Melbourne," Alou recounted. "He wouldn't let us walk." At the ice cream parlor, in the dormitory lobby, and wherever he could bend their ears, he shared his knowledge. What he had to say was invaluable for Alou. "He used to explain to us the rules of the game and also the rules for blacks. It was very important to have a man like him who knew the society so well to explain to us the limitations we had. You know, to protect us from falling into a problem of some sort."[31]

A sense of obligation motivated Pompez to share the lessons he himself had come to learn and accept: of working within the system, of understanding the ways race mattered, and of having to make the adjustment in order to first survive and then succeed. Since his Negro-league days he had witnessed many talented Latinos not making it in professional baseball in the States due to their inability to handle the cultural adjustment. Of the Giants' Latino prospects he told journalist Robert Boyle: "When they first come here they don't like it. Some boys cry and want to go home. But after they stay and make the big money, they accept things as they are." Given their challenge, his "main thing" was to help the prospects. "They can't change the laws."[32]

Evidence of the wily baseball man's successful work was all around the big leagues by the end of the 1950s: Cepeda, Marichal, Alou, and

McCovey, among others, had come through the Giants' minor-league camp to become stars. That success inspired Robert Boyle to examine the case of "Latin Negroes" in the big leagues in a lengthy 1960 *Sports Illustrated* article. Through the study Boyle came to understand why Latinos such as Felipe Alou would declare that Pompez was "king to us." "Alex was like a father to all of us," recalled Manny Mota, "He took us under his wing . . . He prepared us in what to expect in a different country and a different culture."[33] San Francisco–based sportswriter Bob Stevens concurred with the assessment that Pompez was more than just a scout. Pompez was "judge advocate and advisor to all Negroes and Latinos," Stevens observed. "He helped with contracts, told them about haircuts, manicures, neckties and shoeshines. He instructed them in the use of language and their place in 'beisbol.' He explained wages and work rights."[34]

A typical spring training scene found Pompez holding court with Latino players in the lobby of the Giants' hotel. He regaled them with tales from the Negro leagues and of greats who had played in the Cuban League. Felipe Alou recalled how the young players working their way through the minors would gather around Pompez. The impromptu sessions were one of the few times they had someone speaking Spanish to them; it reminded many of home, giving them a sense of familiarity.[35] The lessons he sought to impart touched on all subjects: baseball, race, food, sexual relations, and being a foreigner in a new land. Alou shared a story about his first spring training in 1956. A Giants prospect had whistled at a group of high-school-age white girls passing by the complex. This was the spring following the discovery in Mississippi of the brutalized body of Emmett Till, a Chicago black teenager savagely murdered for committing the offense of whistling at a white woman. A modern-day lynching for infringement of a sexual more, Till's murder shook the nation. Word of the Giants' own "whistling incident" spread through camp and got to Pompez. Incensed, he gathered all the Latinos at the complex that evening. "I don't know who that person was," he intoned, "[but] don't ever whistle to those girls anymore. Don't even look at them anymore." When the Latino players protested that none of them had committed the offense, he snapped back, "I am not asking if any of you did. But don't even look."[36]

Such matters weighed heavily on Pompez. He didn't sleep much at night, aware of the potential pitfalls awaiting his young charges beyond the Melbourne complex, a former naval base. These prospects were mere teenagers; for many, this was their first time out of their native countries. "He was our guardian," recalled pitcher Julio Navarro of those spring days in Melbourne. Navarro first attended Giants spring training camp in 1955 with prospects Orlando Cepeda, José Pagán, and dozens of other hopefuls. The native of Vieques, Puerto Rico, enjoyed a relative advantage compared to his peers: he was bilingual, having been raised mostly in the U.S. Virgin Islands alongside English- and Spanish-speaking neighbors and schoolmates. He could move quite easily between the black and Latino circles, acting as a communication bridge between them. However, he and even those who were returning to Melbourne as "experienced" minor leaguers had to be reminded that this was the Jim Crow South, not "home." Their conduct as black men took on different meaning here. The Giants took precautionary measures. A bus shuttled players from the complex to town; it dropped them off at the movie theaters, local eateries, and even church on Sundays. There was also a 9:00 p.m. curfew to ensure they returned early enough to stay out of trouble. Pompez worried nonetheless; he was always ready to hop into his Packard and pull one of his players out of a dicey situation.[37]

A multinational contingent of Latinos continued to gather around Pompez at the Casa Grande Hotel after the Giants moved their spring training to Arizona in 1961. In the lobby one could find the Dominican brothers Felipe and Matty Alou along with Juan Marichal, Manny Mota, and Dan Rivas; Puerto Ricans Orlando Cepeda, José Pagán, and José Calero; Panamanian Gil Garrido; Cuban José Cardenal. The players soaked up the words of wisdom that often turned to issues of professionalism and deportment. The sight of Cardenal spread out, relaxing on one of the hotel lobby's easy chairs, was a common occurrence. At one of their impromptu lessons Pompez snapped at the young Cuban whom he had signed out of Matanzas a year earlier. "José Cardenal, you have not sat up straight once all morning." Cardenal got into his act, falling out of the chair and rolling about the floor, peeking out after each roll at Pompez. Everyone laughed. The teenager was well on his way to establishing himself as a jokester, someone who kept his fellow players loose.[38]

"We have long talks," Pompez told reporters Art Rosenbaum and Bob Stevens, San Francisco–area sportswriters who regularly observed his interactions with Latino players. Pompez believed the talks had their positive effects, informing the sportswriters that he and his scouts sought out prospects capable of thriving in their new environment. "These are good boys. They marry their childhood sweethearts and they don't go wild when they earn so much money." Pointing across the hotel lobby, he continued: "Look at Felipe Alou's wife over there . . . a lovely, lovely girl. He adores her and she thinks of him as a hero. The same for Cepeda's wife, and the others." But the road for success was not easy for them; neither was it easy for the U.S.-born blacks he signed. "These boys, many of them, have come from the lowest economic strata, and from parents with no education. They get a few dollars and they lose their heads. They won't listen."[39]

Latino players tended to heed Pompez's advice more closely. Perhaps they listened because of his paternal, almost grandfatherly appearance, because he was someone who offered words of wisdom while understanding their necessary maturation process. Pompez explained to Bob Stevens: "We can discover a boy and talk with him, but he is the baseball player, and one day he must be on his own. As he grows in years he needs my advice less and less. So it is my business to find another bright young star; always another one."[40] Or perhaps it was the knowledge that he had been in the game long enough to have signed some of their heroes of the Negro leagues, such as Martín Dihigo, Horacio Martínez, and Lefty Tiant. It may have been that he had also scouted some of their older relatives and, in the case of Orlando Cepeda, his father, Puerto Rican baseball legend Pedro "Perucho" Cepeda. Pompez had known the Cepeda family since his days operating the New York Cubans and had attempted to recruit Perucho Cepeda. He came close, including Cepeda's name on the Cubans' 1942 roster submitted to the NNL office.[41] But the elder Cepeda, who had a legendary career in Latin American baseball in the 1930s and 1940s, opted against going north to the States to play in a segregated profession. He had heard the stories of the social conditions that Negro leaguers encountered from black baseball greats Satchel Paige, Josh Gibson, and Cool Papa Bell on their visits to his home in Puerto Rico. Long bus rides, segregated hotels, and restaurants that refused to serve them as they traveled around the States because they were black did not appeal to him. As the younger Cepeda recalled, even when told that much of the racial discrimination had dissipated, his father "would not set foot in the States."[42]

A Noble Pursuit

A handful of major-league owners actively pursued black players, whether U.S.- or foreign-born, once the process of integration unfolded. A piecemeal approach ensued whereby organizations did not focus on signing the best black players available but rather tried to develop their own young black and Latino prospects. In so doing, most eschewed the years of player development and scouting that had been undertaken in the international domain of the Negro leagues where Pompez and others had initially operated.

Pompez's recruitment of Latin American talent depended on a network of scouts and contacts in the sports world to alert him to emerging talent. Current players served as informal scouts, just as José María Fernández and Martín Dihigo had when they played for his Cuban Stars, offering recommendations about which players merited a close look. That practice stretched back to the 1920s. Shortstop Emilio "Millito" Navarro, who played several seasons for Pompez's Cuban Stars, noted that pitcher Pedro San recommended him to Pompez: the first Dominican in the Negro leagues thus put into motion the signing of the first Puerto Rican to play in that circuit.[43] This practice of local contacts serving as "bird dog" scouts spotting up-and-coming players would continue in baseball's new era, as would Pompez's regular trips throughout the Caribbean.

The transition to playing in baseball's integrated era presented distinct challenges for Latinos. Black Latino players were no longer subject to being summarily bounced from organized baseball upon "discovery" of their racial roots. Talented Afro-Latino players such as Orlando Cepeda, José Cardenal, and Felipe Alou—who a generation or two earlier would have most likely played for Pompez's New York Cubans or some other Negro-league team—were now able to sign directly with major-league organizations. For the first time in the history of Latino participation in the majors, darker-skinned Latinos could openly acknowledge their black ancestry and their Latino cultural heritage. This, of course, did not come without its hiccups: most organizations were not prepared to handle this influx of talent or their peculiar issues, and even those that did make accommodations would still encounter cultural conflicts among players, between players and management, and with the press. Pompez would attempt to stave off some of these concerns, but he was not the guiding voice for the organization, as he had been with the New York Cubans: others chose the managers and filled the big-league rosters.

The Giants would become all too familiar with the complications that arose with having a diverse roster in the generation that was making integration a reality. In fact, no team's roster was more diverse in the 1950s and 1960s than the Giants'. Due to Pompez's active work behind the scenes, the story of baseball's Latino Giants would be much different than that of Papa Joe Cambria and Washington's Cuban Senators. Washington's acquisition of African American and Latin American talent captured the uneven pursuit of racial integration in organized baseball. A few had envisioned Washington as a potential trendsetter in baseball integration. The Senators' home, Griffith Stadium, was located in one of the nation's most elite black neighborhoods (near Howard University) and had served as the second home for the Homestead Grays for much of the 1940s. Additionally, the Senators had been the major leagues' most active pursuer of Latino talent during its segregated era. Yet Washington held out when it came to signing U.S.-born blacks. The first black player to appear in a Senators uniform was Cuban-born Carlos Paula, who debuted in 1954. The team's first African American player did not appear until three years later, making the Senators the third-to-last big-league team to place an African American player on the field. All the while Joe Cambria continued to mine the sugarcane fields of Cuba for talent.

Integration would proceed one-way as major-league organizations actively plucked players from the Negro leagues even as they refused to incorporate black-owned teams into organized baseball at any level. Jackie Robinson and Larry Doby marked the beginning of a massive talent drain from the Negro leagues into organized baseball. Desegregation was not a collaborative project between Negro-league franchise holders and organized baseball's league and team officials. Major League Baseball's unwillingness to engage in two-way integration ensured the inevitability of black baseball's disintegration. Additionally, organized-baseball officials took advantage of the wide support that racial integration enjoyed within African American communities, offering black baseball owners purchase prices far below what talented Negro-league players merited—and would have been offered if they had been white. The sell-off resembled a liquidation sale of a business destined for closure. In this sense, those who had imposed the color line drew the greatest profit from its dismantling—not those who had suffered exclusion and had built an institution to offer the racially excluded a league of their own. The major leagues' piecemeal approach to integration effectively sapped the energies of Negro-league owners and team officials who had scouted, signed, and developed the once-excluded talent. Often positioned as "race" men and women, black baseball officials could not protest too vehemently that the major-league teams were stealing or underpaying them for their best players. The public and the sporting press could easily interpret such protest as black baseball owners placing their own financial interests ahead of the civil rights cause that baseball integration represented.

The employment of Pompez by the Giants was the closest the Negro leagues came to a stakeholder emerging out of its executive ranks. First as a scout and then as its director of international scouting, he would impact the pace of the Giants organization's incorporation of previously excluded talent. This position enabled him to select a number of the players who would literally be the pioneers of integration in different minor leagues. From his decades in the Negro leagues, Pompez knew the barriers that could prove to be stumbling blocks to prospects. He sought to mentor the young men who became his charges and implemented innovations such as language instruction at the Giants minor-league camp to help with cultural barriers and thereby facilitate their transformation into "Latin" Giants.

9

FROM CUBAN STARS TO DOMINICAN GIANTS

When you think of the power, drive and ability of a team which can present such talents as those of Mays, McCovey, Cepeda, and others, you would expect a consistency of the first order. But how can this be possible when, behind his perfectly legitimate attitude of fair play, these guys have to work with a man who has strange cobwebs in his mind about people of color? —Jackie Robinson on Alvin Dark's Giants

In the fall of 1959, the journalist Robert Boyle traveled with Alex Pompez and the Black All-Stars on their barnstorming excursion through Mexico. Boyle's aim on this assignment was "to understand what life was like for Robinson's 57 'successors'" as he prepared to write an article for *Sports Illustrated*. Organized in collaboration with Joe Tubiolo of Sports Attractions Inc., a Washington, D.C.–based company, the 1959 tour marked the first time Pompez had the Black All-Stars play against a team of white major leaguers—a squad that featured the Washington Senators' power-hitting Harmon Killebrew along with the all-stars Jim Lemon, Frank Bolling, and Jim Bunning. Boyle gained an inside look at the world of black ballplayers during the two-week tour that started on October 27 in Monterrey, with stops in Mante, Tampico, Poza Rica, San Luis Potosí, Mexico City, Veracruz, Córdoba, Puebla, Celaya, León, and Aguascalientes, before finishing in Guadalajara on November 8.[1]

Willie Mays was the original headliner for the 1959 tour, until

Horace Stoneham removed the Giants superstar. That forced Pompez to rework his publicity angle: Hank Aaron was substituted on the posters and placards to advertise the individual games and the overall tour. This revised marketing plan also went awry. When the Black All-Stars squad gathered to begin their Mexican journey, Aaron was a no-show. It was too late to change the publicity materials again; the tour had to go forward. Fans at the first few stops were oblivious to Aaron's absence. As was customary at the time with many teams, the uniforms lacked players' names. Thus, Mexican fans had to rely on their own familiarity with the Black All-Stars players to discern among the group that included Willie McCovey, Junior Gilliam, Bill White, Johnny Roseboro, Don Newcombe, and Bob Gibson, among others.

Hopeful of gaining an interior view of their world, the Ivy League–educated Boyle decided to travel on the team bus transporting the black major leaguers. The sportswriter sat down next to Bill White on his first ride-along. The big first baseman jokingly told the white sportswriter: "Well, I'll get to sleep tonight." Boyle asked why. He simply replied: "Because you're on board." White, of course, was right: The white journalist's presence altered the dynamic on the Black All-Stars' bus. The players watched their words; Boyle observed that they "had little or nothing to say when I sought to interview them."[2]

Then they arrived at San Luis Potosí. Aaron's name had been prominently displayed on advertising distributed in the lead-up to the game. An overflow crowd entered the ballpark grounds to witness the exhibition. They grew impatient as the game proceeded to the third inning; they noticed who was missing. A chant started: "Aaron! Aaron! Aaron!" The chant grew increasingly louder over the next half inning. Seated a number of rows behind the first-base dugout with Bennie Daniels (a pitcher with the Black All-Stars not slated for action that day), Boyle grew nervous. Shortly thereafter, racial epithets began to fly from the mouths of fans, the sportswriter recalled. The *n* word and other offensive slurs followed. Alarmed, Boyle and Daniels headed down to the dugout housing Pompez and the Black All-Stars.

"It's bad, and it's only going to get worse. We've got to get out of here fast," Boyle informed Pompez as the two conferred in the temporary sanctuary of the dugout. "These people are going to riot." Pompez talked with the others in the dugout. A decision was reached: the two barnstorming squads would make a run for their buses in deep center field as soon as the current half inning ended. After the last out was recorded, the players spilled from both dugouts, carrying whatever equipment they could, and joined those on the field in sprinting for the waiting buses beyond the center-field fence. Once fans realized what was happening, they poured out of the stands and gave chase to the escaping barnstormers.

The bus carrying Harmon Killebrew and the white barnstormers took off in haste. Boyle jumped aboard the bus with Pompez and the Black All-Stars. Their terrified driver could not start the bus; its harried riders became unnerved as the angry fans drew closer. Pitcher Don Newcombe readied the team for battle, passing out bats to his teammates, exclaiming: "Jesus Christ! . . . going to die in baseball's Alamo!" The fans began rocking the bus to and fro. At last the bus started, and the driver sped down the road out of San Luis Potosí.

Respecting Boyle's decision to ride with them, players on the Black All-Stars began to open up to him; the white sportswriter had placed his lot with them when he could have easily hopped on the other bus with white major leaguers when the fans gave chase. The rest of the time he spent touring with the black players provided special insight about intergroup dynamics between the U.S-born blacks and the Caribbean-born players. A window into the world of those who were Robinson's successors was being cracked open for him; it was a world to which not too many of Boyle's journalist ilk—particularly those from mainstream publications—had yet to enjoy this type of access.[3]

Fortunately for Boyle, "Pomp" had remained his loquacious self, always ready to talk on a variety of subjects: the big-league prospects of the tour's players, his work as a Giants scout, and his time as an owner in the Negro leagues. He shared stories from the mundane to the fantastic as the barnstorming travels continued through Mexico. He regaled Boyle with tales of using a *brujo* (witch doctor) to aid him in signing Orestes Miñoso for the New York Cubans. "He wouldn't even talk to me," Pompez recalled; the young infielder seemed to elude him throughout this scouting trip in Havana. That's when Pomp supposedly contacted a local santero priest, whom Boyle referred to as a *brujo*, and the two brokered an agreement. "Okay, you get Miñoso, and I will bring you to the United States the year after next as coach," proposed the Cubans owner. Pompez informed him where he would be the next night so Miñoso could sign the contract. And the next evening, there was Miñoso, knocking on his door: Pompez got his man.

True to his word, the season after signing Miñoso—who put together an all-star 1946 campaign—Pompez brought the "*brujo*" north to serve as a coach. "I give him a uniform. He is now my coach," Pomp explained, recounting to Boyle what happened in 1947.

"Now in all my years in the Negro National League I have never won a pennant. The *brujo* comes up to me and he says: 'Hey, Pompez, is it true that you have never won the pennant?'

"'That's right. In all these years I've never won the pennant.'"

Looking at Pompez, he told the longtime Negro-league owner, "Don't worry, Pompez. This year you win the pennant."

"And you know what?" the Cubans owner said to Boyle. "We won the pennant! We won the pennant!" Twelve seasons of futility as the New York Cubans came to end.[4]

Traveling through Mexican towns, interviewing Pompez and the Black All-Stars during the 1960 season, provided Boyle special insight into what he would call "The Private World of the Negro Ballplayer." Resentment occasionally flared between the U.S.-born "Negro" and the "Latin Negro," although both were counted among Jackie's successors. Players noticed that team officials, sportswriters, hotel managers, restaurateurs, and gas attendants, among others, perceived and often treated blacks who were U.S.-born and those who were foreign-born differently. That difference spurred resentment and riled "American Negroes." It fueled perceptions that "Latin Negro" teammates thought of themselves as superior to U.S.-born blacks, that they were indifferent to their plight, or that they attempted to avoid them in the clubhouse or in interactions beyond the playing field. Boyle observed that, with occasional exceptions, "Latin Negroes do not willingly mingle with American Negroes . . . The reason is simple and painful," the sportswriter noted. "To be a Negro in the United States is to be socially inferior. Therefore, Latin Negroes are not Negroes, at least as far as they are concerned." A noticeable rift occurred on many teams: African Americans socializing in one clique and Latinos off in another or moving in between their white teammates or black teammates. Some U.S. blacks interpreted this behavior as evincing an "attitude" among black

Latinos. "I don't think I'm any better than they are," one player complained to Boyle, "but I'm not any worse either. They think they're better than the colored guy." "Latin Negroes cry when they encounter segregation for the first time," another told Boyle. "I don't cry . . . We don't cry, and we have it a hell of a lot worse than they do," he added, discounting the challenge of cultural adjustment and the foreign-born Latinos' unfamiliarity with the Jim Crow segregation they encountered.[5]

Competition for roster spots spurred ambivalence if not animosity. The slow pace of integration did not help matters: twelve years had lapsed from when Jackie Robinson broke in with the Dodgers and when the Boston Red Sox became the last major-league team to field a black player. At the start of the 1959 season, U.S.-born blacks hovered around 10 percent of all major leaguers; Latinos amounted to approximately 5 percent of the forty-man spring training rosters.[6] These numbers hid the uneven pace of incorporation of formerly excluded players across the major-league organizations. The Dodgers were at the forefront of a handful of teams that heavily recruited African American talent from the earliest days of integration; they, however, were not as successful developing Latino talent. The Giants organization signed players out of both the U.S.-born and foreign-born talent pools largely due to their black baseball inside man who was also their Latin American connection. The Washington Senators continued to sign players from Latin America but neglected to acquire U.S.-born blacks. Thus, while the Senators had five Latinos and just one African American among the forty players who performed for the team during 1959, the Giants had six African Americans along with four Latin Americans among its thirty-seven players.[7]

This generation entered a profession in the midst of a sea change. A generation earlier most of these same players would have plied their skills on Negro-league diamonds, staying together in segregated hotels, being denied service at gas stations and restaurants as their teams traveled, and facing other racially discriminatory practices. Now that they were thrust into the role of integration pioneers, the results were decidedly mixed when it came to intergroup relations, regardless of whether the players entered straightaway into organized baseball or came via the Negro leagues. On the one hand, a black Latino like

Puerto Rican Felix Mantilla might form a tight bond with Hank Aaron as they moved through the minors to the Braves' big-league club. In other situations a U.S.-born black like Harry "Suitcase" Simpson openly questioned the blackness of Cuban native Orestes Miñoso for his decision to take a different tack when it came to dealing with racial matters in the States—this in spite of the fact that the two had both performed in the Negro leagues before becoming teammates on the Cleveland Indians. Indeed, neither routes nor origins determined the tenor of these relationships. Individual personalities shaped their interactions and whether they envisioned each other as fellow sojourners confronting the same racial barriers or acknowledged challenges peculiar to their origins.

As baseball's most racially and culturally diverse team, the Giants had to directly engage the issues involved in incorporating U.S. blacks and Latinos onto their big-league and minor-league squads. Encounters with American race relations and its multiple local permutations could be quite perplexing. That was how Puerto Rican pitcher Rubén Gómez, a member of the Giants from 1953 to 1958, felt on noticing the different treatment extended to him versus his African American teammates in most towns that hosted spring training in Florida. After an incident in which he was allowed to eat at a restaurant and a black teammate who entered after him was denied service, the Puerto Rican Gómez exclaimed, "How crazy the whole question of race is in America—if you speak Spanish you're somehow not as black." That reality proved as divisive a force between U.S.-born and Caribbean-born blacks as their own actions within and beyond the playing field.[8]

From Cuban Stars to Dominican Giants

The opening of the Dominican Republic, which became even more important once Cuba was closed off, enabled the Giants to supplant the tight fisted Washington Senators as the top importers of Latin American talent, especially in terms of quality. The two organizations had long had different scouting and player development philosophies. Rather than sign players in numbers as the Senators did—most signees had little hope of making it onto the major-league diamond or of handling the cultural adjustment—the Giants organization opted for a more hands-on, culturally aware approach. The hiring of Pompez involved not only casting his scouting net to capture talent throughout the Americas but also roaming among minor-league affiliates to check on the progress of his organization's Latino prospects.

Evidence of Pompez's work was sprinkled throughout the Giants lineups: the names Alou, Cepeda, Gómez, Marichal, Mota, and Pagán. Their prominence in the Giants organization and in Major League Baseball as a whole signaled the circuit's ongoing transformation, indicative of both its racial integration and of its Latinization. This influx of Latino talent propelled the Giants into a first division National League team. The organization's dynamic scouting in Latin America figured significantly in this sustained transformation from also-ran in the 1940s into perennial contenders throughout the 1950s and into the mid-1960s.

Hiring his former Negro-league shortstop Horacio Martínez ranked among Pompez's most significant decisions. The Dominican native was himself a telling indication of Pompez's ability to evaluate talent. He had first witnessed the slick-fielding shortstop when his New York–based Negro-league team toured the Dominican Republic in the winter of 1933–34. Impressed with Martínez's glove, his ability to wield his bat, and his overall bearing, the Negro-league entrepreneur signed the Dominican infielder to his New York squad. In so doing, Martínez joined fellow Dominicans Juan "Tetelo" Vargas and Enrique Lantigua on the soon-to-be-named Negro National League franchise. Competing on the New York Cubans between 1935 and 1947, Martínez appeared six times as a selection in the Negro leagues' East-West Classic. Primarily a reserve on the 1947 Negro League World Series–winning Cubans squad, he retired after that season and returned to his native land.[9]

Martínez would quickly make his mark on the future of Dominicans in the major leagues from two posts: as a coach in the Dominican professional league and as the head baseball coach at the University of Santo Domingo.[10] He coached up-and-coming Dominican players at both the amateur and professional ranks, notifying Pompez whenever he spotted a player with the potential to make the jump to the States. Theirs was a relationship built on trust: Pompez placed his trust in

Martínez's initial assessment of Dominican prospects—that they were truly capable of handling the on-field and off-the-field challenges and were not unruly suspects. The roots of that trust came from their years in the Negro leagues, of Martínez observing what his New York Cubans boss looked for in a player, of knowing what was required in terms of physical skills and mental acuity for a foreign-born Latino to make the grade in the States.

Together Martínez and Pompez created the Dominican pipeline into the majors that produced the Alou brothers, Manny Mota, and, most notably, Juan Marichal—the first generation of big-league heroes for Dominicans. The general lack of awareness of Pompez and Martínez's role in recruiting Dominican Giants and the shift in the Latinization of baseball from Cuba to the Dominican Republic are part of the cloak of invisibility that envelops the contribution of Latinos to baseball history in the States. Martinez is respected across the Dominican Republic as one of the game's elder statesmen, and his scouting laid the groundwork for what would become the major leagues' most significant source of foreign-born talent by the end of the twentieth century. However, his contribution to the development of the Dominican pipeline remains—to extend sportswriter Marcos Bretón's metaphor about the awareness of Dominican baseball in U.S. baseball circles—"lost in the translation from Spanish to English."[11]

For his part, Pompez started to gain notice for his scouting success within and beyond the baseball public in the late 1950s. Ironically, his work would largely be overlooked by historians in their accounts of integration, the Negro leagues, and the Latinization of baseball, especially in the decades after his death in 1974. On the heels of the Giants christening their new ballpark, Candlestick Park, Pompez appeared on the popular television game show *What's My Line?* on April 17, 1960. The show's first game involved contestants attempting to ascertain an individual's occupation by asking them a series of questions. The first contestant successfully surmised that Pompez was a scout for the Giants. In the postgame interview, Pompez remarked that he had participated in the Giants' signings of Monte Irvin, Hank Thompson, Willie McCovey, and Orlando Cepeda. The success these players enjoyed with the Giants increased the attention Pompez received within the sporting world.

The big splash Willie McCovey made through his slugging prowess during his rookie campaign in 1959 prompted sportswriters to search for the scout who signed the Giants' slugging first baseman. In mid-August that search led one magazine photographer to the "high hills of deepest Cuba," where he found Pompez on a scouting expedition—this in the months before the island was closed off to U.S. commercial activity.

"We want your picture because you discovered Willie McCovey," the photographer informed the Giants scout. "McCovey? I have discovered many ballplayers . . . and what is so special about McCovey?" Pompez replied. The Giants scout had been traveling the far reaches and had not yet heard the news of McCovey's exploits until the photojournalist broke the news to him. The Giants had called McCovey up from the minors and within weeks he had made his mark. Now "everything must be known about McCovey," the photographer remarked.

McCovey's success story followed that of Cepeda (1958) and preceded the breakthrough of the "Dominican Dandy," pitcher Juan Marichal, in 1960. Other accolades followed for Pompez's scouting work and for his role in the signing of all three superstars (and future Hall of Famers). In 1963 he twice received the "Topps Also Salutes" recognition from *The Sporting News* for having been the scout who signed the National League's player of the month.[12] These players were part of the bounty of talent drawn from the baseball circuit that Pompez had traveled since his Negro-league days that extended from the playing fields of the U.S. South to the islands of the Caribbean and the Latin American countries that bordered the sea.

The collective success of these star players belied the challenging management issues involved in dealing with diversity within the clubhouse and between the players and the front office. Integrating Latinos and blacks from such disparate places meant team officials had to figure out minor-league assignments that best gave the organization an accurate indication of each player's development to predict future success. After all, these were for the most part teenage prospects thrust into an alien culture who had to undergo the transition into manhood while in the minor leagues. In addition to hormonal changes, there was the hobgoblin of race in U.S. society, the rules of which changed according to location, region, or what kind of "Negro" one was, and were at times bewildering even to native-born blacks. By the late 1950s the Giants realized that although they could assign African American players to certain minor-league affiliates in the South, they could not necessarily do the same with darker-skinned, foreign-born Latinos. Jim Crow was yet another alien culture for them, and the assessment of their development as players required addressing this reality. "A few clubs are beginning to realize that the Latin Negro comes from a different world," observed journalist Robert Boyle after his study of Robinson's successors. The worry for the Giants' minor-league officials was that "segregation might sour a foreign Negro on the U.S. as a whole."[13] That matter is what Pompez aspired to mediate in creating more formal classes in which he and Horacio Martínez taught cultural literacy to the prospects in addition to rudimentary English-language skills.

The Giants' relocation of their minor-league spring training complex to Casa Grande, Arizona, in 1961 meant dazzling new amenities. The player dormitories came complete with a meeting space that would double as a classroom for Pompez and his charges. Everywhere one looked, one saw evidence of his scouting. The attendees when the 1961 minor-league camp opened included fifteen Dominicans, ten Cubans (with two more awaiting visas to enter the States), seven Venezuelans, six Panamanians, five Mexicans, three Puerto Ricans, and one Costa Rican. Seeing the fruit of his labors, *The Sporting News* labeled Pompez a "super sleuth." The publication, moreover, acknowledged the additional responsibilities he took upon himself. "Kids come into this camp who can't say 'hello' in English," he boasted to its sportswriter, "but after mixing with American boys on the field, in the clubhouse and social hall, they leave here six weeks later speaking fluently."[14]

A hands-on approach to aiding prospects with their acculturation process featured prominently in Pompez's recruitment pitch to parents and guardians. He highlighted his status as a Latino familiar with U.S. cultural dynamics and emphasized the care he would personally provide. "I go to the mothers and fathers and I say, 'Every team has money to offer. But no team has a man like me!'" he explained to a *Sports Illustrated* journalist. He concluded his pitch: "Your boy go with the Giants, and I will look after him. Your boy gets sick, I see he get better. With the other clubs no one speaks Spanish.'"[15] The sight of the balding gray-haired man who spoke in their native tongue and also addressed their concerns about their sons heading off to a distant land no doubt assured many parents that the Giants were indeed the organization with which to sign.

Of course, not every player the Giants scout recruited signed with the organization. There were myriad reasons that inspired particular individuals to pursue a different life's journey. Fidel Castro was no different. Like many Cuban boys in the early twentieth century, Castro developed a passion for baseball and its history and perhaps even fancied pursuing a big-league career. Historians have debated the extent of Castro's talent—specifically, whether he had big-league potential; their pronouncements on his professional prospects prior to becoming a revolutionary are typically colored as much by their individual political stances as by any evidence in accessible archives or from the oral testimony of those who profess to be contemporaries.

Both Joe Cambria and Pompez get caught up in the tales of Castro the baseball prospect and of what might have been in the course of political relations between the United States and Cuba. Tales first circulated in the months after Castro's takeover in 1959. In June, *Baseball Digest* ran a brief item quoting Cambria: "I saw Fidel Castro pitch at Havana University. I gave him a long look and then decided he'd never get higher than Class B ball—or at best struggle up to 'A' ball." Eleven issues later, the baseball magazine ran a different version of the scout's assessment: this time Cambria assessed him as "Class D material only."[16] Literary scholar turned Cuban baseball historian Roberto González Echevarría believes not a word of the accounts of Fidel Castro the baseball prospect. In his tome *Pride of Havana* the scholar attempts to emphatically refute them. He notes that Castro was not a member of the Havana University varsity baseball team and the only box score he located with an *F. Castro* was an intramural game between the university's law school and business school teams.[17] Decades later, assessments of Castro from former classmates at his high school (El Colegio de Belen) and at Havana University appeared in the *Miami Herald*. Their overall evaluation: "an average pitcher at best"; "he could be terrible," offered one Belen teammate.[18] This, along with the lack of creditable living sources attesting to any pitching prowess on Castro's part, places the accounts of Castro as a baseball prospect in the realm of fantasy for González Echevarría—the creation of overactive North American imaginations.

If there is one individual that deserves much of the credit for this persistent, ever-evolving tale, Joe Cambria is that person. Time and again he told sportswriters about his encounter(s) with Fidel the potential Senators prospect in prerevolutionary Cuba. And U.S. sportswriters went with what Cambria gave them. "The rejected baseball prospect" who had been "turned down by Washington scout Joe Cambria" became "a key figure" in the 1961 major-league season, declared the *Pasadena Independent* on January 5, following the breaking of U.S.-Cuban diplomatic relations. Two months later in Florida, Cambria was working his charm again, recounting to those gathered the time when someone tipped him to look at a sandlot pitcher: "The guy didn't have much," he informed them, "and I figured he'd never go above Class C ball. His name was Fidel Castro."[19]

Pompez's name also gets interjected into the tale of Castro as a baseball prospect, courtesy of his former boss Horace Stoneham and the overactive imagination of several journalists. In a conversation with the sportswriter Roger Angell, an eighty-four-year-old Stoneham, suffering from Alzheimer's, recalled a scouting encounter his Giants had with Castro. According to his recollection, Pompez had submitted a scouting report after witnessing Castro play in Cuba. After Castro's revolution, Stoneham had the Giants' personnel search their scouting files to check whether it was the same guy. "It was the same Castro," he informed Angell. "A good ballplayer. I think if he'd have stayed in the game, he'd have made it to the majors." Stoneham reportedly told another journalist, "We had our top people evaluate him, as did several other teams. Castro was a real prospect." The Giants' top executive was not alone in recalling such an encounter between his scout and the Cuban ruler. Four scouting reports in J. David Truby's article "Castro's Curveball" included one purportedly filed by Pompez in 1948. That report stated that the Cuban pitcher had "good control and should be considered seriously." The positive evaluation was followed by Pompez's allegedly extending a contract offer complete with a $5,000 signing bonus, an offer the future Cuban revolutionary refused.

Jack Schwarz, Stoneham's own former director of scouting and Carl Hubbell's successor, disputed Stoneham's recollection. "I don't think Alex even saw him," Schwarz told a *Miami Herald* sportswriter in 1987. "If he did see him, he never thought anything of him. I'm sure I would have heard of it if that wasn't the case."[20] In a 1991 interview, Schwarz was even more emphatic: "I heard this years ago, looked in our files and can assure you we had no scouting report on a Fidel Castro." Other details don't fit either. Pompez was not yet officially scouting Latino prospects in Cuba or elsewhere for the Giants in 1948; the organization hired him in 1950 after the Mays signing. Prior to that Pompez mainly advised the Giants on the acquisition of Negro-leaguers or sold prospects from his own Negro-league club to the organization; his scouting for players remained focused on stocking his New York Cubans roster. Additionally, the reported $5,000 signing bonus Pompez supposedly offered Castro seems exorbitant, especially given the paltry signing bonuses of $500 Pompez later negotiated in the mid-1950s for Orlando Cepeda, Willie McCovey, and Felipe Alou as prospects at the Giants' minor-league complex. Indeed, Juan Marichal received a $4,000 signing bonus as a strong pitching prospect in 1957, almost a full decade after Castro was supposedly offered a $5,000 bonus.[21]

Fleeing Castro's Cuba

Baseball prospect or not, Castro's assumption of power in Cuba altered the flow of talent between the two baseball-loving societies. Broken diplomatic ties had raised the question of whether Castro would permit Cuban players such as Orestes Miñoso, Camilo Pascual, and Pedro Ramos, among others, to leave Cuba and play the 1961 season. The U.S.-backed Bay of Pigs invasion worsened political relations, as did the discovery by U.S. spy planes of the installation of Soviet missiles on the island in October 1962. From minor leaguers Rigoberto "Tito" Fuentes and Luis Tiant to established veterans Miñoso, Tony Taylor, and Sandy Amoros, all Cuban players faced the same quandary: to stay on the island and potentially be cut off from a major-league career, or to go to the States and possibly be forever separated from family and loved ones.

The story of how Pompez managed to make Tito Fuentes a Giants farmhand vividly captured the impact of the closing off of Cuba, for individuals as well as for organizations. Major-league organizations scrambled to secure safe passage for their Cuban players. A seasoned traveler within the Americas, Pompez was uniquely able to navigate political channels and cultural territory others dared not or could not traverse; this was most clear in his snatching up of Tito Fuentes. The Cuban infielder originally caught the eye of a Kansas City Athletics scout at the 1961 Pan-American Games held in Costa Rica. Unfortunately for the A's, the Bay of Pigs invasion occurred in the days following the games. Political fallout from the failed invasion threatened the flow of talent out of Cuba. Fuentes feared what would become of his parents and turned down the chance to sign a contract with Kansas City to return to the island. "I was thinking only of them at the time," said Fuentes. "I went home, found my family was okay and waited." The Kansas City scout had warned Fuentes that he might not be able to arrange for the Cuban to leave the island if he did not sign immediately after the Pan-Am games; the Athletics scout was right and the team would suffer for it.

The A's needed an inside man who knew Cuba and how to operate within such exigent circumstances; Kansas City needed what the Giants had in Pompez. Involved in Cuban baseball since 1916, he had built a network of contacts there and elsewhere in Latin America that could literally make the seemingly impossible happen. Fuentes recounted how the Giants signed him: "At the time, Alex Pompez, the famous Giant scout in Latin America, worked the Cuban area, but the Bay of Pigs made it impossible to come back to Havana. So, he had a bird dog [former player Lázaro Ruiz] follow me. He said the Giants could get me out of Cuba, through Mexico, so I signed with the Giants." Thus, at a moment when other organizations failed (or dared not try) to obtain an exit visa from Cuba to travel to the United States, Pompez's network secured Fuentes a passport that allowed the promising shortstop entry into the States. After the 1962 season, Fuentes returned to Cuba. The following year Pompez again used his international contacts to arrange for Fuentes's safe passage out of Cuba. This time Fuentes left Cuba for good; years would pass before he would see his family members or his native Cuba. In becoming a major leaguer in 1965, he acquired the appellation "the last ballplayer to escape from Cuba."[22]

The closing off of Cuba created a personal dilemma in which

players faced a choice between career, country, and family. Such was the case with Tito Fuentes. So it would be for the son of Lefty Tiant, one of Pompez's former New York Cubans pitching aces. A Negro-league standout in the 1930s and 1940s, Lefty Tiant had a career that included professional stints in the United States, Mexico, the Dominican Republic, and Cuba. His travels exposed him to the best and worst aspects a professional baseball career offered a black Cuban. He finished his career in the States on a high note: an undefeated season climaxed by the New York Cubans' winning the 1947 Negro League World Series. However, life off the field—the realities of dealing with the racial divide—soured him on professional baseball in the States. He hoped his only son would choose a different career path from the one he had chosen for himself. Instead, there would be two pitchers named Luis Tiant who would come north out of Cuba.

The second Luis Tiant's path to the major leagues was not a direct route, but it was one where the son realized that which had been denied to the father. Starting his career in Mexico in 1959, after three seasons pitching in the Mexican League he faced the difficult choice of returning home to Cuba and giving up his big-league dream or signing with a major-league organization and possibly not returning to Cuba again. Tiant vacillated: his father had encouraged him to pursue his education, not a career on the diamond. In fact, he outright discouraged his son. Drawing on his own experience in traveling baseball's backwaters in the days of Jim Crow, Lefty told his teenage son that "there was no place in baseball for a Black man."[23] "I didn't want Luis to pitch," the elder Tiant would later tell sportswriters. "I didn't want him to come to America. I didn't want him to be persecuted and spit on and treated like garbage like I was."[24] However, young Luis's mother intervened and convinced the father to allow their son to pursue professional baseball in the States. His signing with the Cleveland Indians organization in 1961 meant leaving Cuba behind; another forty-six years passed before he again set foot on Cuban soil.

The Tiant family was clearly not alone in suffering the separation from one another. Other young Cubans, such as Bert Campeneris, Tony Oliva, and Zoilo Versailles, faced that dreaded decision of whether to place their individual professional aspirations over remaining with their families in Cuba. Making that choice was all the more difficult for those in big-league organizations that were not as attentive to the issues of cultural adjustment that foreign-born Latinos encountered under the best of circumstances, much less when a return to their native land was not possible due to the widening political gulf between the United States and Cuba.

Dark Days by the Bay

Formerly excluded black and Latino players undertook organized baseball's most dramatic transformation, starting with Jackie Robinson in 1947. Together they literally and figuratively changed its color. Their very presence challenged its culture, which had been established in a time of segregation. Organized baseball had to adjust its practices and accommodate racial and cultural differences to truly maximize the influx of talent. That was a lesson Alvin Dark could not quite grasp when he took his first managerial job directing the San Francisco Giants.

With the Giants the majors' most diverse ball club as the 1960s opened, Stoneham's decision to hire Dark as the manager in 1961 did not match up with the forward thinking exhibited in hiring Pompez to comb the Negro leagues and Latin American fields for talent a decade earlier. The Giants never realized their goal of winning the World Series under Dark; the clubhouse dynamic never quite jibed. And that was the result as much of the team's leadership in the clubhouse as it was of team management. Baseball may have entered into a new era as to the composition of its teams, but racial ideas that had sustained segregation in organized baseball, and in much of American life, proved enduring.

Jackie Robinson understood the psychological dimension involved in being a pioneer in the majors as the first to participate in the demolition of the color line that had stood in place over six decades. The Dodgers second baseman well comprehended the necessary elements of team chemistry and the importance of the team's manager and front office. When Robinson broke in with the Dodgers in 1947, team president Branch Rickey promised to trade away any of the team's white players who grumbled about Robinson's arrival, which Rickey did in the cases of Dodgers veterans Bobby Bragan and Dixie Walker after they publicly expressed reservations about being forced to participate in an integrated club. Rickey also handpicked the manager for the 1947 season, naming Burt Shotton to the post.

The precautions Rickey took aimed to ensure that the talent on the field would ultimately determine the team's success and not latent resistance, public griping, or outright hostility to Robinson and integration. They worked on multiple levels. The 1947 Dodgers won the National League pennant and made it to the World Series, which they dropped to crosstown rivals the New York Yankees. Robinson was selected 1947 Rookie of the Year. And over the next decade the Dodgers remained perennial front-runners in the National League as its pioneering black stars Robinson, Roy Campanella, Don Newcombe, and Junior Gilliam continued to shine.

The San Francisco Giants of the late 1950s and early 1960s expanded the promise of integration; their success and failure on the diamond attested to how properly managing diversity truly mattered. Whereas the Dodgers had initiated baseball's project of integration, the Giants set a new standard for diversity by internationalizing integration, as evident in the team's multinational contingent of black and Latino players. That diversity had much to do with the terrific scouting system developed under former pitching great Carl Hubbell's direction and with the impact of Alex Pompez's work.

Directing this veritable melting pot was Alvin Dark. In a Giants tradition that harkened to the days of John McGraw being named player-manager in 1902, owner Horace Stoneham hired the former Giants standout shortstop Dark to manage the team in 1961; it was the first managerial post Dark ever held. The talent-laden team enjoyed regular-season success, although the World Series crown proved elusive.

The Giants came awfully close in 1962. An all-star cast of African American and Latino players led the Giants to the World Series against the New York Yankees. Five of the Giants players that year appeared as National League All-Stars: Felipe Alou and Juan Marichal (Dominican), Orlando Cepeda (Puerto Rican), Willie Mays (African American), and Jim Davenport (white American). These men were joined by future Hall of Famers Willie McCovey (African American) and Gaylord Perry (white American) and all-star-caliber players Matty Alou (Dominican), Manny Mota (Dominican), Harvey Kuenn (white American), and Mike McCormick (white American). For the *Baltimore Afro-American* sportswriter Sam Lacy, the 1962 squad was "still reaping a harvest from their employment of Alex Pompez ten years ago"—he credited the Cuban-American for discovery of all the team's "colored" players and proclaimed that he had "as keen a knowledge of baseball talent as anyone in the game."[25] But the squad did not obtain the World Series title, losing a classic seven-game series that ended with a leaping Yankees second baseman Bobby Richardson snaring a bases-loaded line drive struck by Willie McCovey; a foot in either direction, the Giants would have claimed the championship.

Dark thought the root of the Giants' failure to accomplish their ultimate goal lay partly in the team's culturally diverse roster. His approach to this problem varied: he imposed a ban on players speaking Spanish in the clubhouse, in the dugout, or on the field; he attempted to motivate his players with traditional manager's tactics such as flipping over the clubhouse table with the postgame spread; he spoke directly with his players, *hombre* to *hombre*. The underlying issues seemingly came out in a 1964 interview with *New York Newsday*, an interview Dark later alleged misquoted him. *Newsday* sportswriter Stan Isaacs quoted the Giants manager's sentiments on the impact of race and cultural difference on his team's chemistry, players' individual performances, and his squad's overall success: "We have trouble because we have so many Spanish-speaking and Negro players on this team. They are just not able to perform up to the white ball players when it comes to mental alertness. You can't make most Negro and Spanish players have the pride in their team that you get from white players."[26]

Published in the days before the Giants visited New York for a series against the Mets, the comments sparked a firestorm within the New York media and the black press. Copies of the offending *Newsday* article were placed by an unidentified individual in the lockers of the Giants' Latino and black players prior to the team's arrival. Once at Shea Stadium, Dark held a news conference in the visiting manager's office; this followed a meeting with Commissioner Ford Frick earlier that day. At the tense press gathering, with Isaacs in attendance, Dark "denied vigorously the views attributed to him," wrote *The New York Times*'s Leonard Koppett. The comments attributed to Dark nonetheless prompted calls for Stoneham to fire Dark. The Giants owner refused. Instead, he gave his manager a vote of confidence, after two days of silence, insisting "Alvin was misquoted in some cases, and in some cases the writer elaborated on what he [Dark] did say."[27]

Black sportswriters were not surprised at the controversy; Dark had a spotty record at best on racial matters. The *Pittsburgh Courier* columnist Wendell Smith remained unconvinced Dark had been misquoted. Smith found one part of the Giants manager's defense particularly unconvincing: Dark accusing Isaacs of taking it for "granted I said those things because I am a Southerner and they are Negroes" and his referring to "the six Negro and Spanish speaking players" on the Giants roster as evidence of his lack of derogatory views toward blacks or Latinos. Smith knew, as did others, that these players (Mays, Cepeda, McCovey, Marichal, Felipe Alou, and José Pagán) represented a vital part of the team's core and had joined the Giants before Dark was named manager. Smith instead pointed to comments Dark had reportedly made when asked about civil rights and racial discrimination as evidence that Dark was a less-than-forward-thinking man and surely not a friend of "the Negroes." In speaking about the ongoing civil rights movement, Dark opined: "I think Negroes are pushing too hard. I think they are rushing things." For Smith and others, such as the *Los Angeles Sentinel* scribe Brad Pye, Dark's statement, which appeared in a version of Jackie Robinson's *Baseball Has Done It*, "branded" him as someone entirely capable of uttering the words that Isaacs quoted in *Newsday*. Even Jackie Robinson offered his opinion, writing in the days after Isaac's article appeared that he was "not too surprised that Dark has put himself on the spot as a result of his having expressed patronizing opinions about Negro and Latin American ballplayers." While the Dodgers great hesitated to label Dark as "either deliberately biased or bigoted," he acknowledged that Dark had openly told him "things that amazed me as to their patronizing tone."[28]

Dark's managerial style arguably presented the biggest hurdle to a fully functional team dynamic during his tempestuous four-season managerial stint. However, contrary to what many assumed at the time, it was not Dark's relationship with the team's southern-born black players, including Willie Mays and Willie McCovey, that would determine the team's ultimate ability to realize its championship aspirations, but rather how he related to the Giants' Latino players.

Dark's policies and actions as manager constantly antagonized the team's Latino contingent, who in actuality constituted the majority of the team's "colored" players. The rookie manager attempted to address the team's diversity at his first spring training by changing the locker assignments in the Giants clubhouse to inspire more intermingling among the team's white, black, and Latino players. The players grumbled. Dark also instituted an English-only policy that spring— another misstep. Although his team had eleven Latinos at its spring training camp and its starting lineup for much of the regular season would be over half Latino, the manager posted a sign that said SPEAK ENGLISH, YOU'RE IN AMERICA.[29] The English-only policy infuriated Orlando Cepeda, who confronted Dark: "Listen, I'm Puerto Rican and I'm proud of my language. I would feel foolish if I talked to Pagán in English . . . First of all, we won't be able to communicate because we don't speak [English] that well, and secondly, I'm Puerto Rican and I'm going to speak my language." The edict against speaking Spanish also placed the Alou brothers in an odd position, forbidden to talk to each other in their native tongue. What Dark's policy did do was protect the feelings of his English-speaking players, white and black. That is the rationale Felipe Alou and Cepeda saw in their manager's policy. "They feel that the moment we begin speaking in Spanish that we are talking about them. This is not so," Alou declared. Cepeda took the policy personally: "He treated me like a child. I am a human being, whether I am blue or black or white or green. Dark did not respect our differences."[30]

Alvin Dark's inability to master managing a thoroughly integrated squad contributed to his being fired immediately following the 1964 season. Horace Stoneham's decision to replace him with Herman Franks pleased Orlando Cepeda; Franks had managerial experience in Puerto Rico's winter league, meaning he had already dealt with a diverse, multicultural locker room. The hire also meant the Giants' top brass better understood that the handling of the team's clubhouse dynamics mattered, giving careful attention to the balance of talent and psyche of those on its big-league roster. However, the dismantling of the team's roster had already begun. The Giants club that lost the 1962 World Series in dramatic fashion had included three Latino everyday starters; all three would be traded away. The strongest Latino voice, Felipe Alou, was sent packing to the Milwaukee Braves in 1964. The next year José Pagán was shipped off to Pittsburgh. A season later Cepeda was sent to St. Louis; the Cardinals would win the 1967 World Series. The lone Latino standout from the 1962 World Series team to remain with the Giants was the Dominican pitching ace Juan Marichal.

Fade into the Shadows

Politics had intervened in the work of Pompez in the early 1960s. The end of U.S.-Cuban diplomatic relations cut off the main source of foreign talent for the major leagues. Organizations shifted their scouting focus in Latin America, first to Puerto Rico in the mid-1960s; then by the late 1970s many moved to combing the sugarcane fields of the Dominican Republic, and in the early 1980s a few, led by the Houston Astros, began to scout Venezuela intensely. By the 1990s the Dominican Republic would claim the title Cuba once held as the top producer of foreign-born talent to the majors.[31]

Notably, the flow of Dominican talent into organized baseball started in the mid-1950s after Pompez hired Horacio Martínez. The two would sign the first wave of Dominicans to enter the minors and to star in the majors. But by the time Sammy Sosa was launching tape-measure home runs and Pedro Martínez (no relation) was lancing knee-buckling curves and stupor-inducing changeups from the mound in the 1990s, Pompez and Martínez were largely forgotten figures in the United States. The Negro leagues from whence the two came to so impact organized baseball after integration had faded into the far recesses of the minds of the sporting public. Negro leaguers who had played for Pompez's Cuban Stars or New York Cubans had likewise retired to the shadows, where they led quiet lives as school security guards, hospital workers, or machinists. Martínez was an exception, spending the rest of his years involved in baseball, coaching in the Dominican amateur and professional levels, and scouting for the Giants, for whom he remained on the payroll until his death in 1993. Rodolfo Fernández, Rafael Noble, and Armando Vásquez all would settle in New York City, their former baseball exploits unknown to most who interacted with them. Fellow workers at St. Luke's Hospital did not know that a former

Negro-league pitcher labored among them; most just knew "Rudy" as a sweet elder, always willing to help his coworkers. The closest of "Ray" Noble's neighbors knew him as a bear of a man, strong and hardworking; little did they know he had participated in the championship series of the Negro leagues, the major leagues, and the Caribbean. Most who filed through the doors at the intermediate school in Manhattan where Vásquez worked were surprised to learn that the vigilant security guard working the front door once occupied a different post, anchored at first base to receive throws from a young shortstop, Henry Aaron. It would be Alex Pompez who would enjoy another moment in the baseball spotlight when he was drafted to participate in the National Baseball Hall of Fame's first effort to honor the legacy of the Negro leagues. That service would again seat him at a table where those gathered exercised the power to determine the fate of baseball players. Over the span of twenty-five years, he had gone from a Negro-league owners' table, where those gathered were pondering how to deal with the new reality of baseball integration, to one convened to determine access to baseball's Valhalla.

10

INTO THE SHADOWS

The truth of the matter is that, were it not for Pompez,
American baseball would not now have the large number of
black Latin American players presently on the major league
rosters.   —Sam Lacy, 1975

"I'm a very lucky guy to have been able to wear a baseball uniform. I'm only sorry that many of the great Negro players didn't have this chance. I hope some day there will be plaques for Satchel Paige and others who have done so much for baseball." Such recognition, the speaker continued, would serve "as a symbol of the great Negro players that are not here only because they were not given a chance." No one expected Ted Williams to utter these words during his acceptance speech at the 1966 Hall of Fame induction ceremony.[1] The stance he took that day was fully within character for the man who had served two wartime military tours during his big-league career. He did not mince words or suffer fools; he spoke what he believed. The figurative tipping of his cap to the "great Negro players" in the speech by the Red Sox great, known for his reluctance to do so for adoring Boston fans during his playing career, surprised the estimated crowd of seven thousand gathered on the Hall's grounds that late July afternoon. Indeed, rather than bask in the glory of his induction, Williams chose to expose one of baseball's lingering shames and how those forced to play in the shadows had yet to receive their due from the baseball establishment.

The Hall of Fame lacked any presentation of the Negro leagues or of the sordid tale of organized baseball's color line put into place by a gentleman's agreement to bar all blacks and virtually all Latinos from the late 1880s until Jackie Robinson's 1947 arrival. Williams's induction speech made clear that truly honoring baseball's history involved more than recognition of the great black players who entered the majors after integration occurred, starting with Jackie Robinson. His declaration that those who had played in the Negro leagues deserved recognition made Williams the first insider to call out the Hall of Fame and the Baseball Writers Association of America (BBWAA) for their failure to acknowledge Negro-league greats. This lack of acknowledgment was not the product of sheer ignorance; rather, it was rooted in choices made by human actors; decisions to exclude and to neglect to tell the full story. A number of major-league greats already enshrined in the Hall, such as Bob Feller and Dizzy Dean, had barnstormed against Negro leaguers during baseball's Jim Crow era. A number of major leaguers had personally battled Satchel Paige's lances from the pitcher's mound on barnstorming tours and in Latin American leagues. They had stood on the field as Josh Gibson strode into the batter's box or watched in awe when the fleet-footed Cool Papa Bell ran the bases. And they had also faced Cuban greats such as Martín Dihigo and Luis Tiant in their tours through the Caribbean. Even Jackie Robinson, veteran of a single season in the Negro leagues but of several barnstorming tours, had not made such a bold declaration as to call for the Hall to honor Negro-league greats alongside major leaguers when he was inducted four years prior to Ted Williams.

Williams's call for acknowledgment spurred formal recognition of Negro-league greats and of the story of segregation. The Hall of Fame initiated a process of addressing organized baseball's daunting legacy of segregation, and it is here that the story of Pompez intersects once more with the larger story of baseball, race, and American history. The former numbers king completed his transformation from once-scorned outsider to an insider valued for his knowledge of Negro-league baseball. That Major League Baseball commissioner Bowie Kuhn would select him to participate on this blue ribbon committee attested to his well-regarded reputation within professional baseball circles. A man redeemed from his days as a numbers king would participate in the redemption of the greats from the circuit that had been disparaged as being like a racket.

The Hall Opens

Hall of Fame and major-league officials debated a series of proposals about how to properly recognize Negro-league greats. A plan for a separate gallery dedicated to black baseball and its stars was an early favorite. Black sportswriters voiced concerns that the plan would re-create the racial divide by segregating Negro-league greats from the plaque gallery where all the enshrined major leaguers resided: No separate but equal gallery, they insisted.

The black press's campaign to have Negro leaguers honored in the Hall predated Jackie Robinson's 1957 retirement and his 1962 induction. Black journalists pointed to the unique situation of Negro leaguers and baseball's integration pioneers. In a January 1953 column, Joe Bostic noted that the careers of a number of top black players bridged baseball's two racial eras. Those, like Sam Jethroe and Monte Irvin, who had performed at their peak in the Negro leagues had "little chance" to gain election into the Hall as eligibility rules stood. Only major-league players were eligible for inclusion on the election ballot for BBWAA voters. Thus those who had their glory days in the Negro leagues were all ineligible, from the slugging Josh Gibson to the versatile Martín Dihigo, as were pitching aces Smokey Joe Williams and José Méndez. Until a new apparatus was created, those like Satchel Paige who spent the majority of their careers in the Negro leagues but enjoyed a few seasons in the majors would likewise fall short of the criteria for consideration.[2] The lack of progress in the revision of eligibility criteria after Ted Williams's 1966 speech frustrated a cadre of black sportswriters. In December 1970, *Chicago Defender* writer Lee Jenkins bemoaned that the BBWAA had made little advancement in the two years since it approved a resolution that recommended a section dedicated to the Negro leagues in the Hall. Instead, that resolution languished in the "talking stage."[3]

Finally, on February 3, 1971, Commissioner Bowie Kuhn announced a process for election of Negro-league greats into the Hall of Fame. "A

ten-man committee composed of eight Negroes and two white men
will name one player a year from the days before 1947," *The New York
Times* reported. The committee's charge was to vote on candidates
worthy of enshrinement from among those who had played ten or
more years in the Negro leagues prior to 1947. The committee, whose
composition was later criticized for being overly slanted toward Eastern representation, would convene once a year: eight votes out of the
ten committee members would be required to qualify for induction.
Those elected would enter the Hall of Fame "as part of a new exhibit
commemorating the contributions of the Negro leagues to baseball,"
their plaques to be kept separate from the 117 major leaguers inducted
over the previous thirty-three years. Progress came in spurts: a door
to the museum had been opened, but entry to the main gallery was still
being denied.

Commissioner Kuhn and Hall of Fame president Paul Kerr were
joined at the February 3 press conference by the former Negro leaguer
and major-league standout Monte Irvin (then employed as special assistant to the commissioner), sportswriter Sam Lacy, and former Negro-
league owners Eddie Gottlieb and Alex Pompez. Questions hurled by
journalists made those gathered at the dais squirm. Why a different
section of the museum from the major leaguers for the old Negro-
league stars? the reporters asked. "The Hall of Fame is not segregated," the commissioner responded. "In addition to being a brick
building, it's a state of mind." That answer was the type of spin that
would make most politicians and their handlers proud. Monte Irvin
stepped in to take a hack at the query. "I can't see any adverse reaction
at all," Irvin stated. "The only hesitation I've met was in substantiating
the records of the old Negro league players. That's why the committee
is made up of players, writers, and owners who were familiar with
them." Another scribe questioned the people on the dais whether
those elected would actually be Hall of Famers. Was this a compromise? inquired another. "I wouldn't call it a compromise," Kuhn responded to the query about the special category created to allow Negro
leaguers into the Hall. "The rules of the Hall of Fame are very strict,"
he reiterated, "and through no fault of their own these stars of the Negro leagues didn't have major league exposure." Kuhn expanded on his
answer: "The purpose here is to recognize the great contributions

made by the Negro leagues and I think the stars should be identified and recognized by the public." Eddie Gottlieb then elaborated on the standard: "The players who would be recognized would have been of major league caliber if there had been no color line at the time they were playing."[4]

Reactions to the commissioner's announcement on the Hall of Fame were mixed. Certain quarters rejoiced: at long last Satchel, Josh, Cool Papa, and others would have a chance to be recognized in the Hall. *Los Angeles Times* writer Charles Maher spoke for many in wondering why they would be placed in a separate section. "It's a commendable gesture," Maher wrote, "but it would have been better, it seems here, if the committee had been empowered to make players such as Gibson and Paige full-fledged members of the Hall of Fame instead of putting them in a 'special category.' "[5]

In naming Pompez to this blue-ribbon committee, Commissioner Kuhn granted the onetime Harlem numbers king access to organized baseball's inner sanctum, a space where individuals possessed the ability to decide which greats were to be forever memorialized in the pastime's most hallowed ground. Later asked about the inclusion of Pompez on the committee, the retired baseball commissioner explained that he had surveyed a number of baseball insiders about individuals who possessed knowledge about the Negro leagues: "Alex Pompez was one of the names nearly everyone mentioned." Did the commissioner know about Pompez's days as a numbers king? "No. I knew nothing of that," he replied. However, his informants did express high regard for Pompez's decades of work with the San Francisco Giants, his temperament, and his knowledge of Negro-league baseball, which few living sources could match.[6]

On February 9, 1971, the full committee—which also included Negro-league official Frank Forbes, sportswriter Wendell Smith, retired Negro leaguers Judy Johnson and Roy Campanella, along with former major leaguer Eppie Barnes—announced its unanimous choice: Satchel Paige. The controversy over a separate section for Negro leaguers had yet to be resolved. "I'm proud to be in wherever they put me in the Hall of Fame," Paige told reporters after receiving word of his election.[7] *Chicago Defender* writer "Doc" Young was more circumspect about the "special section." "It sounded like the back seat of a bus,

separate dining rooms, water fountains marked 'white' and 'colored,'"
Young offered. Jesse Peters from *The Pittsburgh Courier* was blunt,
calling the separate section "an insult to all of Black America." Seven
years after the Civil Rights Act had been signed into law and seventeen
years after the *Brown v. Board of Education* decision, the plan was a
stark reminder that inclusion still did not mean equality.[8] The protest
was heard. In early July the Hall of Fame and the commissioner announced a reversal in their plan: the plaques of Satchel Paige and other
Negro leaguers inducted would not be segregated; baseball's most hallowed space would not be the last stand of Jim Crow.[9]

Pomp and Circumstances

From 1971 until his death in March 1974, Pompez participated on the
Hall of Fame's special Negro-leagues committee. During those three
years black baseball's greatest pitching star was joined in the Hall by
Josh Gibson and Buck Leonard (1972), Monte Irvin (1973), and James
"Cool Papa" Bell (1974). For Pompez, these were years of declining
health. A stroke had slowed him down, limiting his travels beyond
New York City. "I am feelong [*sic*] much better but not quite as good as
I would like to be," he wrote to Giants scouting department secretary
Jack Schwarz in July 1972. "I am able to get about fairly good and my
speech is only slightly improved." His failing health did not prevent
him from seeing Monte Irvin, the man he had recommended to the
Giants in 1948 and who had barnstormed on the Black All-Stars, enshrined in 1973.

Pompez cast one final vote in the 1974 deliberations, when Cool
Papa Bell was elected. The Cuban-American would not be in Cooperstown to personally witness Bell's induction that summer. Shortly after
the committee's 1974 gathering, his health took a decidedly bad turn.
On Thursday, March 14, he succumbed to complications due to stroke
at St. John's Hospital in Queens; he was survived by his wife, Ruth Seldon Pompez. The Frank E. Campbell Funeral Home at Eighty-first
Street and Madison Avenue in Manhattan hosted the visitation the
following Monday and Tuesday. Over the years Campbell Funeral
Home would develop into a prime choice for hosting funeral services

of celebrities in entertainment and politics: among those whose services were held there were Judy Garland, Jacqueline Kennedy Onassis, and New York Yankee Billy Martin, as well as Latino musical legends Hector Lavoe, Tito Puente, and Celia Cruz. Pompez's funeral service was held March 20; he was interred in the family plot he had purchased in 1931 at Woodlawn Cemetery alongside his sister Leonora, brother-in-law Pedro Rodríguez, and younger brother Oscar.[10]

Obituaries celebrated Pompez's baseball accomplishments; few recalled his reign as a Harlem numbers king. Instead he was remembered as the man who had scouted twenty-five years for the Giants and who had previously owned a Negro-league team. *The New York Times* highlighted his service on the Hall of Fame's special committee and observed that his contribution to the Giants organization came "in the early days of integration on the diamond" and listed notable players he had directly signed or had aided the Giants in acquiring: the three Alou brothers, Juan Marichal, Manny Mota, Tito Fuentes, José Cardenal, Orlando Cepeda, José Págan, Hank Thompson, Monte Irvin, Willie Mays, and Reubén Gómez. The *Sporting News* obituary, which wrongfully listed Pompez's first name as Alessandro, acknowledged that his scouting work had started in his Negro-league days, including Orestes Miñoso along with Willie McCovey, Tony Taylor, and Marshall Bridges in their list. His personality as much as his deft ability as a talent evaluator drove his success, the obituary claimed, describing him as "affable and soft-spoken" and "a convincing talker" able to persuade prospects to sign with the Giants. Sam Lacy illumined a long view, cast from the Negro leagues to the present, stating that the majors owed much to Pompez for the prominence and presence of black Latin American players in its ranks. The *Amsterdam News* sportswriter Les Matthews offered a Harlem insider's perspective, informing readers that the stretch from 110th Street to 116th Street on Lenox Avenue that had once been labeled "Pompez Boulevard" served as the base of operations for his New York Cubans and other businesses for decades. This and his willingness to invest a great deal of his own money to field a competitive Negro-league team made him "a man of the street" in Matthews's estimation.[11]

For much of his redemptive path from Harlem numbers king operating outside the law to respected insider within America's pastime,

Pompez was accompanied by his second wife, Ruth Seldon. Married in 1934, she was there when he reached the apex of Harlem's numbers scene. She stayed behind in their 409 Edgecombe Avenue apartment when he fled Tom Dewey's 1937 indictment, awaiting his return. She stood by his side when he testified as state's evidence in the two Hines trials and as he rebuilt his Negro-league baseball operations in the years following. Ruth had lived the heights and the depths: the coup of bringing Babe Ruth to Dyckman Oval (1935) and the triumph of winning the Negro League World Series championship (1947) as well as the loss of Dyckman (1937), the Negro National League's collapse (1948), and the disbanding of the New York Cubans (1950).

The presence of Senator Edward Brooke cast an official air of respectability over the proceedings at the Campbell Funeral Home. "A funny, good-natured, kind man," the senator recalled in his 2007 memoir, "everyone liked Uncle Alex." Knowledge of Uncle Alex's involvement in the numbers racket did not deter Brooke's parents from sending him and his older sister Helene to Harlem to spend part of their summers with Aunt Ruth and Uncle Alex. These were the Depression days, but not for Pompez, who was riding high atop Harlem's numbers scene out of the clutches of Dutch Schultz and not yet under the intense scrutiny of Tom Dewey. Uncle Alex and Aunt Ruth doted on their nephew and niece. They took the pair on vacations down to the Jersey shore, where they stayed in exclusive resorts. Aunt Ruth bought Helene expensive dresses and fashionable clothes for Edward. The extravagance extended to Uncle Alex's giving him a twenty-dollar bill for running an errand. Uncle Alex and Aunt Ruth did not try to hide the proceeds from the numbers operations from their nephew but rather ostentatiously counted their money, Brooke recalled. The man who lay at the front of the Campbell Funeral Home was no violent mobster to the standing senator: it was Uncle Alex, the person who loved his Aunt Ruth and who had lavished him and his sister with affection. Even to that point, Senator Brooke confessed, he had yet to "fully appreciate his saga" as a Harlem numbers king and sports impresario who had to undertake an incredible personal makeover to gain respectable standing in the world of professional baseball.[12]

Ruth continued to reside at the brick ranch home they had bought on Forty-fourth Avenue in Woodside, Queens, until Senator Brooke decided to bring his aunt south to Tiber Island, a neighborhood in southwest Washington, D.C. Once she was there, the senator, family members, and friends looked in on Ruth. Among these friends was the granddaughter of Juan and Onelia Valdes, longtime family friend of the Pompez's. The two families had known each other since their days in Key West and Tampa in the early twentieth century. Juan Valdes had migrated from Ybor City to Harlem in 1931 hoping to find work as a cigar maker. He and his wife, Onelia, established their home in the Little Ybor section at 15 West 107th Street, in the same building as Rodolfo and Matilda Fernández and a few blocks south of one of Pompez's business offices. In Harlem, Valdes and Pompez struck up a personal friendship that lasted decades. Their families shared holiday visits; Pompez's players visited the Valdeses' home for some of Onelia's Cuban cooking. In the 1950s Juan and Alex vacationed together several times, including a Cuban excursion in 1955. Not surprisingly, those trips turned into working vacations, if one counted catching a few baseball games while Alex assessed local talent and checked in on former players as work. The Valdes family members maintained the bonds of affinity after Alex's death; Ruth would spend the remainder of her days under the watchful eyes of family and friends, including the Valdeses' granddaughter, Lesley Rankin-Hill Valdes, then an anthropology professor at Federated College in the District. Ruth died in July 1985 at the age of eighty-five; she was laid to rest next to Alex in the Pompez family plot in Woodlawn Cemetery.[13]

Baseball had been a constant in Senator Brooke's departed uncle's life. As a teenager Brooke had visited Harlem while his uncle operated Dyckman Oval as Harlem's premier sporting center and his New York Cubans were playing to acclaim as "Harlem's Own." The senator himself got involved in baseball about a year after his Uncle Alex died. Judge Buddy Schreiber, one of Brooke's clerks while he was Massachusetts attorney general, contacted the senator's office seeking for his intervention on behalf of a friend, the Boston Red Sox pitcher Luis Tiant. Schreiber inquired whether Senator Brooke could pull some political strings and arrange a visit for Tiant's parents from their native Cuba. The Cuban ace had enjoyed quite a renaissance in Boston while his parents languished in Cuba. However, the pitcher's Boston friends worried that his big-league career had entered its decline: wait too long and his parents would never get the joy of watching their son perform as a major leaguer. Tiant had not spent any time with his parents since 1960 except for a weeklong visit with his mother in Mexico City in 1968. The last time the baseball public had seen Lefty Tiant in the States was in 1947, celebrating with his New York Cubans teammates their Negro League World Series triumph.

Early in 1975, Senator George McGovern, a Democrat representing South Dakota, sensed a possibility for reopening U.S.-Cuban relations and planned an unofficial visit to Cuba to see Fidel Castro. Hearing of his Senate colleague's impending Cuban visit, Senator Brooke decided to intercede on his constituent's behalf and pen a personal letter to Fidel Castro and to have McGovern personally deliver it to the Cuban leader. Brooke's letter opened expressing a hope for normalization of relations; the senator then turned to his letter's central purpose. "My specific interest in writing you is to seek your assistance on a matter of deep concern to myself and one of my constituents, Mr. Luis Tiant. . . . He has not had the chance to spend any significant time with [his parents] for many years. Naturally, he has a great desire to do so," Brooke continued, after explaining Tiant's circumstances. The senator noted that the younger Tiant's career was "in its latter years" and that "he is hopeful that his parents will be able to visit him during this current baseball season."[14]

Arriving on the island in May, Senator McGovern's first encounter with the Cuban leader was an impromptu one. Castro appeared after having attended a *liga nacional* playoff game—an opportune moment for McGovern to pass Brooke's letter to Castro. The Cuban leader read the letter and told McGovern he would mull the matter over. Castro was in his true form at their next encounter, hosting a marathon twelve-hour meeting with the senator. But the good news came early: the visas for Tiant's parents to visit their son in the States would be granted; moreover, they could stay as long as they liked.

They arrived in Boston to much fanfare in late August. Lefty Tiant would finally witness his son as a major leaguer, observe his son's contorting windup, his glance toward the outfield or toward the sky before whirling to deliver the ball to the plate. Their son had amazed the Red Sox faithful that season with his guile and determination on the mound. However, as the summer began to turn into fall, Tiant had seemingly lost whatever zip he had left on his fastball. He then proceeded to get batters out on his pitching know-how and a vast collection of junk pitches: the son had become the right-handed reincarnation of the father. Everyone rejoiced and quite a few wept openly at the on-field ceremony before the August 26 game, when Lefty Tiant stood on the Fenway Park mound to throw the first pitch. There stood the two Luis Tiants, reunited on the diamond, the dream deferred of the father realized by the son, in the park where Jackie Robinson had had a sham tryout over three decades earlier. The lanky lefty wound up as the crowd buzzed "Loo-ie, Loo-ie." He hurled the sphere to the Red Sox catcher as the crowd roared. Senator Brooke's intervention had made it happen. Uncle Alex would certainly have been proud.[15]

Buoyed by the emotional reunion of the Tiants, Boston enjoyed a magical run to claim the American League pennant and face the Cincinnati Reds in the 1975 World Series. Lefty Tiant watched once more the mastery of his son against the powerful and heavily favored Reds. The younger Tiant won two games and almost willed the Red Sox to the series victory. As this dramatic scene played out, the *Baltimore Afro-American* writer Sam Lacy reminded his readers of Alex Pompez's role in this storyline. "Tiant's presence in the 1975 World Series is welcomed here mainly because it produces nostalgia," Lacy wrote. "The nostalgia involves [Tiant's] father, who watched his son as he gained hero status in the waning days of the campaign and in the playoffs." Lacy connected the multiple storylines: that of the father and the son, the Negro leagues and the current World Series. "Pompez paved the way for the Tiants—senior and junior—and countless others."[16]

Legacy Like No Other

Pompez's impact on U.S. professional baseball continued to manifest itself on the diamond and in the Hall of Fame. Three years after his death, the greatest player from the land of his father, Martín Dihigo, entered the Hall of Fame as part of the 1977 induction class. Three major leaguers whom he had signed—Juan Marichal (1983), Willie McCovey (1986), and Orlando Cepeda (1999)—also were enshrined in the Hall of Fame over the next two decades.

Pompez's legacy in America's game was more than as a scout, however. He made the transition from baseball's Jim Crow era into its integrated era more successfully than any other Negro-league team official. Horace Stoneham and the Giants organization provided him a new context in which to operate. For the Giants, he was a conduit to a world of which the organization had little direct knowledge. And the Giants gave Pompez wide rein to do his scouting in Latin America, which he did by extending his talent search to the Bahamas, Costa Rica, and other previously untapped lands.

The Giants' decision to hire Pompez as a scout represented another dimension of baseball integration. In the 1950s, no other major-league organization had a bilingual, U.S.-born Latino in charge of scouting Latin America; this put the Giants at a competitive advantage in the procurement of Latin American talent. His experience in the Negro leagues, moreover, enabled the Giants to compete in acquiring the very best the Negro leagues had to offer. Monte Irvin, Willie Mays, and Hank Thompson were the first fruits of his work; Orlando Cepeda, Felipe Alou, Juan Marichal, and Willie McCovey were the finer picks of the second harvest. This, in conjunction with his work as a Negro-league team owner, cements Pompez's place as the most significant importer of Latino talent into U.S. professional baseball, particularly in terms of quality.

There was no one quite like Pompez in baseball—not in the States, not in the Caribbean. As he demonstrated in his Negro-league days while operating the Cuban Stars and New York Cubans, he maneuvered between the English- and Spanish-speaking worlds with great facility. Joe Cambria could not move so easily between these two worlds. And despite the "Papa Joe" moniker that Cubans granted Cambria, the professional associate and friend of Pompez was from a different world. The son of Italian immigrants gained his love of baseball in the States; it was learned, not a cultural inheritance passed down from his elders. But that was what baseball was in Pompez's life, something that island-born Cubans and their U.S.-born descendants shared in common. Baseball had given his forebears a context in which to struggle for self-identity and, yes, national independence; for him the game had been a refuge, the place where he ultimately found redemption.

The inability of other major-league organizations to replicate the approach Pompez and the Giants had created came at a tragically steep and wasteful price, limiting the fullest development of Latino talent in the 1950s and 1960s. Baseball has often celebrated the success stories of Roberto Clemente, Cepeda, Marichal, and the Alou brothers. Those players were survivors of a flawed structure within organized baseball, one that did not fully account for the culture differences of foreign-born Latinos. Felipe Alou published an article in *Sport*, "Latin Ballplayers Need a Bill of Rights," in November 1963 that outlined the grievances of Latinos. Written from the perspective of having experienced the highs and lows of how league and team officials dealt with difference, Alou's article suggested reforms that were born out of seeing its affirmative possibilities in the work of Pompez and Horacio Martínez—and its polar opposite: the cultural clashes of the Latino Giants with manager Alvin Dark.

Attention to this element of difference in the baseball world was part of what had always made Pompez unique: he was black and Latino. Moreover, he had lived what it meant to be seen as foreign in both the United States and Cuba. He was not betwixt and between, he was both: Latino and American, black and Latino. His experience provided him a reservoir of insight into how to survive in professional baseball and in a society that was once openly divided along racial lines but was much more subtly so as he headed into his later years.

The key to his success was an ability to adapt to new situations by using the entirety of his background. His affable and caring personality made him a favorite; he took care of his current and former players and his friends. And as the network of players, journalists, and local contacts made evident, they likewise took care of him. These relationships stretched back to his days operating in the Negro leagues. That was evident when Dave García, a former Giants farmhand hired to scout for the organization, tagged along to scout the Cuban winter league in 1959 shortly after Fidel Castro's takeover. The pair made several unannounced visits, one to an aging Miguel Angel González, a longtime big leaguer and third base coach for the St. Louis Cardinals, and another to the home of Martín Dihigo.[17] The Cubans had remained part of Pompez's network that had offered formal and informal assessments of prospects; they had also remained among the friends he regularly checked in on to see their well-being. A similar lasting relationship occurred with Horacio Martínez, whom Pompez had hired as a bird-dog scout in the Dominican Republic and who evolved with the

Giants into a full-fledged scout who ultimately became the organization's key figure internationally after Pompez's 1974 death. His relationship with Gil Garrido, a reserve New York Cubans infielder in the mid-1940s, paid dividends twice over: Garrido helped arrange tour stops in Panama for the Black All-Stars in 1957, and three years later Pompez signed his son, Gil Jr., for the Giants.

Stateside, a similar pattern of fostering friendships and professional relationships was established. First, his Negro-league connections enabled him to influence the Giants' acquisition of talented players Monte Irvin, Willie Mays, and Hank Thompson, among others. Then there were acquaintances that developed from decades as a Negro-league owner and as an organizer of barnstorming tours. Joe Cambria was the most significant such professional associate; the two met in the early 1930s as fellow owners in the Negro leagues and would collaborate on a number of signings that got several racially ambiguous Cubans into organized baseball before the color line's official end. There were others he met along the way, friends of his players and family relatives. Such was Jesse Thomas, the brother of former New York Cubans first baseman Showboat Thomas, who convinced Pompez to try out a tall, lanky sixteen-year-old, Willie McCovey. McCovey linked the stories of Thomas, Pompez, and Jackie Robinson in his 1986 Hall of Fame induction speech, thanking them each for their roles in helping him realize his big-league dream. "There are some other people I can't help but to remember fondly on this day," McCovey stated. "I am thinking of Jackie Robinson, who broke the color line and made our dreams of becoming a major leaguer a reality . . . I am thinking of Jesse Thomas, a playground director in Mobile who arranged a tryout in front of the Giants scouts down in Melbourne. And the late scout Alex Pompez and Mr. Jack Schwarz, who together signed me to my first contract."[18]

Indeed, the network Pompez built through the friendships and relationships he fostered over his decades in the game was instrumental in his changing the face of modern baseball. Some scouting experts and baseball insiders contest the description of Pompez as a "shrewd" talent evaluator, as his Hall of Fame plaque reads. Their criticism hinges on the finer points of what a baseball scout traditionally does in assessing talent. "There are different skill levels in being able to spot a player," observes the baseball historian John Klima, also an experienced scout. A scout takes pride in being able to "walk up to 100 players he had never seen before, pick one, and say, that's the big leaguer."[19] This exceptional ability to locate the one prospect out of the thousands of players they observe and to stake their reputation on that claim is what scouts take the ultimate pride in and what a few insist Pompez lacked—the ability to pull the sparkling needle (prospect) out of the (talent) haystack. To them, he was a master network builder who could bring them hay.

The critique of Pompez's scouting ability is partly semantics: it is the degree of his ability to discern the finest talent, rather than whether he could discern it or not, that is debated among the more knowledge-able talent evaluators. That debate involves differentiating between the process of evaluating amateur talent in the United States, where scouts for major-league organizations first strictly evaluated white tal-ent and then, after baseball's color line fell, any ballplayer, versus the task of finding talent in Latin America's amateur and professional ranks who might handle the transition to professional baseball in the States, first in the Negro leagues and then as part of baseball's generation of integration pioneers. It was in the latter context that Pompez operated, needing to fill the rosters of his Cuban Stars and then New York Cu-bans teams during his Negro-league days and later acquiring black and Latino prospects for the Giants organization.

The on-field success and the financial viability of Pompez's baseball operations were dependent on Pompez's deciding which Latino players could make the grade in the black baseball circuit. And during his Cuban Stars days, when his finds failed to pan out or suffered serious injury during the Negro-league season, he would have to dip back into Cuba or elsewhere in Latin America to locate a replacement; his fellow Negro-league owners simply found new players stateside. And it was from 1916 into the late 1920s when Pompez showcased his ability to find stellar talent. Shut out by the likes of Abel Linares and Tinti Mo-lina from acquiring the most established talent in the Cuban profes-sional circuit, Pompez found a teenage Martín Dihigo, Alejandro Oms, and José María Fernández, among other talented Cubans. Dihigo and Oms would become stars in the Negro leagues. In Fernández, Pompez found a smart player to whom he could ultimately entrust the manage-rial reins of his New York Cubans franchise upon the numbers king's retiring from that racket in 1938 to dedicate himself to his various sporting endeavors.

Pompez's development as a talent evaluator while operating as an owner in the Negro leagues is indispensable to any assessment of his place among the game's best scouts. For certain, Negro-league owners relied on their network of contacts to point them in the right direction. Importantly, they also invested money into the finds that filled their team's roster. In this regard, Pompez put more at risk than scouts who were then working in organized baseball who staked their reputation on an individual's being a surefire prospect; Pompez risked his own money as a Negro-league owner, and too many failures damaged the viability of his baseball operations. And while the traditional Negro-league division of labor involved the team's manager making the decision as to who made the club after spring tryouts, Pompez spent about a decade filling that role before hiring Martín Dihigo as his player-manager in 1935 and then selecting José María Fernández as Dihigo's replacement in 1938.

The practices that Pompez used to secure prospects for the Giants from the Negro leagues and out of Latin America remained rooted in what he had done previously as a Negro-league owner. For Pompez, success in acquiring talent always involved investing in maintaining good relations with his contemporaries in black baseball, those such as Tom Hayes of the Birmingham Black Barons who were formerly fellow owners, or his former players, such as Horacio Martínez, with whom Pompez opened the Dominican talent pipeline into organized baseball. Significantly, Pompez did not discover the talent pipeline because of Martínez; the retired Negro-league shortstop was one of its initial products, having been signed by Pompez in 1933. And that is a vital part of Pompez's legacy as a talent evaluator and network builder; he opened the door of opportunity for Latinos and many blacks throughout the Caribbean, Latin America, and parts of the United States where others had yet to roam or lacked the ability to maneuver the cultural intricacies of race and discrimination.

Scarcely could Alex Pompez have imagined as he defended his reputation from a Mexico City jail cell in 1937 that his approach to operating in U.S. professional baseball would presage the changes that America's game would undergo in the late twentieth century. That day he was merely fighting for his reputation, hoping one day to again be free to operate in the game he loved. Even wilder still, he would not have divined a dream wherein his contribution to baseball would have landed him in a place like the Baseball Hall of Fame; no such place yet existed and the game was not even integrated. That day he was merely a man desperate to stay out of the hands of those who wielded more power or had access to more power in American society: former (higher) associates within the Schultz syndicate, Schultz's collaborators who operated on the legitimate side of the law, and the ever determined special prosecutor Tom Dewey, bent on ridding New York city of its racketeers.

Pompez's life story is more than the redemption song of a criminal mastermind, a recuperation narrative that unveils the flawed humanity of a criminal forged out of a violent urban culture typically depicted in Hollywood films about Harlem. Pomp and his circumstances were much more complicated than trite stereotypes. His life story illustrates the promise of America and its lived contradictions during the twentieth century, especially when it comes to how the color line influenced just about every aspect of American life: where one worked, lived, worshipped, and even played. His was a life that involved overcoming challenges of a racially divided profession and society as someone who was twice different, black and Latino. Rather than see this as necessitating a choice—whether to be black or Latino—he embraced both aspects of his identity to successfully fashion a path different from the one his contemporaries in the numbers and professional baseball had followed. As a result he was a trailblazer. His broad vision and transnational approach enabled him to pursue possibilities that contemporaries overlooked and to maneuver through racial and cultural terrain others dared not or could not navigate. Over a half century in professional baseball that spanned from black baseball's informal professional circuits through organized baseball's generation of integration pioneers, his work demonstrated that diversity truly mattered, not just on the playing field but also throughout the organization.

Latinos now represent organized baseball's largest minority population: over a quarter of all major leaguers and almost half of all minor leaguers are either foreign-born or U.S.-born Latinos. Moreover, the talent pipeline from the Dominican Republic, which Pompez first tapped into as a Negro-league owner in 1926 and later as a Giants scout, is more productive than ever. And it is no longer just on the field where they participate. At the start of the 2009 Major League Baseball season, the circuit featured a bilingual Mexican-American owner (Arturo Moreno, Los Angeles Angels), a bilingual, multicultural general manager (Omar Minaya, New York Mets) born in the Dominican Republic and raised partly in New York City, and a Venezuelan manager (Ozzie Guillen) who led the Chicago White Sox to the 2005 World Series championship.

The significance of Pompez's life story also moves beyond the baseball diamond. It provides insight into the experience of first-generation U.S.-born Latinos, a generation that directly encounters the quandary of growing up in a society different from that of their parents yet still dealing with matters of cultural maintenance and change. In Pompez's case, it was a story of dealing with the legacy established by his father's—and a generation's—fervent commitment to Cuban national independence, a commitment that left his family almost destitute and forced him to carve his own path. As a black Latino, he dealt with the racial and cultural cleavages that marked social interactions as much in the urban North as they did in the Jim Crow South, despite popularized notions of a melting pot, cultural pluralism, or multiculturalism. His experience gave substantive meaning to life in between two hyphens, Afro-Cuban-American. Equally important is how he carved a singularity of out that multiplicity of identity that unveils part of the promise of integration. Instead of seeing the hyphens as divisions, markers that separated his past and present, he forged an approach to life in the Americas that maximized his place as a bilingual, multicultural actor; that approach would benefit not only his numbers enterprise during the Depression but also his Negro-league franchise and later make him attractive to the Giants as someone who could aid their full entry into baseball's integrated era.

Pompez's success in brokering access for so many significant figures within baseball's generation of integration pioneers—Miñoso, Irvin, Cepeda, Felipe Alou, among others—attests to the importance of the inclusion of Latinos in off-the-field capacities. His attention to the particular issues that foreign-born Latinos encountered upon their entry is likewise instructive of the ways diversity mattered, then as now, on and off the playing field. The approach he undertook to scouting the Americas represented a consistent outlook on life in the Americas, one in which being bilingual and possessing the ability to comfortably move within multiple cultural settings represented the promise of the diverse societal mixture in the United States. This latter point is all the more relevant as U.S. society progressed in the early twenty-first century with Latinos as its majority minority and its youngest overall population. His success demonstrated that, rather than the transnational practices of Latinos having a deleterious effect on American culture, they offered a new means of more fully capitalizing on all available resources.

The terrain in which Pompez operated as a baseball entrepreneur was not limited or defined by nation-state boundaries. His migrations throughout the Americas as he searched for talent unveil a circuit that transcended national lines and that was multilingual, international, and culturally diverse. Being personally versed in the workings of multiple Latino cultures proved greatly beneficial to him as he attempted to convince players and, in some cases, their families to sign with his New York Cubans and, after 1950, with the Giants organization. In this sense, his travels geographically and culturally simulate those of Harlem's perhaps best-known black Latino, Arthur Schomburg. Both would hear time and again questions about whether they were black or Latino, when the fact that being both opened as many doors as it closed and proved a key ingredient to their individual outlook and success. In the case of the Afro–Puerto Rican Schomburg, his insistence on recognizing both dimensions to his identity—that he was black and Latino—drove his life's work in collecting published materials and ephemera that reconstituted the history of African-descended peoples and resulted in an irreplaceable archive of the African Diaspora. Schomburg's concept of the "Negro" people as a "nation in theory" spoke to the possibility of recasting the lines of affiliation among people of African descent within and beyond the Americas. This conceptualization did not place African-descended people within the dominion of a nation-state but rather positioned them as members of a transnational community where membership emanated from their shared ancestry and history of displacement to (and within) the Americas, as well as cultural practices that evolved from African origins.[20]

Whether Pompez ascribed to such a specific articulation of being black and Latino cannot be ascertained through the bits of evidence that reveal parts of his political ideology or openly offer his self-identification. Newspapers and sporting periodicals from throughout the Americas that document his works and the words of the players he signed represent the richest, most accessible archive available. But at minimum, what we can find enlightens how he was an actor who did not limit himself by the definitions others set as to his identity; in this way, he lived what José Martí had espoused in his vision for Cuba, *mas que blanco, mas que negro*, more than white, more than black. His wrinkle to this was that he lived his life as more than black and Latino, more than Cuban and American; he was all those and used this identification with both for his personal benefit and to impart that lesson to those whose lives he touched. It is in that life lesson that Pompez sought and ultimately claimed his redemption, even as he stood in the shadows.

NOTES

ACKNOWLEDGMENTS

INDEX

NOTES

PREFACE

1. *New York Times*, March 12, 2006, p. C13.
2. David Kindred, "O'Neil Injustice Must Be Rectified," *Lawrence Journal World*, March 9, 2006; transcript, *Countdown*, aired February 28, 2006.
3. Rufus Schatzberg, *Black Organized Crime in Harlem: A Social History* (New York: Garland Publishing, 1996), p. 115.
4. *San Jose Mercury News*, July 30, 2006; *San Francisco Chronicle*, July 30, 2006, p. C-6; *New York Daily News*, July 31, 2006; interview with Orlando Cepeda, July 2006, Cooperstown, NY.

PART I: RISING STAR

1. The Cuban Giants initiated a practice within the U.S. baseball circuit that associated Cuban with nonwhite racial identity, one which continued through the arrival of Linares's team of actual Cubans. *New York Freeman*, August 8, 1886. On the Cuban Giants' formation, see Sol White, *Sol White's History of Colored Baseball: With Other Documents on the Early Black Game* (Lincoln: University of Nebraska Press, 1995); Alvin Harlow, "Unrecognized Stars," *Esquire* (September 1938), p. 75; and Jerry Malloy, "The Birth of the Cuban Giants: The Origins of Black Professional Baseball," *Nine* 2:2 (Spring 1994), pp. 233–46. On interactions between African American and Cuban teams, see Lisa Brock and Bijan Bayne, "Not Just Black: African-Americans, Cubans, and Baseball," in *Between Race and Empire: African-Americans and Cubans Before the Cuban Revolution* (Philadelphia: Temple University Press, 1998), pp. 168–204.
2. Newspaper clipping, n.d., Luisin Rosario, "El Diamante Negro," Luis Alvelo Personal Collection (scrapbook), Caguas, Puerto Rico.
3. Ibid.

1. ROOTS AND ROUTES

1. Consuelo Stebbins, "The Insurgents of Key West and Expedition of 1895," *Florida Keys Sea Heritage Journal* 15:1 (Fall 2004): p. 11.

2. C. Neale Ronning, *Cubans and the Émigré Colony in Key West: Leadership and State Formation* (Westport, CT: Greenwood Publishing, 1990), pp. 43–45.
3. Gerald E. Poyo, "Cuban Revolutionaries and Monroe County Reconstruction Politics, 1868–1876," *Florida Historical Quarterly* 55: 4 (April 1977), p. 409.
4. Ancestry.com. *Philadelphia, 1789–1880 Naturalization Records* [database online]. Provo, UT: Generations Network, 2003. Original data: P. William Filby, ed. *Philadelphia Naturalization Records.* Detroit, MI: Gale Research, 1982.
5. Adrian Burgos, Jr., "Entering Cuba's Other Playing Field: Cuban Baseball and the Choice Between Race and Nation, 1887–1912," *Journal of Sport and Social Issues* 29: 4 (November 2005), p. 20; Louis A. Pérez, Jr., *On Becoming Cuban: Identity, Nationality, & Culture* (Durham: University of North Carolina Press, 1999), p. 82.
6. Louis A. Pérez, "Between Baseball and Bullfighting: The Quest for Nationality in Cuba, 1868–1898," *Journal of American History* (September 1994): pp. 493–517.
7. Story reported in *Diario de la Marina* in a January 1924 article. González Echevarría, *Pride of Havana: The History of Cuban Baseball* (New York: Oxford University Press, 1999), p. 90.
8. Team names drawn from nineteenth-century U.S. and Cuban newspapers: *New York Clipper, Sporting Life, Sporting News, New York Age,* and Tampa's *El Score;* from Cuba, *El Score, El Pitcher,* and *El Figaro.* On early Key West baseball, see Pérez, *On Becoming Cuban,* p. 75; Burgos, "Entering Cuba's Other Playing Field," p. 15.
9. Pérez, "Between Baseball and Bullfighting," pp. 493–94.
10. Stebbins, "The Insurgents of Key West and Expedition of 1895," p. 1.
11. Ibid., p. 10.
12. Alex Antón and Roger E. Hernández, *Cubans in America: A Vibrant History of a People in Exile* (New York: Kensington Publishing, 2003), p. 85; Gonzalo de Quesada, "The Cuban Revolutionary Party," *Independent,* December 5, 1895, p. 7.
13. Gonzalo de Quesada, *Martí, Hombre* (Miami: Editorial Cubana, 1998), p. 205, cited in "José Martí at the San Carlos Institute," www.institutosancarlos.org/jose_marti.php, last accessed June 5, 2009. Document, "Bases del Partido Revolucionario Cubano, 5 de Enero 1892," www.exilio.com/Marti/Cuba/Cu1/Cu1_basesPRC.html. Last accessed January 1, 2006.
14. Letter from Jose Martí to Serafin Bello, Febrero 1892. www.exilio.com/Marti/Cuba/Cu1/Cu1_1892-2-2.html. Last accessed January 1, 2006; Document, "Patria, 3 de Septiembre, 1892," www.bnjm/efemeridas_martianas. Last accessed January 2, 2006. "Cuban Newspapers," fcit.usf.edu/florida/docs/c/cubanews.htm, last accessed August 29, 2004.
15. "Key West: The Old and the New," fcit.usf.edu/florida/docs/c/cubanews.htm. Last accessed January 1, 2006. Browne mistakenly states that in the fall of 1892 Cubans elected Pompez (R) and Morúa P. Delgado (D) to the statehouse. However, state records indicate that 1889 was when Delgado and Manuel Moreno served; in 1893 Pompez was the lone Cuban elected from Key West. *Membership for the Florida House of Representatives, 1845–2009,* p. 196. www.myfloridahouse.gov/FileStores/Web/HouseContent/Approved/Public%20Guide/Uploads/Documents/house_counties_final.pdf#xml=http://search/texis/search/pdfhi.txt?query=Pompez&pr=PROD_MFHMain&rdepth=0&order=r&mode=admin&cq=&id=49c3e26f3. Last accessed June 11, 2009.

16. *Journal of the Proceedings of the House of Representatives of the Session of the Legislature of the State of Florida* (1893), www.uflib.ufl.edu/UFDC/UFDC .aspx?b=UF00027834 &v=00008.

17. *Tampa Tribune*, September 27, October 26, and November 22, 1888; Tony Pizzo Collection, Special Collections Library, University of South Florida.

18. Drew would also build the three-story Céspedes Hall in West Tampa, a local landmark for the Cuban community. Arsenio M. Sanchez, "Incentives Helped to Build West Tampa," p. 3; "West Tampa Cigar Factories Reminders of Area's Past Boom," *Sunland Tribune* 7: 1 (November 1981), p. 2.

19. L. Glenn Westfall, "Florida's Cultural Legacy: Tobacco, Steam & Stone," *South Florida History* 23: 4 (Fall 1995/Winter 1996), part 3, www.historical-musuem .org/history/tobacco/tobacco3.htm. Last accessed June 12, 2006; Armando Méndez, *Ciudad de Cigars: West Tampa* (Tampa: self-published, 1994), p. 35.

20. José Alvarez de la Vega, "Pompez Affectionately Remembers His Trip to Puerto Rico," *Puerto Rican Deportivo* 4: 7–8 (July–August 1947), p. 16. (Hereafter, "Pompez Affectionately Remembers.") Author's translation.

21. Pérez, "Between Baseball and Bullfighting," p. 514. The Cuban insurgent army included numerous soldiers and officers who previously played amateur baseball in the provinces, in émigré communities, or in the professional league in Havana, or had served on the directorial boards of baseball clubs.

22. Molina allegedly hit a home run with Martí present at a game in Florida. This claim comes from an obituary published in the February 11, 1961, edition of *Revolución*. González Echevarría, *Pride of Havana*, fn. 2, p. 410.

23. *New York Times*, July 27, 1897, p. 2.

24. *Sporting Life*, January 25, 1896, and January 23, 1897; *New York Times*, November 24, 1897, p. 3; *Chicago Tribune*, November 24, 1897, p. 3.

25. Susan Greenbaum, *More than Black: Afro-Cubans in Tampa* (Gainesville: University Press of Florida, 2002), p. 70; Narciso E. Ferrer Aguilar, "La Historia del Béisbol en Cienfuegos entre los años 1888–1920," *Trabajo de Diploma de Instituto Superior Técnico de Cienfuegos, Facultad de Cultura Física: 1991–1992*, pp. 2, 7. Burgos, *Playing America's Game: Baseball, Latinos, and the Color Line* (Berkeley: University of California Press, 2007), p. 75.

26. *Tampa Tribune*, October 26, 1888, Tony Pizzo Collection, Special Collections Library, University of South Florida, Tampa; and Susan Greenbaum, *More Than Black*, p. 83.

27. Greenbaum, *More Than Black*, p. 12.

28. Ibid., p. 81.

29. Ibid., p. 12.

30. Ibid., pp. 12, 149, and en. 4, p. 347. On schism within Tampa's Cuban community, see pp. 103–110; and Mirabal, "Telling Silences and Making Community," in *Between Race and Empire*, pp. 49–69.

31. Greenbaum, *More Than Black*, p. 193.

32. Burgos, *Playing America's Game*, pp. 81–82.

33. 1910 U.S. Census, Tomas Mendoza et al., Key West Ward 5, Monroe, Florida; Roll: T624 Roll 165; p. 1A; Enumeration District: 127; Image 1060.

34. *Tampa Tribune*, October 26, 1888, Tony Pizzo Collection, Special Collections Library, University of South Florida, Tampa; and Greenbaum, *More Than*

Black, p. 83; Alvarez de la Vega, "Pompez Affectionately Remembers," pp. 14, 16.

35. Alvarez, "Pompez Affectionately Remembers," p. 14; Greenbaum, *More Than Black*, en. 4, p. 347. 1910 U.S. Census entry, Alejandro Pompe[z], completed March 25, 1910, Florida, 6-WD Tampa Series T624, Roll 162, p. 61.

36. Aline Helg, *Our Rightful Share: The Afro-Cuban Struggle for Equality, 1886–1912* (Durham: University of North Carolina Press, 1995), p. 225.

37. Greenbaum, *More Than Black*, p. 63.

38. On the work involved in being a *lector*, see Pérez, Jr., "Reminiscences of a *Lector*: Cuban Cigar Workers in Tampa," *Florida Historical Journal Quarterly* 53 (April 1975), pp. 443–49.

39. Greenbaum, *More Than Black*, pp. 112–13, 118.

40. Pam Iorio, "Political Excess Shaped by a Game of Chance: Tampa, *Bolita*, and the First Half of the Twentieth Century," *Sunland Tribune* 26:1 (August 2000), p. 4.

41. "The Cigar Industry in Tampa," www.tambabayhistorycenter.org/cigar.htm, last accessed November 26, 2004; Durwood Long, "Labor Relations in the Tampa Cigar Industry, 1885–1911," *Labor History* 12:4 (1971), p. 552.

42. Greenbaum, *More Than Black*, p. 63. On Cuban immigration to the States and the process of community formation, see Nancy Mirabal, "*De Aqui, De Alla*: Race, Empire, and Nation in the Making of Cuban Migrant Communities in New York and Tampa, 1823–1924" (Ph.D. diss., University of Michigan, 2001). On political alliances forged in New York between Cubans and Puerto Rican nationalists in the late nineteenth century, see Mirabal, "No Country but the One We Must Fight For," *Mambo Montage: The Latinization of New York* (New York: Columbia University Press, 2001), pp. 57–72.

43. For more on the rise of Jim Crow in communities in northern and central Florida stretching down to Tampa, see Paul Ortiz, *Emancipation Betrayed: The Hidden History of Black Organizing and White Violence in Florida from Reconstruction to the Bloody Election of 1920* (Berkeley: University of California Press, 2005).

44. Evelio Grillo, *Black Cuban, Black American: A Memoir* (Houston: Arté Publico Press, 2002), p. 12.

45. Greenbaum, *More Than Black*, en. 4, p. 347; Schatzberg, *Black Organized Crime in Harlem*, p. 115.

2. MAKING HARLEM HOME

1. *New York Age*, January 28, 1928, p. 1 (emphasis added in epigraph).

2. Irma Watkins-Owens, *Blood Relations: Caribbean Immigrants and the Harlem Community, 1900–1930* (Bloomington: Indiana University Press, 1996), p. 4.

3. Watkins-Owens, *Blood Relations*, p. 2.

4. *New York Amsterdam News*, February 10, 1979, p. 25.

5. *Baltimore Afro-American*, February 22, 1936, p. 14; *Chicago Defender*, May 25, 1940, pp. 13, 15; Shane White, Stephen Garton, Stephen Robertson, and Graham White, *Playing the Numbers: Gambling in Harlem Between the Wars* (Cambridge, MA: Harvard University Press, 2010), p. 61.

6. Greenbaum, *More Than Black*, p. 199; *Chicago Defender*, May 25, 1940, pp. 13, 15; Schatzberg, *Black Organized Crime in Harlem*, p. 115.
7. *Chicago Defender*, August 27, 1938, p. 2.
8. Claude McKay, *Harlem, Negro Metropolis* (New York: Harcourt Brace Jovanovich, 1968), p. 109; *New York Times,* August 24, 1938, p. 14. According to Claude McKay, "Each collector was remunerated with 10% of monies collected . . . The controller's reward was 5% of the total sum turned over to the banker."
9. Winthrop D. Lane, "Ambushed in the City: The Grim Side of Harlem," *Survey Graphic* 6:6 (March 1925), p. 692.
10. *Amsterdam News*, May 14, 1938, p. 7.
11. *New York Times*, August 18, 1938, p. 1.
12. Alvarez, "Pompez Affectionately Remembers," p. 15.
13. *New York Times*, March 2, 1907, p. 10; Lawrence D. Hogan, Adrian Burgos, Leslie Heaphy, Neil Lanctot, Michael Lomax, James Overmyer, Robert Peterson, Robert Ruck, and Lyle Wilson, *Shades of Glory: The Negro Leagues and the History of African-American Baseball* (New York: National Geographic, 2005), p. 101.
14. *Warren* (PA) *Evening Times*, June 4, 1915, p. 7.
15. Hogan et al., *Shades of Glory*, p. 230.
16. *Baltimore Afro-American*, May 23, 1924, p. 14.
17. *Amsterdam News*, October 5, 1927, p. 20.
18. Rose C. Feld, "Harlem Riot Attributed to Many Economic Ills," *New York Times*, March 1935, Claude Barnett Papers, Chicago Historical Society.
19. *New York Age*, January 28, 1928, p. 1.
20. Robert A. Hill, ed., *The Marcus Garvey and Universal Negro Improvement Association Papers*, vol. 1 (1826–August 1919), (Berkeley: University of California Press, 1983), note 3, pp. 211–12; Colin Grant, *Negro with a Hat: The Rise and Fall of Marcus Garvey* (New York: Oxford University Press, 2008), pp. 190–98. For an overview of Grey's testimony, see *Amsterdam News*, May 23, 1923, pp. 1, 6; Hill, *The Marcus Garvey and Universal Negro Improvement Association Papers*, p. 211.
21. Watkins-Owens, *Blood Relations*, p. 83.
22. *New York Age*, January 28, 1928, p. 4.
23. New York Municipal Archive, Magistrates' Court Docket Books, Twelfth Court, Roll 9, January 24, 1923.
24. *New York Age*, January 27, 1923, p. 6.
25. *Amsterdam News*, February 10, 1979, p. 25.
26. James Bankes, *The Pittsburgh Crawfords* (Jefferson, NC: McFarland, 2001), p. 78. Johnson played for Greenlee's Crawfords in the 1930s and later served with Pompez on the National Baseball Hall of Fame's blue ribbon committee on the Negro leagues (1971–74).
27. *New York Times*, August 20, 1938, p. 9.

3. LAUNCHING THE CUBAN STARS

1. *New York Times*, March 25, 1921, p. 24, and May 9, 1921, p. 13.
2. *New York Age*, December 23, 1922, p. 7.

3. *New York Times,* January 10, 1923, p. E1.
4. New York Municipal Archive, Magistrates' Court Docket Books, Twelfth Court, Roll 9, January 24, 1923.
5. *New York Age,* April 21, 1923, p. 6.
6. "Primeros Pasos en el Professionalismo," p. 21. Thanks to Jim Riley for sharing this chapter by Dihigo from his personal collection.
7. *New York Age,* March 7, 1925, p. 6; *Amsterdam News,* March 11, 1925, p. 4. Standings for the Eastern Colored League and the Negro National League can be found in Appendix A in Robert Peterson, *Only the Ball Was White* (New York: Oxford University Press, 1992).
8. *Chicago Tribune,* October 17, 1924, p. 25; *Baltimore Afro-American,* July 4, 1924, p. 15, and December 5, 1924, p. 10.
9. *Baltimore Afro-American,* August 7, 1926, p. 9; *Amsterdam News,* August 4, 1926, p. 13. The news was not as good for the Brooklyn Royal Giants, who were dropped from the league the following season.
10. *Baltimore Afro-American,* August 28, 1926, p. 9.
11. Ibid.
12. *Baltimore Afro-American,* September 4, 1926, p. 9.
13. Ibid.
14. For more on the squabbles over San (1926) and Montalvo (1927), see *Amsterdam News,* March 3, 1926, p. 6, and March 17, 1926, p. 6; and *New York Age,* May 21, 1927, p. 6, and July 2, 1927, p. 6.
15. *Amsterdam News,* March 3, 1926, p. 6, and March 17, 1927, p. 7.
16. *Baltimore Afro-American,* April 30, 1927, p. 14.
17. *Baltimore Afro-American,* January 22, 1927, p. 14.
18. *New York Age,* May 21, 1927, p. 6.
19. Ibid.; *Amsterdam News,* June 29, 1927, p. 10; *Baltimore Afro-American,* July 2, 1927, p. 15.
20. *Amsterdam News,* April 6, 1927, p. 14.
21. *Baltimore Afro-American,* May 14, 1927, p. 14.
22. *Baltimore Afro-American,* August 28, 1926, p. 9.
23. *New York Age,* April 9, 1927, p. 6.
24. *Amsterdam News,* September 14, 1927, p. 11.
25. *Chicago Defender,* September 10, 1927, p. 8; *Baltimore Afro-American,* September 10, 1927, p. 15; *Washington Post,* September 25, 1927, p. M19.
26. *Baltimore Afro-American,* February 25, 1928, p. 12.
27. Ibid.
28. *Baltimore Afro-American,* March 24, 1928, p. 12
29. *Pittsburgh Courier,* March 24, 1928, p. A15.
30. *Baltimore Afro-American,* March 31, 1928, p. 13, and August 14, 1926, p. 14.
31. *Chicago Defender,* April 21, 1928, p. 8; *Pittsburgh Courier,* April 21, 1928, p. A4; *Amsterdam News,* April 25, 1928, p. 10.
32. *Chicago Defender,* May 5, 1928, p. 11, and April 28, 1928, p. 9.
33. Daliana Muratti, *Millito Navarro: Una Leyenda Centenaria* (San Juan, Puerto Rico: Orbis, 2007), pp. 46, 47.
34. Muratti, *Millito Navarro,* p. 48; interview with Emilio Navarro by the author, June 3, 2010, Ponce, Puerto Rico.

35. *Amsterdam News*, May 2, 1928, p. 10, and May 30, 1928, p. 7; *Baltimore Afro-American*, June 2, 1928, p. 12; *Chicago Defender*, April 28, 1928, p. 9; *Pittsburgh Courier*, June 2, 1928, p. A4.
36. Hogan, *Shades of Glory*, p. 230; Pompez's statement originally appeared in the *Pittsburgh Courier*, July 28, 1928, p. A4.
37. *Amsterdam News*, June 26, 1929, p. 8; *Chicago Defender*, June 29, 1929, p. 9; *Pittsburgh Courier*, June 29, 1929, p. A4.
38. *Amsterdam News*, July 31, 1929, p. 8; *Pittsburgh Courier*, August 3, 1929, p. A5.
39. *Amsterdam News*, August 7, 1929, p. 9; *Chicago Defender*, August 10, 1929, p. 9.
40. Neil Lanctot, *Negro League Baseball: The Rise and Ruin of a Black Institution* (Philadelphia: University of Pennsylvania Press, 2004), p. 15.

4. THE RISE AND FALL OF A NUMBERS KING

1. The authors of *Playing the Numbers* provide a misleading statement: "After all, it was the wagering of only some $115 that had caused Pompez's devastating loss." The dollar amount they cite refers to the amount in winning bets on that number alone. As the authors note, there were several ways of scoring a winning wager on variations of 527. White et al., *Playing the Numbers*, p. 178.
2. Watkins-Owens offers a succinct description of the genesis of the numbers game and the role of Caribbean individuals within the development of Harlem's number game in her chapter "The Underground Entrepreneur" in *Blood Relations*, pp. 136–48.
3. Schatzberg, *Black Organized Crime in Harlem*, p. 115.
4. Paul Sann, *Kill the Dutchman! The Story of Dutch Schultz* (Cambridge, MA: Da Capo Press, 1991), chapter 13, p. 11, republished online at www.killthedutchman.net/chapter_XIII.htm. Last accessed January 1, 2006.
5. *New York Times*, May 30, 1931, p. 15.
6. *New York Times*, August 18, 1938, p. 1, and August 20, 1938, p. 1.
7. "Harlem Doesn't Consider Game Wiped Out by Big Raid," Associated Negro Press news release, January 18, 1937, Box 339, Folder 6, "Crime—Organized Crime—'Policy,'" *Claude Barnett Papers*, Chicago Historical Society (hereafter "Harlem Doesn't Consider"). The Associated Negro Press was a subscription news service founded by African American Claude Barnett for black newspapers in the United States. For a history of the press service, see Lawrence Hogan, *A Black National News Service: The Associated Negro Press and Claude Barnett, 1919–1945* (Cranbury, NJ: Associate University Presses, 1984).
8. *New York Times*, August 20, 1938, pp. 1, 7.
9. "Harlem Doesn't Consider"; *Chicago Tribune*, August 20, 1938, p. 1; *New York Times*, August 20, 1938, p. 1; Sann, *Kill the Dutchman!*, chapter 13, pp. 10, 11.
10. *New York Times*, August 20, 1938, p. 1; *Chicago Tribune*, August 20, 1938, p. 1.
11. "Harlem Doesn't Consider."
12. *New York Times*, August 20, 1938; Schatzberg, *Black Organized Crime in Harlem*, p. 115.
13. *Chicago Defender*, March 19, 1938, p. 1.

14. *New York Times*, August 18, 1938, p. 1.

15. *Amsterdam News*, August 27, 1938, p. 1.

16. On the ways the struggle against segregation affected the civil rights movement in New York City, see Martha Biondi, *To Stand and Fight: The Struggle for Civil Rights in Postwar New York City* (Cambridge, MA: Harvard University Press, 2003).

17. *Chicago Defender*, May 25, 1940, pp. 13, 15; Sann, *Kill the Dutchman!*, chapter 13, p. 9; McKay, *Harlem*, pp. 107–109; *New York Times*, August 20, 1938.

18. *New York Times*, January 15, 1937, p. 1; *Amsterdam News*, January 16, 1937, p. 1.

19. *Chicago Tribune*, "2 Policy Kings Admit Giving to Fund for Hines," August 20, 1938, p. 1.

20. *Amsterdam News*, February 7, 1934, p. 1.

21. *Chicago Tribune*, August 23, 1938, pp. 1, 2; *New York Times*, August 23, 1938, p. 11.

22. Edward Brooke, *Bridging the Divide: My Life* (New Brunswick: Rutgers University Press, 2007), p. 10.

23. Larry Lester, *Black Baseball's National Showcase: The East-West All-Star Game* (Lincoln: University of Nebraska Press, 2002), p. 12; Bankes, *The Pittsburgh Crawfords*, p. 23. On Gus Greenlee's place within Pittsburgh's sporting world, see Rob Ruck, *Sandlot Seasons: Sport in Black Pittsburgh* (Urbana: University of Illinois Press, 1993), especially chapter 5, "Gus Greenlee, Black Pittsburgh's 'Mr. Big.'" In a 1980 interview with historian Rob Ruck, Gus Greenlee's brother Charles claimed that Gus and Alex Pompez "had discovered the game while vacationing in Cuba." This seems a product of faulty memory, especially given the first arrest of Pompez for "policy violation" in 1923. "Policy" was another name for the numbers game.

24. *Amsterdam News*, May 19, 1934, p. 10.

25. Donn Rogosin, *Invisible Men: Life in Baseball's Negro Leagues* (New York: Kodansha, 1995), p. 104.

26. Ibid., pp. 106–107.

27. *Amsterdam News*, November 24, 1934, p. 11; *Amsterdam News*, December 1, 1934, p. 11.

28. *Amsterdam News*, December 22, 1934, p. 11.

29. *Amsterdam News*, December 15, 1934, p. 11.

30. *New York Age*, December 22, 1934, p. 5.

31. *Amsterdam News*, December 8, 1934, p. 11, and December 29, 1934, p. 11.

32. *New York Times*, January 11, 1935, p. 23.

33. *Chicago Defender*, January 19, 1935, p. 17; *New York Age*, January 26, 1935, p. 5; Lanctot, *Negro League Baseball*, pp. 24, 41.

34. *Pittsburgh Courier*, January 26, 1935, p. A5; *Chicago Defender*, February 2, 1935, p. 17.

35. *Atlanta Daily World*, January 23, 1935, p. 2; *Chicago Defender*, January 19, 1935, p. 17; *New York Age*, January 19, 1935, p. 5.

36. *New York Age*, January 19, 1935, p. 5, May 25, 1935, p. 5, and April 2, 1938, p. 8; *Amsterdam News*, December 8, 1934, p. 11, and February 23, 1935, p. 11; *New York Times*, June 26, 1935, p. 40; and interview with Mauricio Valdes and Lesley Rankin-Hill Valdes by the author, tape recording, Bronx, NY, July 30, 2006.

37. *Chicago Defender*, August 27, 1935, p. 24; *New York Age*, August 24, 1935, p. 8.

38. Bankes, *The Pittsburgh Crawfords*, p. 105.

39. *Amsterdam News*, July 13, 1935, p. 13; *New York Age*, October 19, 1935, p. 6.

40. *Amsterdam News*, July 13, 1935, p. 13, and July 20, 1935, p. 15.

41. *Amsterdam News*, February 2, 1935, p. 11.

42. *New York Age*, March 23, 1935, p. 5.

43. *New York Age*, May 25, 1935, p. 5.

44. *Pittsburgh Courier*, June 1, 1935, p. A4; *Amsterdam News*, June 1, 1935, p. 11.

45. *Amsterdam News*, August 31, 1935, p. 13; September 7, 1935, p. 13; *New York Age*, September 7, 1935, p. 8.

46. *Amsterdam News*, September 21, 1935, p. 12; *Pittsburgh Courier*, September 21, 1935, p. A4.

47. *Amsterdam News*, September 7, 1935, p. 13, and September 28, 1935, p. 12; *New York Age*, September 14, 1935, p. 8, and September 28, 1935, p. 8.

48. *New York Age*, June 8, 1935, p. 8, and June 22, 1935, p. 8. On Dial's proposed teams, see *New York Age*, July 27, 1935.

49. A broader understanding of the struggles of black folks everywhere served as a driving force in the formation of Harlem's black community into what historian Irma Watkin-Owens labels an "intra-racial ethnic community," which she offers to explain black Harlem's heterogeneity: see *Blood Relations*, chapter 10.

50. Rose C. Feld, "Harlem Riot Attributed to Many Economic Ills," newspaper clipping. *New York Times*, March 1935, Claude Barnett Papers, Chicago Historical Society.

51. *New York Age*, October 5, 1935, p. 8; *Amsterdam News*, October 5, 1935, pp. 5, 12; *New York Times*, September 30, 1935, p. 22.

52. Leigh Montville, *The Big Bam: The Life and Times of Babe Ruth* (New York: Anchor, 2007), p. 345.

53. *Amsterdam News*, October 5, 1935, p. 12.

54. Ibid.; *New York Age*, August 10, 1935, p. 8, August 24, 1935, p. 8, and August 31, 1935, p. 8; Alvarez de la Vega, "Pompez Affectionately Remembers," p. 16.

55. *Chicago Tribune*, October 24, 1935, pp. 1, 8. *New York Times*, October 25, 1935, p. 17.

56. *Chicago Tribune*, February 28, 1935, p. 7, and March 3, 1935, p. 17.

57. *Amsterdam News*, March 2, 1935, p. 1; *Washington Post*, March 5, 1935, p. 9.

58. *Atlanta Daily World*, March 12, 1936, p. 5; Lanctot, *Negro League Baseball*, p. 51; *Chicago Defender*, June 27, 1936, p. 13.

59. *Philadelphia Tribune*, May 28, 1936, p. 1; *New York Age*, May 30, 1936, p. 1; *Pittsburgh Courier*, June 6, 1936, p. A4.

60. *New York Age*, December 7, 1935, p. 8; *Amsterdam News*, March 14, 1936, p. 15.

61. *Philadelphia Tribune*, November 5, 1936, p. 12; *Chicago Defender*, November 14, 1936, p. 14.

5. WITNESS FOR THE STATE

1. "Harlem Doesn't Consider."

2. *Baltimore Afro-American*, January 23, 1937, p. 14; *Pittsburgh Courier*, January 23, 1937, p. 4; "Harlem Doesn't Consider"; *Chicago Defender*, April 15, 1939,

p. 13; *Norfolk Journal and Guide*, November 6, 1937, p. 10; and Rogosin, *Invisible Men*, p. 111; Bankes, *Pittsburgh Crawfords*, p. 92.

3. "Harlem Doesn't Consider."
4. Lanctot, *Negro League Baseball*, pp. 59–60; *Pittsburgh Courier*, April 3, 1937, p. 1; *New York Times*, March 30, 1937, p. 2; James Overmyer, *Queen of the Negro Leagues* (Lanham, MD: Scarecrow Press, 1998), p. 276.
5. *Amsterdam News*, February 6, 1937, p. 19, and March 27, 1937, p. 16.
6. *New York Age*, October 17, 1936, p. 8.
7. *New York Age*, April 17, 1937, p. 8.
8. *Chicago Defender*, April 3, 1937, p. 1; *Pittsburgh Courier*, April 3, 1937, p. 1.
9. *Chicago Defender*, April 3, 1937, p. 1; *Amsterdam News*, April 3, 1937, p. 23.
10. *New York Times*, March 30, 1937, p. 2.
11. *Amsterdam News*, April 3, 1937, p. 1.
12. *New York Times*, March 31, 1937, p. 7.
13. *New York Times*, March 30, 1937, p. 2.
14. *Pittsburgh Courier*, April 3, 1937, p. 1; *Norfolk Journal and Guide*, April 10, 1937, p. 1; *New York Times*, March 30, 1937, p. 2.
15. *Amsterdam News*, April 10, 1937, p. 1; *New York Times*, April 7, 1937, p. 9, April 8, 1937, p. 13, and April 15, 1937, p. 8.
16. *Amsterdam News*, April 17, 1937, p. 1.
17. *New York Times*, April 30, 1937, p. 12, and May 7, 1937, p. 11.
18. *New York Times*, July 23, 1937, p. 38.
19. *Chicago Defender*, May 29, 1937, p. 21; *Amsterdam News*, July 24, 1937, p. 1, and July 31, 1937, p. 1.
20. *Amsterdam News*, September 4, 1937, p. 6.
21. John Virtue, *South of the Color Barrier: How Jorge Pasquel and the Mexican League Pushed Baseball Toward Racial Integration* (Jefferson, NC: McFarland Press, 2008), pp. 56–57.
22. *New York Times*, October 27, 1937, p. 19; *Pittsburgh Courier*, November 6, 1937, p. 1.
23. *Amsterdam News*, October 30, 1937, p. 1; *Norfolk Journal and Guide*, October 16, 1937, p. 3.
24. *Norfolk Journal and Guide*, October 16, 1937, p. 3.
25. *Amsterdam News*, October 30, 1937, p. 1.
26. *New York Times*, October 31, 1937, p. 2.
27. *Pittsburgh Courier*, November 6, 1937, p. 1; *Amsterdam News*, November 6, 1937, pp. 1, 5.
28. *New York Times*, October 30, 1937, p. 10, and November 1, 1937, p. 3.
29. *New Yorker*, March 25, 1939, pp. 14–15; *New York Times*, February 3, 1938, pp. 1, 8.
30. *New York Times*, February 12, 1938, p. 1; *Baltimore Afro-American*, April 16, 1938, p. 2.
31. Schatzberg, *Black Organized Crime in Harlem*, pp. 115, 116; *New York Times*, February 3, 1938, p. 1.
32. Schatzberg, *Black Organized Crime in Harlem*, p. 116.
33. Ibid.
34. *Amsterdam News*, April 9, 1938, p. 1, 5.

35. *Chicago Defender*, June 4, 1938, p. 1; *Amsterdam News*, June 4, 1938, p. 4.

36. *New York Times*, August 18, 1938, p. 13; *Chicago Tribune*, August 20, 1938, p. 1; *Baltimore Afro-American*, April 16, 1938, p. 2; *Chicago Defender*, June 10, 1939, pp. 1, 2.

37. *Pittsburgh Courier*, April 10, 1937, p. 16. Thanks to Rob Ruck for sharing this document.

38. *New York Times*, May 30, 1931, p. 15; Watkins-Owens, *Blood Relations*, pp. 143–44. Langston Hughes was one of the early recipients of the Casper Holstein Award and its $1,000 cash prize. On West Indian and Afro-Caribbean migrations to the United States and their political and social movements, see Winston James, *Holding Aloft the Banner of Ethiopia: Caribbean Radicalism in Early Twentieth-Century America* (New York: Verso, 1998).

39. *Amsterdam News*, August 20, 1938, p. 1; *Chicago Defender*, June 18, 1938, p. 4.

40. Mary M. Stolberg, *Fighting Organized Crime: Politics, Justice, and the Legacy of Thomas E. Dewey* (Boston: Northeastern University Press, 1995), p. 227.

41. Ibid., p. 233.

42. *Chicago Tribune*, August 20, 1938, p. 1; Stolberg, *Fighting Organized Crime*, p. 226.

43. *New York Times*, August 18, 1938, p. 13

44. *New York Times*, August 18, 1938, pp. 1, 12.

45. *Wisconsin Rapids Daily Tribune*, August 20, 1938, p. 10; *New York Times*, August 20, 1938, p. 7.

46. *New York Times*, August 20, 1938, p. 7.

47. *New York Times*, August 20, 1938, pp. 1, 7.

48. *New York Times*, August 20, 1938, p. 7.

49. Ibid.

50. *Chicago Tribune*, August 23, 1938, p. 2; *New York Times*, August 23, 1938, p. 11.

51. *Chicago Tribune*, August 23, 1938, p. 2.

52. Shane White et al., pp. 196–98; *New York Times*, August 23, 1938, p. 11.

53. *New York Times*, August 24, 1938, p. 14; *Washington Post*, August 25, 1938, p. 5.

54. *Washington Post*, August 25, 1938, pp. 1, 5.

55. *Amsterdam News*, August 27, 1938, p. 1; *Chicago Defender*, August 27, 1938, p. 1, and October 8, 1938, p. 1.

56. *Amsterdam News*, September 17, 1938, p. 10, October 1, 1938, p. 1, October 8, 1938, p. 1, and October 15, 1938, p. 1; *Chicago Defender*, October 8, 1938, p. 1, and November 19, 1938, p. 1.

57. *Amsterdam News*, October 8, 1938, p. 1, and October 15, 1938, p. 1; *Chicago Defender*, October 8, 1938, p. 1.

58. Stolberg, *Fighting Organized Crime*, p. 245; *New York Times*, February 26, 1939, p. 74.

59. *Amsterdam News*, May 20, 1939, p. 1; *New York Age*, June 10, 1939, p. 1; *Chicago Defender*, June 10, 1939, pp. 1, 2.

60. *Amsterdam News*, September 17, 1938, p. A12.

61. Rogosin, *Invisible Men*, p. 112.

62. Stolberg, *Fighting Organized Crime*, p. 232.

63. *New York Age*, April 2, 1938.

PART II: A WORLD MADE NEW

1. *Chicago Defender,* September 3, 1938, p. 8; Lanctot, *Negro League Baseball,* p. 81. The Dyckman Housing Projects, complete with a basketball court and a children's playground, now stand on the grounds where Dyckman Oval once stood.
2. *New York Age,* February 28, 1939, p. 15; *Chicago Defender,* March 4, 1939, p. 8.

6. REBUILDING THE "LATINS FROM MANHATTAN"

1. *Amsterdam News,* November 19, 1938, p. 1; *Chicago Defender,* November 26, 1938, p. 1.
2. Lanctot, *Negro League Baseball,* p. 82.
3. *Amsterdam News,* April 15, 1939, p. 18.
4. *Chicago Defender,* February 19, 1938, p. 8, and March 19, 1938, p. 8.
5. *Chicago Defender,* June 10, 1939, p. 1; *New York Age,* June 10, 1939, p. 1.
6. *New York Age,* June 3, 1939, p. 8, September 9, 1939, p. 8, and November 4, 1939, p. 8; *Amsterdam News,* October 7, 1939, p. 14.
7. *Chicago Defender,* November 4, 1939, p. 22, and November 11, 1939, p. 23.
8. *Amsterdam News,* June 10, 1939, p. 14.
9. *Washington Post,* August 17, 1932, p. 9. Mulo Morales was not alone in moving from the Cuban Stars into organized baseball. Tomás "Tommy" de la Cruz followed suit in 1934. However, the first of Pompez's finds to go from the black circuit into the majors was Oscar Estrada, who pitched for the Cuban Stars in 1924 and 1925 before being signed by the Boston Braves in 1926 and appearing with the St. Louis Browns in 1929. Estrada's ascent into the majors unveils the possibilities for lighter-skinned and even medium-toned Cuban and Latino players— and how much difference place of birth made when it came to being a nonwhite ballplayer. Upon his signing with the Braves in March 1926, the *Baltimore Afro-American* noted, "Estrada is a colored Cuban, but can easily pass for white." *Baltimore Afro-American,* March 6, 1926, p. 8; *Chicago Defender,* December 25, 1943, p. 13.
10. *Washington Post,* August 19, 1932, and December 13, 1932.
11. *Washington Post,* March 11, 1936, p. 19.
12. Peter C. Bjarkman, *Baseball with a Latin Beat: A History of the Latin American Games* (Jefferson, NC: McFarland, 1994), p. 119.
13. Snyder, *Beyond the Shadow of the Senators,* pp. 70, 73.
14. Rogosin, *Invisible Men,* p. 92; Lawrence Hogan, "The Gift of Alvin White," *Commonweal,* February 10, 1983.
15. Rodolfo and Matilda Fernández, interview by the author, tape recording, Harlem, NY, February 1995 (hereafter Fernández interview); Rafael Noble, interview by the author, tape recording, Brooklyn, NY, February 24, 1995; Armando Vásquez, interview by the author, tape recording, New York, NY, February 23, 1995.
16. Valdes and Rankin-Hill Valdes interview; Fernández interview; Nick Wilson, *Early Latino Ballplayers in the United States: Major, Minor and Negro Leagues, 1901–1949* (Jefferson, NC: McFarland Publishing Co., 2005), pp. 47–48.
17. *Chicago Defender,* June 24, 1939, p. 10.

18. *Chicago Defender,* June 24, 1939, p. 10, and October 21, 1939, p. 8; *Amsterdam News,* November 4, 1939, p. 19.

19. *Amsterdam News,* May 1, 1937, p. 15, and May 8, 1937, p. 14.

20. *Chicago Defender,* May 7, 1938, p. 8.

21. Virtue, *South of the Color Barrier,* p. 4; *New York Age,* April 12, 1941.

22. *Baltimore Afro-American,* July 24, 1943, p. 22; Ruck, *Sandlot Seasons,* p. 174.

23. "Here in Mexico, I Am a Man!," geocities.com/jonclark500/blackslmb.html.

24. *Chicago Defender,* April 20, 1940, p. 22.

25. *Chicago Defender,* September 26, 1942, p. B18.

26. *New York Age,* October 19, 1935, p. 6, and July 3, 1937, p. 17; *Cleveland Call and Post,* September 10, 1936, p. 9.

27. *Chicago Defender,* August 1, 1942, pp. 1, 2; *New York Times,* July 29, 1942, p. 20.

28. *Chicago Defender,* September 26, 1942, p. B18.

29. *Chicago Tribune,* July 17, 1942, p. 21; *Chicago Defender,* July 25, 1942, p. 20; *Atlanta Daily World,* July 22, 1942, p. 5.

30. *Atlanta Daily World,* December 31, 1941, p. 5; *Chicago Defender,* January 3, 1942, p. 24.

31. Rogosin, *Invisible Men,* p. 92, 148; Lanctot, *Negro League Baseball,* pp. 108, 227. Pompez was originally quoted on the clowning issue in the *Pittsburgh Courier,* June 28, 1941, and May 30, 1942.

32. *Baltimore Afro-American,* May 12, 1942, p. 21; *New York Age,* April 17, 1948, p. 8.

33. *New York Age,* August 24, 1935, June 21, 1945, and April 17, 1948.

34. *New York Times,* April 16, 1944; "Selective Service Rules Cubans Resident Aliens," undated newspaper clipping, and "Griffs Lose 3 Mainstays as Latins Go," newspaper clipping, July 1, 1944, Mike "Fermin" Guerra Player File, National Baseball Library & Archive (hereafter NBLA); Dan Daniel, "Daniel's Dope" column, newspaper clipping, *New York World-Telegram,* August 3, 1944, Roberto Ortiz Player File, NBLA.

35. Lanctot, *Negro League Baseball,* p. 119; *Chicago Defender,* February 6, 1943, p. 20, and March 13, 1943, p. 21; *Baltimore Afro-American,* March 13, 1943, p. 27, March 20, 1943, p. 22, and April 3, 1943, p. 22.

36. *Chicago Defender,* February 6, 1943, p. 20.

37. Everard Marius, interview by the author, tape recording, Harlem, NY, July 16, 1996; *Cleveland Call and Post,* September 8, 1945, p. 7B.

38. Thanks to Scot Mondore, then a researcher at the National Baseball Library & Archive in Cooperstown, NY, for locating the admission costs for the Giants' games.

39. *New York Age,* September 11, 1937, p. 16.

40. *New York Age,* October 19, 1935, p. 6.

41. British scholar Raymond Williams first coined the term *structure of feelings.* Fellow British scholar Graeme Turner expounded on the meaning of the term: "Williams suggests that all cultures possess a particular sense of life, a 'particular and characteristic colour': 'this structure of feeling is the culture of a period' . . . Williams's own description of the term is notoriously slippery; Tony Bennett's (1981) is more accessible if still tentative: 'The general idea . . . is that of a shared set of thinking and feeling which, displaying a patterned regularity, form and are

formed by the "whole way of life" which comprises the "lived culture" of a particular epoch, class or group.'" Turner, *British Cultural Studies: An Introduction*, 2nd ed. (New York: Routledge, 1996), p. 53.

42. See Table 5.1 in Lanctot, *Negro League Baseball*, p. 123.

43. Overmyer, *Queen of the Negro Leagues*, p. 135.

44. *Chicago Defender*, February 24, 1940, p. 24, and March 2, 1940, p. 24; and Overmyer, *Queen of the Negro Leagues*, pp. 129, 135–36. The Jewish Gottlieb was quite familiar with discrimination in dealing with major-league officials: in 1942 those officials denied him an opportunity to explore the potential purchase of the Philadelphia Phillies as part of a consortium of Jewish businessmen.

45. *New York Age*, March 9, 1940, p. 5; Overmyer, *Queen of the Negro Leagues*, p. 141.

46. *Amsterdam News*, January 11, 1941, p. 15; *Cleveland Call and Post*, August 21, 1943, p. 11A.

47. *New York Age*, March 9, 1940, p. 5; *Baltimore Afro-American*, February 13, 1943, p. 22.

7. GLORY DAYS

1. *New York Times*, January 7, 1947, p. 35; *New York Age*, January 11, 1947, p. 11; *Richmond Afro-American*, January 11, 1947, p. 18; *Norfolk Journal and Guide*, January 11, 1947, p. 18.

2. Press release, statement by John H. Johnson, "On the Status of the Negro in Baseball," *Sporting News* Archive, Negro Leagues, Folder 1.

3. The history of the East-West All Star Classic is wonderfully captured in Larry Lester, *Black Baseball's National Showcase*.

4. *New York Age*, January 23, 1943, p. 11.

5. *Atlanta Daily World*, June 10, 1944, p. C18; *Cleveland Call and Post*, June 24, 1944, p. 9B; Overmyer, *Queen of the Negro Leagues*, p. 173; Lanctot, *Negro League Baseball*, p. 148.

6. *Pittsburgh Courier*, June 23, 1945, "The Sports Beat" by Wendell Smith, Smith Papers, NBLA; *Cleveland Call and Post*, May 23, 1946, p. 13.

7. *Pittsburgh Courier*, June 23, 1945, Wendell Smith Papers, NBLA.

8. *Baltimore Afro-American*, September 23, 1944, p. 18.

9. *Norfolk Journal and Guide*, June 26, 1943, p. B19.

10. The journalist Bruce Brown, who cites the Cuban sportswriter Edel Casas as his source, provides perhaps the earliest published account of the García-Rickey interaction: "Cuban Baseball," *Atlantic Monthly* (June 1984), p. 112. Not seeking to prove or disprove the story, Peter Bjarkman discusses anecdotal accounts of the Dodgers' interest expressed in García: See Bjarkman, *Baseball with a Latin Beat*, pp. 148–49.

11. *Cleveland Call and Post*, March 23, 1946, p. 8B.

12. Miñoso and Herb Fagen, *Just Call Me Minnie* (Champaign, IL: Sagamore Publishing, 1994), pp. 25–26, 161; Rogosin, *Invisible Men*, p. 63.

13. *Baltimore Afro-American*, July 27, 1946, p. 26, and August 17, 1946, pp. 1, 27; *Chicago Defender*, August 24, 1946, p. 11; *New York Age*, August 24, 1946, p. 12; and "The Sports Beat," January 11, 1947, Wendell Smith Papers, NBLA.

14. "Pompez Heads N.Y. All-Star Game Committee," July 19, 1947, Wendell Smith Papers, NBLA.

15. *Amsterdam News*, July 26, 1947, p. 10; *Richmond Afro-American*, July 26, 1947, p. 12; "Pompez Heads N.Y. All-Star Game Committee," July 19, 1947, Wendell Smith Papers, NBLA.

16. "Pompez Heads N.Y. All-Star Game Committee," July 19, 1947, Wendell Smith Papers, NBLA; *Chicago Defender*, June 21, 1947, p. 11; *Amsterdam News*, July 26, 1947, p. 10.

17. *Amsterdam News*, August 2, 1947, pp. 1, 11, and August 9, 1947, p. 8; *New York Times*, July 30, 1947, p. 24.

18. *New York Times*, February 21, 1948, p. 16.

19. *New York Times*, October 25, 1945, p. 17, and October 26, 1945, p. 14. That Griffith opposed racial integration is a tale that captured the complexities of human actors involved in overturning formal and informal segregation. For his part, the Senators' owner feared integration's adverse impact on his leasing Griffith Stadium for Negro-league events and, to a lesser extent, how integration would affect the business of his friend Cum Posey.

20. *Chicago Defender*, August 8, 1942, p. 20.

21. *Baltimore Afro-American*, November 17, 1945, p. 30, and December 29, 1945, p. 22; *Chicago Defender*, December 26, 1945, p. 7.

22. Overmyer, *Queen of the Negro Leagues*, pp. 223–24; *Amsterdam News*, October 5, 1946, p. 12; and *New York Age*, March 6, 1948, p. 7.

23. *New York Age*, March 28, 1942, p. 11.

24. For a compelling account of Muchnick's role in Robinson's Red Sox tryout, see chapter three in Howard Bryant, *Shut Out: A Story of Race and Baseball in Boston* (New York: Routledge, 2002).

25. *New York Age*, March 29, 1947, p. 11.

26. *Baltimore Afro-American*, March 15, 1947, p. 13, and August 23, 1947, p. 17; *New York Age*, March 29, 1947, p. 11; *Amsterdam News*, August 2, 1947, p. 10.

27. *New York Age*, April 17, 1947, p. 11; *Baltimore Afro-American*, May 3, 1947, p. 17, and June 7, 1947, p. 17.

28. *Atlanta Daily World*, May 9, 1947, p. 5; *Cleveland Call and Post*, May 10, 1947, p. 8B.

29. *Amsterdam News*, May 2, 1947, p. 13.

30. *Amsterdam News*, July 12, 1947, p. 13.

31. *Richmond Afro-American*, August 16, 1947, p. 12.

32. *Richmond Afro-American*, August 23, 1947, p. 17.

33. *Richmond Afro-American*, September 6, 1947, pp. 12, 13; *Chicago Defender*, September 6, 1947, p. 11.

34. *Amsterdam News*, September 20, 1947, p. 13.

35. *Chicago Defender*, September 27, 1947, p. 20; *New York Times*, September 20, 1947, p. 19.

36. *Amsterdam News*, September 27, 1947, p. 13.

37. *New York Times*, September 24, 1947, p. 31.

38. *Chicago Daily Tribune*, September 25, 1947, p. 50; *New York Times*, September 25, 1947, p. 40.

39. *Chicago Defender*, October 4, 1947, p. 19.

40. *New York Times*, September 29, 1947, p. 25; *Chicago Defender*, October 4, 1947, p. 19.
41. *Chicago Defender*, October 4, 1947, p. 19; *Richmond Afro-American*, October 4, 1947, p. 17; González Echevarría, *Pride of Havana*, pp. 295, 297.
42. *Cleveland Call and Post*, October 11, 1947, p. 8B.
43. *Baltimore Afro-American*, April 20, 1946, p. 31.
44. Quoted in Lester, *Black Baseball's National Showcase*, pp. 316–18.
45. *New York Age*, September 24, 1948; newspaper clipping, "Looping the Loop," *Sporting News*, June 30, 1954, in Claude Barnett Papers, Box 396, Folder 27, "Minnie Miñoso," Chicago Historical Society.
46. *Atlanta Daily World*, February 10, 1948, p. 5.
47. *Chicago Defender*, December 11, 1948, p. 14.
48. Ibid.
49. Lanctot, *Negro League Baseball*, p. 348; *Amsterdam News*, June 11, 1949, p. 27.
50. *Amsterdam News*, June 11, 1949, p. 27; *Chicago Defender*, August 27, 1949, p. 14.
51. *Amsterdam News*, September 10, 1949, p. 24.
52. *Amsterdam News*, April 22, 1950, p. 29.
53. *Amsterdam News*, May 6, 1950, p. 31.
54. *Chicago Defender*, March 4, 1950, p. 17.

8. SCOUTING THE AMERICAS FOR GIANTS

1. *Philadelphia Tribune*, January 27, 1951, p. 11.
2. Gunnar Myrdal, *An American Dilemma: The Negro Problem and Modern Democracy* (New York: Harper and Row, 2009).
3. James Hirsch, *Willie Mays: The Life, the Legend* (New York: Scribner, 2010), p. 63.
4. Letter to *Wall Street Journal*, John S. (Jack) Schwarz, April 11, 1984; Art Rosenbaum, "Senor Scout," *Baseball Digest*, July 1962, p. 59.
5. *New York Age*, January 22, 1949, pp. 1, 8, and February 5, 1949, p. 1; *Sporting News*, November 5, 1958, p. 7. Willard Brown nonetheless was enshrined in the National Baseball Hall of Fame in 2006 based on his Negro-league career.
6. *Atlanta Daily World*, October 6, 1948, p. 5, and October 10, 1948, p. 8; *Los Angeles Sentinel*, October 7, 1948, p. 20; *New York Age*, October 9, 1948, p. 15; *Sporting News*, October 20, 1948, p. 30.
7. *Amsterdam News*, October 7, 1950, pp. 1, 24.
8. *Chicago Defender*, October 14, 1950, p. 16; *Atlanta Daily World*, October 17, 1950, p. 1.
9. *Atlanta Daily World*, October 19, 1950, p. 5, and October 9, 1952, p. 7.
10. *Atlanta Daily World*, September 8, 1951, p. 5.
11. *Atlanta Daily World*, October 14, 1951, p. 7.
12. Allan Pollock, *Barnstorming to Heaven: Syd Pollock and His Great Black Teams*, edited by Jim Riley (Tuscaloosa: University of Alabama Press, 2006), pp. 266–67; John Klima, *Willie's Boys: The 1948 Birmingham Black Barons, the Last Negro League World Series, and the Making of a Baseball Legend* (New York: Wiley, 2009), p. 189.

13. *Atlanta Daily World*, October 18, 1951, p. 5.

14. *Atlanta Daily World*, October 9, 1952, p. 7.

15. *Atlanta Daily World*, October 21, 1950, p. 5; *Amsterdam News*, November 11, 1950, pp. 27–28.

16. *Pittsburgh Courier*, September 12, 1959, p. 14; Glen Dickey, *San Francisco Giants: 40 Years* (San Francisco: Woodford, 1997), p. 26.

17. Klima, *Willie's Boys*, pp. 247–48.

18. This point is missed by Mays's biographer James Hirsch, whose analysis emphasized that Pompez brokered the entry of these players into the Giants organization "on the cheap," noting that Orlando Cepeda, Felipe Alou, and Willie McCovey each received $500 signing bonuses while Marichal received $4,000. By contrast, the white McCormick was given $60,000. Hirsch, *Willie Mays*, p. 283.

19. Hirsch, *Willie Mays*, p. 59. Unfortunately, Hirsch relied mainly on Montague's self-indulgent account of his role in the discovery of Mays.

20. Klima, *Willie's Boys*, pp. 251–52.

21. Ibid., pp. 252 and 253. Klima notes that the negotiated deal that Hayes insisted on involved $15,000, with $10,000 going to Hayes and $5,000 to Mays. However, Mays claimed he received only $4,000, leading to speculation that Pompez may have skimmed $1,000 for his role in the entire affair.

22. Brent Kelley, "How Hank Aaron Almost Became a Giant," *Baseball Digest* 57: 12 (December 1998), pp. 72–73.

23. Interview with Armando Vásquez, July 1, 2005, New York, NY; Lester, *Black Baseball's National Showcase*, pp. 363–65; Pollock, *Barnstorming to Heaven*, pp. 78, 95, 230–34. Notably, Pollock admitted to John Mullen in a May 27 letter that he was asking $15,000 of other big-league clubs to purchase Aaron versus the $10,000 he asked of the Braves.

24. Pollock, *Barnstorming to Heaven*, pp. 269–70.

25. *The Sporting News*, November 17, 1954, p. 18, and October 31, 1956, p. 20; *Atlanta Daily World*, October 14, 1956, p. 8, and October 30, 1956, p. 5; newspaper clipping, "Minor Leaguers Spill Major All-Stars, 4–2," courtesy of Jimmy Robinson Personal Collection.

26. *The Sporting News*, February 19, 1958, p. 32.

27. *New York Times*, August 8, 1957, p. 34, and November 1, 1957, p. 44; *Atlanta Daily World*, October 9, 1957, p. 5, and October 15, 1957, p. 5.

28. Interview with Orlando Cepeda, Cooperstown, NY, July 26, 2006; Wilson, *Early Latino Ballplayers*, p. 119.

29. *Daily Review* (Hayward, CA), March 31, 1974, p. 47.

30. *Chicago Defender*, February 2, 1957, p. 17.

31. Interview with Felipe Alou by Larry Hogan, Phoenix, March 3, 2004.

32. Robert Boyle, "The Private World of the Negro Ballplayer," *Sports Illustrated*, March 21, 1960, p. 18.

33. Mota quoted in Wilson, *Early Latino Ballplayers in the United States*, p. 119.

34. Art Rosenbaum and Bob Stevens, *The Giants of San Francisco* (New York: Coward-McCann, 1963), p. 130.

35. Alou interview.

36. Alou interview.

37. Interview with Julio Navarro by the author, San Juan, Puerto Rico, June 7, 2010.

38. Rosenbaum and Stevens, *The Giants of San Francisco*, p. 131.

39. Ibid., pp. 131–32.

40. Ibid., p. 131.

41. "1942 New York Cubans Player Roster," New York Cuban Stars File, Ashland Collection, NBLA.

42. Orlando Cepeda, *My Ups and Downs in Baseball*, pp. 26–27. The elder Cepeda died at an early age, forty-nine years old.

43. Wilson, *Early Latino Ballplayers*, p. 119; interview with Emilio Navarro by author, Ponce, Puerto Rico, June 2, 2010.

9. FROM CUBAN STARS TO DOMINICAN GIANTS

1. Robert Boyle, "The End Was Near—Almost: When Aaron Didn't Show, Fans Furious," *Freeman's Journal*, December 29, 2006, www.thefreemansjournal.com/ThisWeek.html, last retrieved on January 4, 2007.

2. *Chicago Defender*, October 14, 1959, p. 22; *Sporting News*, October 14, 1959, p. 30.

3. Boyle, "The End Was Near"; interview with Boyle by author, Cooperstown, NY, June 2006.

4. Boyle, "The End Was Near."

5. Boyle, "The Private World of the Negro Ballplayer," *Sports Illustrated*, March 21, 1960, p. 19 (hereafter, "The Private World").

6. Tom Weir and Blane Bachelor, "Spanish-Speaking Players Get Lessons in American Life," *USA Today*, April 13, 2004, www.usatoday.com/sports/baseball/2004-04-13-cover-latinos-x.htm.

7. Boyle, "The Private World," p. 18.

8. Quoted in Samuel Regalado, *Viva Baseball: Latin Major Leaguers and Their Special Hunger* (Urbana: University of Illinois Press, 1998), p. 72.

9. Ruck, *The Tropic of Baseball: Baseball in the Dominican Republic* (Lincoln: Bison Books, 1999).

10. Alou interview.

11. Marcos Bretón, *Away Games: The Life and Times of a Latin Ball Player* (New York: Simon & Schuster, 1999), p. 49.

12. Rosenbaum, "Señor Scout," *Baseball Digest*, July 1962, p. 60; *Sporting News*, October 19, 1963, p. 21.

13. Boyle, "The Private World," p. 74.

14. *Sporting News*, April 12, 1961, p. 2.

15. Boyle, "The Latins Storm Las Grandes Ligas," *Sports Illustrated*, August 9, 1965, p. 26.

16. "Status," *Baseball Digest*, June 1959, p. 82; "He'd Even Be Doing Razor Commercials!" *Baseball Digest*, May 1960, p. 72.

17. González Echevarría, *Pride of Havana*, pp. 6–7.

18. *Miami Herald*, August 12, 1987, p. 1C.

19. *Pasadena Independent*, January 5, 1961, p. 23; *Los Angeles Times*, March 15, 1960, p. C2.

20. *Miami Herald*, August 12, 1987, p. 1C; Milton Jamail, *Full Count: Inside Cuban*

Baseball (Carbondale, IL: Southern Illinois University Press, 2000), p. 25; J. David Truby, "Castro's Curveball," *Harper's*, May 1989, pp. 32–33.

21. *Miami Herald*, August 12, 1987, p. 1C; *Fort Lauderdale Sun-Sentinel*, June 21, 1991; Hirsch, *Willie Mays*, p. 283.

22. *Sporting News*, September 4, 1965, p. 15, and September 17, 1966, p. 6; *Fresno Bee*, April 11, 1967, p. 26.

23. Bill Liston, "The Man: Tiant," *1975 Boston Scorebook*, pp. 8–9; Luis Tiant Player File, NBLA.

24. Newspaper clipping, Luis Tiant, Jr., Player File, NBLA. The newspaper clipping entitled "Of Destiny Man" was written by Maury Allen and published on October 14, 1975.

25. *Baltimore Afro-American*, October 13, 1962, p. 9.

26. Dark quoted in Peter C. Bjarkman, *Baseball with a Latin Beat*, en. 2, p. 138.

27. *New York Times*, August 4, 1964, p. 25, and August 7, 1964, p. 20; *Washington Post*, August 5, 1964, p. D1; *Chicago Defender*, August 6, 1964, p. 40; Hirsch, *Willie Mays*, pp. 417–20.

28. *Pittsburgh Courier*, August 15, 1964, p. 24; *Los Angeles Sentinel*, August 6, 1964, p. B1, and August 13, 1964, p. B1; *Amsterdam News*, August 15, 1964, p. 19; *Chicago Defender*, August 15, 1964, p. 8.

29. Peter C. Bjarkman, *Baseball with a Latin Beat*, p. 229; Hirsch, *Willie Mays*, p. 351.

30. Regalado, *Viva Baseball*, pp. 85, 86, and 98.

31. Historian Sam Regalado charts the composition of each decade of Latin American–born players in *Viva Baseball*; see pp. 7, 40, 117, 140, and 171. Also see Peter Bjarkman, *Baseball with a Latin Beat*, pp. 385–86.

10. INTO THE SHADOWS

1. *Chicago Tribune*, July 26, 1966, p. B1; *Washington Post*, July 26, 1966, p. B1; *Chicago Defender*, July 30, 1966, p. 15.

2. *Amsterdam News*, January 31, 1953, p. 27.

3. *Chicago Defender*, December 19, 1970, p. 33.

4. *New York Times*, February 4, 1971, p. 42; *Los Angeles Times*, February 4, 1971, p. E1; *Chicago Tribune*, February 4, 1971, p. D1; *Washington Post*, February 4, 1971, p. F1.

5. *Los Angeles Times*, February 4, 1971, p. H2.

6. Bowie Kuhn, interview by the author, July 2005, Cooperstown, NY.

7. *Atlanta Daily World*, February 11, 1971, p. 9.

8. *Chicago Defender*, February 15, 1971, p. 24; *Pittsburgh Courier*, February 20, 1971, p. 16.

9. *Chicago Defender*, July 8, 1971, p. 30, and July 15, 1971, p. 28; *Los Angeles Times*, July 8, 1971, p. E1; *Atlanta Daily World*, August 10, 1971, p. 5.

10. *Pittsburgh Courier*, February 16, 1974, p. 25; *New York Times*, March 17, 1974, p. 53; Woodlawn Cemetery, Form 132 (2000 4–29), Affidavit file No. 13574, Deed No. 29393, Area 109.

11. *New York Times*, March 19, 1974, p. 40; *Amsterdam News*, March 30, 1974, p. B8; *Sporting News*, April 6, 1974, newspaper clipping, Alex Pompez File, NBLA.

12. Brooke, *Bridging the Divide*, p. 10.

13. Valdes and Rankin-Hill Valdes interview.

14. Luis Tiant and Joe Fitzgerald, *El Tiante: The Luis Tiant Story* (New York: Doubleday, 1976), pp. 185–86.

15. *New York Times*, May 13, 1975, p. 59; *Washington Post*, August 20, 1975, p. E2.

16. *Baltimore Afro-American*, October 18, 1975, p. 9. The reunion of the Tiant family is powerfully captured in the John Hock film *Lost Son of Havana* (2009).

17. Wilson, *Early Latino Ballplayers*, pp. 102, 112.

18. McCovey induction speech (1986), www.baseballhalloffame.org/hofers/detail .jsp? playerId=118605.

19. Personal communication, John Klima, June 2010.

20. Thanks to Adalaine Holton for sharing her research on Schomburg and his conceptualization of African-descended peoples in the Americas as "a nation in theory." Adalaine Holton, "The Practices of Black Radical Print" (Ph.D. diss., Literature, University of California Santa Cruz, 2005). Jesse Hoffnung-Garskopf's description of Schomburg as "a product of multiple displacements" in discussing his negotiation of his place within New York City and its Puerto Rican communities as someone who was black and Latino is also an apt description of Pompez's life. Hoffnung-Garskopf, "The Migrations of Arturo Schomburg: On Being *Antillano*, Negro, and Puerto Rican in New York, 1891–1938," *Journal of American Ethnic History* 21:1 (Fall 2001), p. 5.

ACKNOWLEDGMENTS

Inspired by the life of one, this book has benefited from the minds and hearts of many. Friends, family, professional associates, and retired players in the United States, Puerto Rico, Cuba, and the Dominican Republic shared their time, stories, and hospitality to allow me to better get a sense of Alex Pompez the man beyond the available documents in the archives. For sharing their stories about how their paths crossed with Pompez and other dimensions of Latino baseball, many thanks to Mauricio Valdes and Lesley Rankin-Hill Valdes, Robert Boyle, Orlando Cepeda, Emilio "Millito" Navarro, Julio Navarro, Armando Vásquez, Monte Irvin, Charlie Rivera, Buck O'Neil, Felipe Alou, Juan Marichal, Albertus "Cleffie" Fennar, Rodolfo Fernández, Rafael "Ray" Noble, Orestes Miñoso, Jimmy Robinson, Luis Tiant, Bowie Kuhn, Willie McCovey, Pedro Sierra, Leo Cardenas, and Lorenzo "Chiquitin" Cabrera. Insight into the Harlem world was gained through interviews with Joe and Claritha "Peaches" Osborne, Everard Marius, and Dr. Jimmy Banks. I would be remiss not to acknowledge the two wonderful days I spent in baseball's Valhalla meeting for the first time with Anthony (Tony) Cromwell Hill, who over a three-hour dinner discussed family history and shared memories of a side of Alex Pompez (his great-uncle) that is inaccessible through the archive.

Family, friends, and associates have hosted research stays, organized lectures, and convened academic conferences while I completed this book. For their hospitality I am much obliged to the Callan family, the Mercado family, Pedro and María Tua, Damaris Quiñones, Mercedes Rivera, my parents, and especially my Harlem connections Millery and

Judy Polyne and Claritha and Joe Osborne. At various times host, intellectual collaborator, and critic, but always friend, Frank Guridy has engaged in countless conversations with me that have shaped how I have thought and rethought the life story of Pompez and its place in American history; his careful reading of this book manuscript made it all the better. Fellow Negro-league historians Larry Hogan, Dick Clark, Rob Ruck, Ray Doswell, Larry Lester, Greg Bond, Jim Overmyer, Leslie Heaphy, Todd Bolton, and Eddie Bedford offered keen insights about the intersections of black baseball, Latino baseball, and U.S. history. Notably, Dick Clark used his encyclopedic knowledge to help me get the names, dates, and events of the Negro leagues right. Tim Wendell, Milton Jamail, Alan Klein, and Bob Heuer suffered my Pompez stories with great humor and sharp wit, and provided compelling insights into Latino baseball history that enabled me to fashion new lines of analysis. John Klima also offered his expertise on scouting and the Negro leagues in helping me think of where Alex Pompez stands among baseball scouts. Another group of collaborators emerged along the way to give me a platform as well as to hone my craft: thanks to Dave Zirin, Teryl Warren, Clemson Smith Muñiz, Dave Winfield, Anthony Salazar, Danny Torres, Mychal Odom, Dan Brown, Bernardo Ruiz, Lou Hernández, Marcos Bretón, and Scott Reifert.

This book benefited from the mentorship and lasting intellectual guidance of Earl Lewis and Fred Hoxie; they are role models as scholars and colleagues. James Grossman served as my mentor during my Ford Postdoctoral Fellowship, offering guidance as I finished one book and launched into producing early chapter drafts of this one and conducting research. I am forever grateful to the late Jules Tygiel for believing in my work, always offering kind words of encouragement, and critically appraising my work. Illinois colleagues challenged me and enhanced this project through our countless conversations and their feedback as I wrote various parts of the book. Thanks again to James Barrett, Antoinette Burton, Vernon Burton, Sundiata Cha Jua, Jason Chambers, C. L. Cole, Ken Cuno, Rayvon Fouché, Kristin Hoganson, Mark Leff, Bruce Levine, Alejandro Lugo, Liz Pleck, Alicia Rodriguez, Leslie Reagan, and David Roediger. Other scholars and intellectual collaborators have lent their intellectual critiques, emotional support, and scholarly expertise: many thanks to George Sánchez, Gina Pérez,

Wilson Valentín, Natalia Molina, Nancy Mirabal, Minkah Makalani, Kathy López, Tom Guglielmo, John McKiernan González, Tim Gilfoyle, Damion Thomas, Lou Pérez, Susan Greenbaum, Gerald Poyo, Samuel Regalado, John Bloom, Michael Willard, Amy Bass, Teresa Runstedtler, and Jose Alamillo.

A historian's work is always the beneficiary of a team of research assistants, archivists, and librarians who offer great assistance in locating materials, alerting us to newly available sources, and making key connections. Thanks for able research assistance on this project to Jennifer Guiliano, Will Cooley, and Melissa Rohde. The research staff at the National Baseball Library has always been in a league of their own. Thanks to head librarian Jim Gates and public service librarian Tim Wiles—aptly nicknamed the "John Stockton of baseball research"—along with their superb team of researchers over the years: John Odell, Scot Mondore, Tom Shieber, Erik Strohl, Bill Burdick, and Bill Francis. Steve Gietschier provided invaluable research guidance in maneuvering the formerly publicly accessible *Sporting News* Archive in St. Louis. Pedro Juan Hernández and the rest of the staff at the Center for Puerto Rican Studies at Hunter College capably assisted me during my visits, as did the Schomburgh Research Library. The staff at the Chicago Historical Society aided me in going through the Claude Barnett Papers, which contained a treasure trove of article drafts from the Associated Negro Press News Service. Mary Stuart of the wonderful History, Philosophy and Newspaper Library at the University of Illinois alerted me to new online databases and newspaper resources that the library had acquired. The Special Collections Library staff at the University of South Florida ensured my research stay in Tampa was extremely productive by pointing me to the Tony Pizzo Collection and other source material.

Research support for this project has been generously extended from the Ford Foundation Postdoctoral Fellowship, the University of Illinois Research Board as well as its Scholars Research Fund. Equally important are those who organized talks where I shared research findings as I finalized my revisions: thanks to Madeleine López and attendees at my lecture at Hamilton College; Ed Muñoz and student organizers Trisha Martínez, J. Robert Trevizo, and Fidencio Simental at the University of Wyoming; and Marisol Negrón at the University of

Massachusetts Boston. Others invited me to share my work as I began to focus more on Pompez's story as a metaphor for Latinos in baseball and U.S. history: Clarissa Cylich at Bartow-Pell Historical Mansion, Karl Lindholm at Middlebury College, and Shelly Jarrett Bromberg at Miami University, Hamilton Campus. Many thanks for audience questions and feedback at those events as well at the Jerry Malloy Negro League Conference (2005, 2008), the Organization of American Historians (2007), the Cooperstown Symposium on Baseball and American Culture (2007), and the American Historical Association (2008). This project benefited immensely from a lecture hosted by La Union Martí-Macéo in Ybor City in 2004 through the auspices of the Tony Pizzo Endowed Lecture on Florida Immigration History.

Working with publisher Thomas LeBien and editor Dan Crissman at Hill and Wang has been a wonderful intellectual collaboration. Their feedback, both editorial and intellectual, consistently pushed me to sharpen my voice, all the while encouraging me to believe that Pompez's life story is a story readers needed to know, sooner rather than later.

Finally, thanks to my strongest advocate and best critic: my wife, Dolly Túa Burgos, who along with our lovely two girls, Miranda and Julia, provides me balance in the often disconcerting world of academia, research trips, and media appearances. Their love, encouragement, and smiles sustain me.

INDEX

Universal Negro Improvement Association
(UNIA), 39
Urban League, 116, 166

Valdes, Juan, 138, 245
Valdes, Lesley Rankin-Hill, 245
Valdes, Manolo, 41, 50
Valdes, Onelia, 245
Vargas, Juan "Tetelo," 59, 65, 221
Vargas, Roberto, 187
Vásquez, Armando, 138, 148, 158, 200,
235, 236
Veeck, Bill, 181
Venezuela, 10, 88, 139, 157, 186, 191, 224,
235, 254
Veracruz, 141
Vernon, Mickey, 202
Versailles, Zoilo, 229

Wagner, Leon, 206
Walcott, Jersey Joe, 133
Walker, Dixie, 230–31
Walker, Jimmy, 41
Walker, Madame C. J., ix, 30
Waller, Fats, 87
Walton, Lester, 40
War for Independence (third), 12, 17, 18, 19
Washington, Chester, 88
Washington, Isaac, 62
Washington Post, 103, 135–36, 156
Washington Senators, xiv, 134, 135, 136,
142, 146, 159, 160, 166, 213, 215, 219,
220, 226, 273n
Wasservogel, Isider, 49
Watkins-Owens, Irma, 265n, 267n
Weinberg, Bo, 70, 71, 72, 73, 74, 121
Weinberg, George, 70, 72–73, 76, 79, 80,
96, 110, 113, 121, 122, 126; courtroom
testimony of, 122–23, 125
Weintraub, Moe, 100

West Indians, 31, 39, 40, 64, 69, 77, 84,
91, 92, 93, 117, 137, 138, 148
West Tampa, Fla., 16–17, 18, 19, 20, 21,
25, 261n
West Tampa Development Company, 16
What's My Line?, 222
White, Alvin, 137
White, Bill, 216
White Citizens' Council, 203
White Municipal League, 25
Wilkinson, J. L., 46
Williams, Chester, 90
Williams, Johnny, 158
Williams, Marvin, 168
Williams, Raymond, 87, 271n
Williams, Smokey Joe, 239
Williams, Ted, 237–38, 239
Wilson, Artie, 165, 197
Wilson, Rollo, 85
Wilson, Tom, 151, 152, 155, 167
winter leagues, 58, 92, 93, 187, 192, 208,
234, 249
Woodlawn Cemetery, ix, 71, 243, 245
World Series, 177, 179, 188, 199, 230, 231,
235, 254; of 1962, 231, 232, 234, 235;
of 1975, 247
World War II, 142, 144, 159; baseball
talent pool drained by, 146–47, 158
Worner, Ted, 193–94, 195, 196, 201,
202–203
Wright, Johnny, 157, 161, 169, 173
Wright, Richard, 68, 82

Yankee Stadium, 34, 66, 132, 147, 149,
150, 151, 175
Ybor, Vicente Martínez, 16, 24
Ybor City, Fla., 16, 19, 20, 23, 25, 26, 30,
136, 138, 245; *bolita*'s popularity in,
31–32
Young, "Doc," 241–42
Young, Frank A. "Fay," 142, 166, 180, 182